BOOMTOWN COLUMBUS

BOOMTOWN COLUMBUS

Ohio's Sunbelt City and How Developers Got Their Way

KEVIN R. COX

TRILLIUM, AN IMPRINT OF
THE OHIO STATE UNIVERSITY PRESS
COLUMBUS

Trillium, an imprint of The Ohio State University Press.

Library of Congress Cataloging-in-Publication Data
Names: Cox, Kevin R., 1939– author.
Title: Boomtown Columbus : Ohio's sunbelt city and how developers got their way / Kevin R. Cox.
Description: Columbus : Trillium, an imprint of The Ohio State University Press, [2021] | Includes bibliographical references and index. |
Summary: "Examines the policies and development politics that have made the Midwestern city of Columbus, Ohio, more like a Sunbelt city, and how Columbus's lessons apply to American cities elsewhere"—Provided by publisher.
Identifiers: LCCN 2020051976 | ISBN 9780814257920 (paperback) | ISBN 9780814281215 (ebook)
Subjects: LCSH: City planning—Ohio—Columbus—History. | Cities and towns—Ohio—Columbus—Growth—History. | Real estate development—Ohio—Columbus—History. | Columbus (Ohio)—Economic conditions. | Columbus (Ohio)—Economic policy. | Columbus (Ohio)—Social conditions.
Classification: LCC HT168.C577 C69 2021 | DDC 307.1/2160977157—dc23
LC record available at https://lccn.loc.gov/2020051976

Cover design by Andrew Brozyna
Text design by Juliet Williams
Type set in Adobe Garamond Pro

∞ The paper used in this publication meets the minimum requirements of the American National Standard for Information Sciences—Permanence of Paper for Printed Library Materials. ANSI Z39.48-1992.

CONTENTS

List of Illustrations		vi
Foreword		ix
Acknowledgments		xv
CHAPTER 1	Out of Place and Out of Step	1
CHAPTER 2	The Annexation Policy and Its Dilemmas	15
CHAPTER 3	Fighting the Image and Trying to Catch Up	45
CHAPTER 4	The "Postindustrial" City Comes to Columbus	75
CHAPTER 5	Property Development and the Pursuit of Rent	107
CHAPTER 6	Scorched Earth	131
CHAPTER 7	How the Developers Get Their Way	165
CHAPTER 8	Whose City?	193
CHAPTER 9	The Contested City	215
Afterword		243
Bibliography		247
Index		251

ILLUSTRATIONS

Figures

FIGURE 2.1	Water and sewer contracts between Columbus and independent suburbs, 1993	19
FIGURE 2.2	Blitzkrieg on the Northern Front: How the annexation policy worked to Columbus's advantage	19
FIGURE 2.3	School districts in Franklin County, 1989	35
FIGURE 4.1	Honda's Central Ohio supply chain	80
FIGURE 4.2	Stretching out the downtown	88
FIGURE 4.3	Median income, 2014	101
FIGURE 4.4	Freight districts in Franklin County	103
FIGURE 5.1	"Wexley" land holdings and their relation to the cancelled water–sewer contract	123
FIGURE 5.2	The annexation of "Wexley" land	125
FIGURE 6.1	Housing values and changes in value	151
FIGURE 6.2	Vacancies and value change	151
FIGURE 6.3	Median income and value change	154

FIGURE 6.4 Median income and vacancies 154

FIGURE 8.1 Distribution of Section 8 housing vouchers by zip code in Columbus, 2015 202

FIGURE 8.2 Poverty and infant mortality for Franklin County zip code areas 205

FIGURE 8.3 Poverty and infant mortality for Franklin County zip code areas projected onto infant mortality rates for select countries of the world 205

FIGURE 8.4 Lack of health insurance and infant mortality rates for Franklin County zip code areas 206

FIGURE 8.5 Poverty and lack of health insurance for Franklin County zip code areas 206

Tables

TABLE 1.1 City population peaks: Sunbelt cities 8

TABLE 1.2 Percentage expansion of jurisdictional area, 1960–2010 9

TABLE 1.3 Retail sales per capita 10

TABLE 1.4 How Columbus is different from its peers 11

TABLE 1.5 Columbus urban area population as a percentage of Cincinnati and Cleveland urban area populations 13

TABLE 2.1 Suburban school district property and pupils in the city of Columbus 34

TABLE 2.2. Changes in school enrollment in Franklin County school districts, 1977–1991 (%) 36

TABLE 2.3 Local economic conditions and bond ratings for Midwestern cities 42

TABLE 3.1 Comparative airline statistics for Columbus and some peer cities, 1990 50

TABLE 3.2 Comparative airline connections for Columbus and a peer group of urban areas 52

TABLE 4.1 Percentage of the labor force employed in manufacturing (urbanized areas) 76

TABLE 4.2	Select location quotients 2012	77
TABLE 4.3	Major private sector employers in the Columbus metropolitan area, 2020	78
TABLE 4.4	Percentage labor force in manufacturing	79
TABLE 4.5	Percentage of employed workers in government employment: Cuyahoga, Franklin and Hamilton Counties	84
TABLE 4.6	Top five office parks, Columbus area, 2015	105
TABLE 8.1	Percentage families under poverty line	204
TABLE 8.2	Percentage of total population under poverty line	204
TABLE 8.3	Comparative statistics for three poorer and three wealthier school districts	208
TABLE 8.4	Educational outcomes across all school districts in Franklin County and "explanatory" variables as measured by coefficients of correlation	209
TABLE 8.5	Census Tract 69.50: Older, white people, living in their own homes and in small households	212

FOREWORD

THIS IS A BOOK about an American city: Columbus, Ohio, a Midwestern city of over 850,000 people set in a metropolitan area of over two million. It is the fourteenth largest city in the US, which comes as a surprise to many and is an aspect of not just its particularity but its peculiarity. But why Columbus? Partly this is because I have lived here for over fifty-six years. I was a faculty member in the Department of Geography at Ohio State. From the '70s on, I became absorbed by urban development and its politics—something hard to avoid given the prominence given to it in local newspapers in the US and an interest sharpened by how different it all was from my native England. Columbus turned out to be a fascinating city to study, and this book should appeal to all those who share my fascination. If you are interested in how Columbus came to be what it is today and why, this book will be of interest.

Urban development and its politics is also an area of interest where there is a large literature shared with sociologists, political scientists, and urban planners. There is theory that generalizes across cities, and there is the particularity of each city. In the US, that particularity is heightened compared with the cities of Western Europe. In the US, a highly decentralized state structure means that there is no single template for urban institutions and subsequent politics. Every city in the US is different in often quite striking ways. This book is about how theory comes into contact with a particular American city, Columbus, and what that instance in turn tells us about US cities taken as a whole. In short: What are the more general issues of urban analysis and theory that the Columbus case can shed light on?

First, the Americanness of Columbus is something that should be emphasized. As I said, American cities and the processes through which they develop are different from what one encounters in, say, Western Europe, and the degree of difference between them is also different—a staggering variety that puts the more monochrome character of municipal government in France, Germany, or Great Britain utterly in the shade. Yes, there is a sense in which all American cities are the same: not least, the sprawl. And there are, to be sure, dominant social relations that apply across all American cities. In contrast to European ones, the property development industry holds pole position. Local government is turned to *its* purpose rather than having to confront a more implacable, West European–style state with its own views as to what development patterns should be: no greenbelts, anxieties about the less well-off, or intrusive central state here, just a local government that seemingly bends to the will of those in pursuit of rent. Part of the reason for this, of course, is the high degree to which the American state is decentralized: a radical federalism—perhaps the most radical in the world—in which states, in their wisdom, have seen fit to delegate a remarkable degree of power and responsibility to local governments. This also means, though, that the particularity of places can assume an enhanced significance, and it does.

The dispersion of formal political power has provided scope for local governments to find their own institutional "solutions" to the contradictions of (capitalist) urbanization as it affects them, and local state representatives have typically been happy to help in securing what turns out to be legislation designed to satisfy the interests of—or interests *in*—particular cities. The fact of the nonpartisan ballot in many cities also helps, for under particular circumstances it can lead to rapid shifts in city policy, particularly in smaller cities where a social movement can grow to the point at which a takeover of city council is possible, as indeed happened in Santa Cruz and Santa Monica, and with very "interesting" consequences. The drama of geographically uneven development also factors into the creation of particularity: Compare Detroit and, say, San Francisco. Local economic bases rise and fall, but there is nothing of the sort that is available in the more centralized states of Western Europe to brake the rise or counter the collapse.

Serendipity can be cruel, as San Bernardino has recently learned. And to drive home the point: There is nowhere in Western Europe that approaches the situation of contemporary Detroit.

There are, of course, many studies of particular cities, but they are dominantly of the larger ones: cities like Atlanta, Boston, Chicago, LA, New York, and San Francisco have all been given their due, and in some cases *ad nauseam*. They are prominent in the public eye, and they command wide interest. They are not just national cities; they are international cities. One might say that they are overstudied and do not reflect the entirety of urban America.

Middling sized cities, like Columbus, Kansas City, Sacramento, Milwaukee, or Austin, or even Portland and San Diego, have been more of a problem. Why bother? Yet they pose interesting questions, and this is my second point of justification. They certainly share things with larger cities, most notably their capitalist dynamic and the fact that federal urban policy leaves a common imprint: urban renewal, busing for racial balance, deregulation of airlines and of railroads, to mention a few. They may share certain things with some of the major metropolises: Those of the Western US are different from those of the East. But they also share certain things that set them apart from the big urban centers, and in some ways they are also distinct from each other.

So what do they share with each other, and in contrast to the larger cities? First, they compete for investment, but the stakes are different than for the bigger cities, the competition all the more intense, whether it be major league franchises, airline connections, or a big corporate headquarters. The big metropolitan centers have advantages that smaller cities lack, not least the relative size of their markets and the diversity of their labor forces. Their advantages have cumulative effects. Because of their markets, they will attract the airlines and be connected both nationally and internationally. That in turn makes them more attractive for corporate headquarters functions—something very clear in the recent decision of Amazon to divide its HQ2 between New York and Washington, even while the former would eventually demur. We should note in passing that this competitive advantage seems to be increasing: With airline mergers and takeovers, there are now fewer hubs to distribute, and the big hubs are monopolizing traffic raised to a power. Middling cities, including Cincinnati, Cleveland, Pittsburgh, and St. Louis, have all lost their hub status.

On the other hand, and orthogonal to this distinction between the major metropolitan centers and more middling, there are issues of history that have imposed a second layer of difference. There are big differences, encapsulated in part by the Coldbelt/Sunbelt contrast: differences in emphasis on mass transit, and in population density, and differences in the relation between central cities and suburbs. The classic fiscal disparities problem of the 1960s and '70s was particularly intense in the older central cities of the Coldbelt since they were typically surrounded by independent suburbs cutting them off from a suburbanizing tax base. Sunbelt (central) cities, overall, have been able to grow by annexation, and this has provided them with a much more favorable fiscal situation. In short, there is what might be called a "second-generation" urbanization that was more automobile based, and in which central cities could learn from the mistakes of an earlier cohort of cities and ensure their future through annexation.

It would, though, be a mistake to reduce second-generation urbanization to broad regional contrasts. There are some Coldbelt cities that are much more like Sunbelt cities: most notably Columbus, Dayton, Indianapolis, and Minneapolis. This is because they share the situation of being relative latecomers, which imposes a further layer of particularity. The classic Coldbelt cities were ones of the steam age. They grew up around heavy industry on the basis of the access to coal afforded by navigable water: the Ohio River, the Great Lakes, the Atlantic. Cities like Columbus and Indianapolis are quite different. In terms of population growth, they did not start to take off until the age of electricity, and then largely on the back of consumer goods–producing branch plants. Columbus and Indianapolis also gained from being state capitals, while Minneapolis benefitted from being cheek-by-jowl with the state capital, St. Paul; this was an important aspect of their economic bases that would help them survive the regional crisis of the '70s. Dayton is the exception that proves the rule.

Accordingly, Columbus lies at the intersection of a number of axes of differentiation among US cities: It is middling, it is a case of second-generation urbanization, and it is a latecomer. Even so, Columbus cannot be read off from this particular intersection. It has the features of a Sunbelt city, but it is in the Coldbelt. Like Sunbelt cities it is a latecomer, but a Coldbelt location makes a difference for it has been a latecomer in a regional environment where there were already cities of substantial size that claimed the major league franchises, the corporate headquarters, and the hubs before Columbus had achieved the necessary thresholds. It is a regional environment therefore, one of more closely spaced cities, that has made an important difference.

Yet how to tackle particularity from a theoretical standpoint? Returning to studies of American cities, there are particular genres. One approach is that of Mike Davis in his widely praised *City of Quartz*: a set of particular slants or angles on the city with no single story to tell. In other cases, like Elizabeth Shermer on Phoenix, Harvey Graff on Dallas, or Richard Gendron and William Domhoff on Santa Cruz, the stories told are more linear and topically focused. But insofar as the particularity of places is concerned, an explicit theoretical undergirding has proven elusive, which makes it harder to bring these sorts of studies into a relation one with another, aside, that is, from the use of a common vocabulary of growth coalitions, developers and landlords, and shifts in the wider space economy. This book, therefore, is one that looks both at a particular city, and how one might theorize cities in their specificity more generally.

At one level, as Massey (2007) would have argued, the particularity of a city is simply the result of a coming together of diverse influences and conditions: ones like government policies, discursive environments, sectoral change, and population movements. The juxtaposition of elements can result in their interactions, with further consequences for what a city is. Some of the forces and conditions so converging may be shared with other cities and some not. As a latecomer in the annals of American urbanization, as we have seen, Columbus bears strong likenesses to some other cities in terms of its conditioning factors and outcomes—which facilitates the posing of questions as to why the cities in question are otherwise different. In a number of respects it is more like Sunbelt cities than those of the surrounding Rustbelt.

There are other commonalities one can point to beyond the idea of Columbus and its suburbs as a Sunbelt city marooned in the Midwest. Wedged in by the once much larger metropolitan areas of Cleveland and Cincinnati, it has a similar subordinate regional status as Milwaukee, San Diego, or Sacramento. Austin and Kansas City have important similarities to Columbus in terms of their size and the recency of their growth, but they have not had to deal with the regional hegemony of a Chicago, San Francisco, or, for Columbus, Cincinnati and Cleveland. On the other hand, what Columbus *does* share with Austin is a very large state university, a state government, and an ability to expand horizontally in all directions with limited topographic hindrance. Unsurprisingly, in both cities housing supply is extraordinarily responsive to changes in demand, which makes it a relatively cheap city in which to live. There are also things that they *do not* share. For a start, respective economic bases vary. Austin has a much stronger concentration of computer and information science researchers, while Columbus is more reliant on the insurance industry.

This is to focus on how cities differ one from another and the complex ways in which things get combined from one to the next. Clearly, this is only part of the story. We need a stronger sense of social process and resort to more general logics of urbanization. Synergies clearly count for something, like that between universities and major white-collar employers. Students come from very different locations, and decide to marry or live together and split the difference by staying where they are, which works to the benefit of employers like Nationwide Insurance in Columbus or IBM or Dell in Austin. In addition, corporations need office buildings, people need housing, and retailers need shopping centers: an extraordinary field of opportunities for the development industry, and one that they further promote through their support of those who are keen, for their own reasons, to expand employment in the area, like the utilities. Developers are a major presence in cities, of crucial significance for the urbanization process, but a process in which they will encounter not just each other, in competition, but those who seek to protect themselves against all the consequences, intended or otherwise, of development. Accordingly, in any study of an American city, developers have to loom large. And in Columbus they have been a major force, with an agenda that city government has found hard to resist.

One final note: It should be clear from this foreword that my geographical perspective on the world is central to how I conceive urban studies. Differences in urban development within major metropolitan areas, between different cities and different countries, all figure in to varying degrees in this book. When a layperson thinks of geography, one of the things that comes to mind is maps. This book contains a number of maps. They are an indispensable tool in following the argument at various points. However, there are still instances in the text where I refer to events, or particular configurations of events, where there is no map. In those instances, I strongly urge using Google Maps. This will not only help in orienting the reader but also, through the Street Scene option, one can achieve an enhanced sense of the Columbus area.

ACKNOWLEDGMENTS

IN THE COURSE of writing this book, I had numerous and helpful conversations with a number of people who have been involved in Columbus development politics over the years. They include Herb Asher, Jonathan Beard, Bill Habigh, Joe Motil, and Joe Sommer. Earlier discussions with Jack Bachtel and Tod Ortlip of Planned Communities, Dean Jeffers of Nationwide Realty Investors, and Ron Huff of Vantage were extremely helpful in understanding the nuts and bolts of the development process and why it tends to be so localized and embedded in particular places. I am grateful to them all for sharing their time with me. The interpretations and conclusions, though, are entirely my own. Another special thanks to Jamie Valdinger, who prepared the maps and figures. The reader will find that I have drawn copiously on news reports, particularly those in the major daily paper, the *Columbus Dispatch.* While it is a paper whose editorial views I frequently quarrel with in this book, their news reporting was, as will be seen, very helpful to this project. Finally, thanks to all those in urban studies who have inspired me over the years and helped me understand how cities, and particularly American cities, work.

CHAPTER 1

Out of Place and Out of Step

Context

The first thing that strikes one about Columbus is how similar, in many respects, it is to other major American cities and in comparison with, say, cities in Western Europe. It is a low-density city in which the automobile dominates personal mobility. Its geographic form is molded by freeways that focus on the downtown and by one that circles the city—the Outerbelt—designed to take through-traffic away from the city center. It is reliant for its external connections on highways and air transport. It has not had a train station for almost forty years: It was closed and demolished in 1977. This is a little bit unusual—its Ohio peers, Cincinnati and Cleveland, still have theirs, albeit with minimal service—but reflects a low level of passenger train transport that is a feature of the US as a whole and that again serves to distinguish it from the cities of Europe.

Columbus, like other of its American counterparts, also experienced a decline in the role of the central city or what is still sometimes called the central business district, or CBD. Historically the downtown everywhere in the US was the major retail and employment generating center. This began to change sometime around the turn of the century with the emergence of branch plant assembly-style manufacturing. In an age of electricity and liberation from the steam engine and systems of belts to provide energy across numerous stories, large factories on a single floor were now preferred. This gave suburban sites an advantage, and Columbus, as we will see, shared in this. After the Second World War, the spread of employment within metropolitan areas became more pronounced, but was then stimulated further by the suburbanization of retailing and office employment. The real estate innovations of the property developers, notably the office park and the suburban shopping center, meant some geographic concentration of activity at points on the urban periphery; something further stimulated by the creation of freeways circling the cities, largely in the '70s. So central cities found themselves competing for retailing and office employment with new suburban nodes. The city was becoming multinuclear: so many nodes of business activity, each surrounded by housing developments. Early instances in Columbus were the office employment clusters at Dublin, Worthington, and Westerville, and more recently, Tuttle, Easton, and Polaris—so, and parenthetically, a definite bias toward the northern rim.

This emptying out from the center has been a common story, but many central cities have risen from seeming ashes into what is commonly now known as the postindustrial city.[1] Urban renewal and the redevelopment of downtown areas in the '50s and '60s, along with a growth in tertiary employment—offices, both public and private, particularly finance, higher education, and health—all helped pave the way for their resurrection as major employment centers. The addition of convention centers, the hotels to serve them, and new stadiums for professional sports would add to the mix. This would then be a condition for the slow conversion of surrounding areas into gentrified neighborhoods. The general white-collarization of employment would be intensified by deindustrialization, the closure of suburban assembly plants, and the relative growth of manufacturing in smaller towns in the wider hinterland. Meanwhile, office employment in the suburbs would expand further, partly in the form of branch offices for the big downtown financial firms. Columbus fits this pattern very well.

One of the forces helping stimulate the suburbanization of employment has been the division of metropolitan areas into numerous municipalities, each competing for the investments of the developers in shopping centers and office parks and then for the tenants. This pattern of territorial fragmentation—a jurisdictionally independent

1. Mollenkopf 1983, chapter 1.

municipality of some considerable size, both in area and population, surrounded by smaller ones—is again one shared by Columbus with other American cities and in sharp contrast to the European instance. There is the relatively large central city and fifteen adjoining independent municipalities. The same pattern repeats itself with the jurisdictionally independent school districts: a big one in the middle, Columbus itself, and sixteen adjoining ones. Again, and to add to the complexity, school district boundaries do not always coincide with municipal ones. And in addition, there are those relics of premunicipal days, the townships, parts of which, as with other American cities, can survive as so many tiny islands surrounded by some city: veritable archipelagoes. It is, in short, a very complex territorial mosaic and one that exists in utter contrast to what is considered normal in Europe but that is typical for the US.

The social forces driving this are historically distinct. Of course, we are talking about a capitalist city, but the concrete form of capitalism has tended to change. A crucial feature of postwar urban development in the US was a broadening out of its division of labor. Previously one had been able to talk about three major divisions: industry that produced the goods, and that paradoxically included agriculture;[2] finance, which through lending helped promote production; and commerce, which distributed the products, often again, drawing on the banks for short-term financing of its purchases from industry. All of these have been revolutionized in their organizational forms, and large firms have come to dominate not just production but also finance and the wholesale and retail sector. This tripartite division is fairly old. But after the Second World War and for various reasons, there was an elaboration on this: This was the emergence of a set of companies that provided premises of various sorts—shopping centers, industrial premises, office parks, and large housing developments, of which the poster child was Levittown. The first three of these would be held for rent or sold on as sources of rent income to insurance companies and pension funds, while a large portion of the housing would be sold.[3]

2. But only paradoxical if one ignores the way in which agriculture has been progressively industrialized through the adoption of new, labor-saving technologies, by specialization, and by its insertion into the production of inputs like fertilizers and agricultural machinery upstream and the processors of what they produce downstream.

3. Though the interest on mortgages can be understood as a form of rent on property.

Hitherto, firms—industrial firms, retail outlets—had tended to own their own premises. When they needed new factories, stores or offices, they would purchase the land, perhaps through a real estate broker, and then hire architects and a construction company to do the necessary. Development, therefore, was to order and more speculative forms a matter for the future. Housing was very similar in terms of the custom element, people buying a lot and then looking for a builder, though larger developments, often with a strong planned element[4] had started putting in an appearance much earlier.[5] On the other hand, there was also a lot of self-built housing where people bought a lot and organized the construction themselves, perhaps contributing most or even all of the labor.

After the Second World War, this would change quite dramatically with a new breed of speculative developers who bought the land, built the structures, and then looked for tenants or final buyers. Every American city had and continues to have them. They have become major agents in the development of cities. In Columbus, one thinks today, among others, of names like Casto, Edwards, Kenney, Solove, Wagenbrenner, Weiler and Wexner, Continental Real Estate and Planned Communities, and the real estate development arms of the newspaper the *Columbus Dispatch*[6] and Nationwide Insurance.[7] In other cities, there are similar companies but the names will be different. Real estate development is very hands-on. A company gets to know a particular market, makes the necessary connections with the real estate

4. In the Columbus area, a notable case was Upper Arlington, which was the brainchild of two developer brothers, Ben and King Thompson, and goes back to 1913. For a discussion, see Blackford 2016, 167–70.

5. Weiss 1987.

6. A note of clarification here: First, the Dispatch was owned by the Dispatch Printing Company. The Printing Company also owned the real estate subsidiary Capitol Square Limited. When the Dispatch was sold to Gatehouse Media in 2015, the Printing Company remained in the hands of the original owners of the newspaper, the Wolfe family. That means that the real estate arm no longer has anything to do with the newspaper. However, my impression is that, regardless, the real estate subsidiary was and remains largely passive, putting up money and not involved in the day-to-day development process.

7. They are at the center of a much more extensive set of interests which depend, in their turn, on the initiatives of the developers. These include the architects; the zoning attorneys; the builders, who are sometimes separate from the developers; the producers and layers of concrete, whether for houses or roads; the electrical and plumbing companies; and many others. For a more theoretical treatment as it applies to housing development, see Buzzelli and Harris (2006).

lawyers and local planning officials, and builds up a reputation with local banks and builders. None of this is portable to other cities. You would have to start again from scratch. That has an important consequence for the subsequent politics of development—and it *is* highly political. In short, there is no escape elsewhere. You have to make it happen in Columbus / Denver / Austin / Charlotte or wherever, or you are in trouble. So developers fight, and they fight tooth and nail. And once you have bought the land and are committed, you are unlikely to back down when some resident group tries to throw a wrench in the wheel and put all that money at risk.

Complementing the postwar development scene have been the local governments and the planners. Local government in the US is different from its counterparts in other countries. It depends heavily for its revenue on local taxes: historically, property taxes, and more recently, sales and income taxes. In Western Europe, local government can be a little more relaxed about things. Functions that are local in the US may be national in Europe, like schools or police in France. Usually there is also a purposively redistributional element in local government finance. Central governments provide aid that is calibrated on some estimate of local need and local (taxable) resources. Among other things, this means that the sort of gulf that exists in the US between the wealthy and the poorer school districts will be much, much more modest. People do not fight over educational finance reform, as they have recently in Ohio,[8] because there is little or no need for it.

Historically in the US, that money would have come ultimately from a fairly stable local economic base of home-grown industry. The deskilling of industry and the emergence of firms with multiple locations, perhaps through takeovers, and thus the possibility of closing down a plant here and opening a new one somewhere else, have tended to put paid to it. It was at this point that local governments and later the developers started talking about "local economic development" as something they had to worry about. What would take shape as the primary vehicle to that end would be trying to attract the investments

8. In Franklin County, per-pupil expenditures vary between the most well- and least well-endowed school districts by a factor of 1.8—almost double, in other words, between Grandview Heights, spending in 2014–15 $14,491 per pupil, compared with $7,902 per student in Hamilton Local Schools. See "School Report Cards: Which districts spend the most on students?" Columbus Business First, March 15, 2016. Available at http://www.bizjournals.com/columbus/news/2016/03/15/school-report-cards-which-districts-spend-the-most.html#g24 (last accessed 10/25/20).

of firms that were now looking for sites for branch plants and later offices, corporate headquarters, research and development facilities, and the like. In other words, a market in locations was beginning to take shape as local governments vied with one another in a beauty contest in which the prize would be something to stabilize or enhance the local tax base. This was supported by the local developers, embedded, as we have seen, in particular cities because their ability to extract rent rested in considerable part[9] on the way in which a new investment by a national corporation would pull value through the area and create demand for their various real estate products.

This has put the planners in a difficult position. As a profession, city and regional planning emerged historically as a response to the dysfunctionalities of nineteenth-century urbanization: problems of sanitation, clean water, transport, and poor housing. It had a strong reformist component with a view to improving conditions for the masses.[10] But in the American instance, the priorities have tended to shift. Because of the dependence of local government on local taxes, the developers have held pole position and been able to a greater extent than might otherwise apply to bend the planning apparatus to their will: the rezoning of land, priorities for investment in public infrastructure, and annexation, among other things. To add to the advantages so enjoyed, there is no supervision on the part of the state: no attempt to subordinate local plans and their implementation to some overriding conception of how things *should* be; what, for example, would be socially just. Local planners, or the local governments and planners to whom they are ultimately responsible, are allowed to do pretty much what they want so long as they stay within the law on things like the right of eminent domain. This is in sharp contrast to the West European model, where land-use planning is organized in a geographically hierarchical manner. Local plans have to adhere to regional plans and regional plans to some national conception. This national conception has emerged through debate about "the good geography": a debate rather than the sort of fait accompli that is the result of the market in locations to which local planners and local governments have tended to be subordinated in the US.

---

9. But not entirely. Developers innovate—new housing models, new forms of shopping centers—and this can attract buyers and tenants away from the older ones that then start declining in value, at best only relatively and at worst absolutely.

10. Haig 1927; Preteceille 1976.

How Columbus Is Different

In many ways, Columbus is utterly predictable when set beside other US cities; at first sight, not much to surprise. But closer inspection suggests something else. In regional terms, Columbus can be identified in a number of different ways. From the US census standpoint, it is a Midwestern city; that is how it is classified, or by the more specific census division, "East Central." In terms of classic notions of the country's economic geography, it sits squarely within the old Manufacturing Belt. And nobody would argue that it is not in that part of the US, the Midwest and the Northeast, that has been identified interchangeably as the Rustbelt / Coldbelt / Snowbelt and in contrast to what has come to be known as the Sunbelt of the South and West. And to be sure, the posterchildren of the Rustbelt are not that far away, places like Cleveland, Detroit and Pittsburgh.

But in a number of ways, it is significantly different from most of the larger cities of its region. For a start, it is far less "ethnic" than what one associates with the major cities of the area. Columbus did receive immigrants from Eastern and Southern Europe during the great migration toward the end of the nineteenth century, but in no way on the scale of Buffalo, Chicago, Cincinnati, Cleveland, Detroit, Pittsburgh, New York, Philadelphia, Newark, or Boston. Columbus has its Hungarian Village as a reminder of that period, but for the most part Columbus is not an "ethnic" city in the classical sense.

A seemingly very different sort of contrast is that Columbus has not had the same fiscal problems as have been typical of Midwestern and Northeastern cities. Its tax base has continued to expand and keep up with that of the suburbs, while the concentration of need that one finds in many central cities of the region, and not just the well-known ones like Detroit and Newark, has not been so apparent. The imbalance between central city and suburb in terms of both public resources and public need—what used to be known as the central city–suburban fiscal disparity[11]—has been much less in evidence. Part of the reason that its tax base has managed to expand in the way that it has is that its population of tax payers has grown. This has manifested itself in the very favorable ratings that the municipal bonds sold by the city to raise money for public works have been able to attract. In all these regards, it has been much more like Western and Southern cities.

---

11. Cox 1973, chapter 3.

Crucially, this is related to another difference: Unlike cities such as Boston, St. Louis, and Chicago, Columbus has not found itself hemmed in by independent suburbs. Rather, like Denver, Los Angeles, Houston, Austin, and some other cities, it has been able to expand by annexing unincorporated land: land of particular interest to developers looking for large sites for their shopping centers, office and industrial parks, distribution centers, and new, innovative, and appropriately large residential developments. In other words, it is a city that has been able to suburbanize rather than being left stranded as the tide went out.

Compared to the wider region, the city has had a very different population trajectory. It has been a relative latecomer and in that regard, and again, more akin to peers further west and even south than those in the old Manufacturing Belt. In contrast to most other Midwestern and Northeastern cities, it is still growing. Table 1.1 gives the census years in which cities reached their population peaks.[12] The final year is 2010, which indicates that as of that date cities with peak populations for that date were still growing. Cities in the regions designated by the US census as in the West or South are indicated in bold. The cities that had stopped growing by 1950 are, with the exception of Washington, DC, entirely in the Northeast or Midwest. Cities continuing to grow in 1990 were almost equally entirely in the West and to a lesser degree in the South: testimony to a shift in the distribution of population in the US over the last sixty years that has been widely noted. Of the twenty-nine cities that were still growing in 2010, only four were in the Midwest or Northeast, and one of these was Columbus.

TABLE 1.1. City population peaks

YEAR	CITIES
1950	Baltimore, Boston, Buffalo, Chicago, Cleveland, Detroit, Minneapolis, Philadelphia, Pittsburgh, St. Louis, **Washington, DC**
1960	Cincinnati, Milwaukee, **New Orleans**
1970	**Atlanta**, Kansas City, Toledo
2000	**Memphis**
2010	**Albuquerque, Austin, Charlotte,** *COLUMBUS*, **Dallas, Denver, El Paso, Fort Worth, Houston,** Indianapolis, **Jacksonville, Long Beach, Los Angeles, Miami, Nashville,** New York, Oakland, **Oklahoma City,** Omaha, **Phoenix, Portland, Sacramento, San Diego, San Francisco, San Jose, Seattle, Tucson, Tulsa**

Note: Sunbelt cities are set in bold. Identified according to Census regions: West and South.

12. The fifty largest cities in the US as of 1900.

Table 1.1 is a little misleading. Some of the cities that reached their peaks prior to 2010 have since staged revivals without ever exceeding that peak. Atlanta is a case in point, and these instances possibly reflect the residential resurrection of many US cities through gentrification and the development of high-rise living for the affluent. It also needs to be emphasized that these are data for cities and not for the metropolitan areas of which they are the centers. The problem here is not only that metropolitan areas are nebulous and often embrace large areas that are undeniably rural, but census attempts to identify them are relatively recent, which limits the period over which population growth can be assessed. As it is, it is clear from other evidence that part of the reason for the continued growth of cities has been their ability to annex. Table 1.2 shows the very different rates at which cities in the Midwest, Northeast, and West have been able to expand by annexation since 1960. Some cities have actually shrunk. What is very evident, though, is that of the ones that have been able to expand, a clear majority have been in the West. And again, Columbus is part of that group. Meanwhile the vast, vast majority of the Midwestern and Northeastern cities have shown minimal rates of expansion.

TABLE 1.2. Percentage expansion of jurisdictional area, 1960–2010

LESS THAN 10%	50–100%	100–150%	OVER 150%
Boston, Buffalo, Chicago, Cincinnati, Detroit, **Los Angeles,** Milwaukee, Minneapolis, Newark, New York, Oakland, Philadelphia, Pittsburgh, San Francisco, **Seattle,** St. Louis, St. Paul	Toledo, **San Diego,** **Portland**	**Anaheim,** *COLUMBUS,* **Denver,** Kansas City, Omaha, **Sacramento**	**Albuquerque,** Indianapolis, **San Jose,** **Tucson**

Note: Sunbelt cities are set in bold. Identified according to Census regions: West and South.

The ability to expand has had other consequences. Cities have been able to retain more of their retailing, and this has redounded to their fiscal health in the form of sales taxes. As retailing has suburbanized and assumed the form of ever larger malls, so, by virtue of annexation, they have found themselves located in the central city and not in an independent suburb. All of Columbus's regional malls are within the city boundary. More generally, table 1.3 contrasts cities with higher retail sales per capita with those with less. Again, Western cities are in bold and the broad regional contrast is evident. But, and again, Columbus is an anomaly, and this due to its ability to annex—testimony to its latecomer status.

TABLE 1.3. Retail sales per capita

LESS THAN $5,000	$5,000–$9,999	$10,000–$14,999	OVER $15,000
Cleveland, Detroit, Newark	**Anaheim,** Boston, Buffalo, Chicago, **Los Angeles,** Milwaukee, Minneapolis, New York, **Oakland,** Philadelphia, **Sacramento,** St. Paul, St. Louis, Toledo	**Albuquerque,** Cincinnati, *COLUMBUS*, **Denver,** Indianapolis, Kansas City, Omaha, Pittsburgh, **Portland,** **San Diego,** **San Francisco,** **San Jose,** **Tucson**	**Seattle**

Note: Sunbelt cities are set in bold. Identified according to Census regions: West and South.

This status has also affected its economic character. Columbus had some heavy industry and assembly plants, but with a time lag in both instances. It was never like Chicago, Cleveland, Detroit, or Pittsburgh, and manufacturing industry never acquired the prominence that it did there. By the time that industry took off in Columbus, labor productivity by virtue of technical advance was way ahead of what it had been in those cities that acquired industry much earlier. So wages were higher and could support a relatively larger service sector of retailing, construction, banking, and transport. In other words, Columbus, even taking out of account state employment in the city, was always more white collar, and this because of its relatively late industrialization.

There is, in consequence, a very important sense in which Columbus is "out of place"; it is unusual among cities of the Midwest and Northeast, though not alone in that regard since it shares some similarities with Indianapolis and Kansas City. But it is also "out of step," whereas they are quite clearly not, and that too is significant in terms of the city's particularity. It is "out of step" in the sense that for a city of its size, it has less than what one might expect. There are two quite different expressions of this: airline service, and professional sports franchises (see table 1.4). Particularly interesting are the comparisons with Kansas City and Indianapolis. So how to shed some light on this?

TABLE 1.4. How Columbus is different from its peers

CITY	2018 MSA POPULATION*	AIRLINE PASSENGER BOARDINGS 2018**	MAJOR LEAGUE FRANCHISES***
Charlotte	2,569,213	22,281,949	1 (NFL)
Las Vegas	2,231,647	23,795,012	0
Cincinnati	2,190,209	4,269,258	2 (NFL, MLB)
Austin	2,168,316	7,714,479	0
Kansas city	2,143,651	5,790,847	3 (NFL, MLB, MLS)
Cleveland	2,057,009	4,701,713	3 (NFL, MLB, NBA)
Columbus	2,106,541	3,976,620	2 (NHL, MLS)
Indianapolis	2,048,703	4,655,847	2 (NFL, NBA)
San Jose	1,999,107	7,032,851	0
Nashville	1,930,961	8,017,347	2 (NFL, NHL)

*Estimates for respective metropolitan statistical areas: "List of metropolitan statistical areas," *Wikipedia*, n.d. Available at https://en.wikipedia.org/wiki/List_of_metropolitan_statistical_areas (last accessed October 25, 2020).

**Federal Aviation Administration: "Passenger Boarding (Enplanement) and All-Cargo Data for U.S. Airports," *Federal Aviation Administration*, Washington DC. Available at https://www.faa.gov/airports/planning_capacity/passenger_allcargo_stats/passenger/ (last accessed October 25, 2020).

***"List of American and Canadian cities by number of professional sports franchises," *Wikipedia*, n.d. Available at https://en.wikipedia.org/wiki/List_of_American_and_Canadian_cities_by_number_of_major_professional_sports_franchises (last accessed October 25, 2020).

A Question of Geohistory

In short, Columbus, in comparison with most other major cities in the Midwest and Northeast, developed late; in that regard, it is similar to most Western and Southern cities. That lateness had advantages and also disadvantages. The major advantage has been that it could learn from the problems that older cities were starting to face in the post-WWII period. The major challenge was that it had to fight for a place in an already highly urbanized part of the country with an existing urban hierarchy.

Columbus is a city of the electricity age. The steam age did not pass it by entirely, but a location away from navigable water, other than the Ohio canal system, was a disadvantage since it made it relatively inaccessible to the coal that drove the steam engines, and also to the sort of access to coal and iron ore that cities on the Great Lakes and northwest Pennsylvania would be able to take advantage of in the development of the iron and steel industry. Only with electricity would Columbus, like two other Midwestern odd cities out, Indianapolis and Kansas City, start to take off industrially, at least beyond the agro-industries of meat packing and flour milling. This meant that Columbus, by and large, missed out on the surge of immigration from Eastern and Southern Europe so that it would never be an "ethnic" city like Buffalo, Chicago, Cleveland, or Detroit.

Columbus also took off in a state that already had major cities. Cincinnati is just over one hundred miles away, and Cleveland short of one hundred and fifty. This is a major reason why Columbus is "out of step." Metro area populations are now very similar, but just fifty years ago, that was by no means the case; the Columbus area had just a third of the population of Cleveland, whereas today it is slightly larger—a big change, something that is not widely recognized, and testimony to how better Columbus has been situated with respect to new growth sectors (table 1.5). Cincinnati and Cleveland have been major cities for a very long time, and this meant that they would be the logical places for professional sport franchise owners to set up shop. Columbus is seen as part of their market, so they have been an important obstacle to Columbus gaining an NFL or NBA franchise.[13] Later, in the 1980s, there would be airline hubs. Cincinnati had a Delta hub and Cleveland was a hub for Continental; to the east, US Air was at Pittsburgh, and somewhat farther afield to the north-northwest, Northwest was at Detroit. Again, Columbus was squeezed out. And while one can argue that it was better off without a hub, since airline fares in the city were always more competitive, that was not how it was seen by the Chamber of Commerce, which identified the absence of direct service

13. Possibly the popularity of Ohio State football has also been a deterrent to someone trying to bring an NFL franchise to the city.

to more cities as a major problem in attracting inward investment, and particular corporate headquarters.

TABLE 1.5. Columbus urban area population as a percentage of Cincinnati and Cleveland urban area populations

CITY	1960	1970	1980	1990	2000	2010	2018*
Cincinnati	62.1	71.1	74.2	77.9	75.4	84.2	96.2
Cleveland	34.5	40.3	47.6	56.3	63.4	78.8	102.4

Note: Urban areas in the US are defined by the US Census Bureau as contiguous census block groups with a population density of at least 1,000/square miles (390/km^2) with any census block groups around this core having a density of at least 500/square miles (190/km^2).

*2018 estimates for standard metropolitan statistical areas.

The comparison with Indianapolis and Kansas City is again telling. While not in the middle of nowhere, the nearest city of any size to Kansas City is St. Louis, and it is 240 miles away. Indianapolis is almost as close to Cincinnati as is Columbus, but to the west, it is almost 250 miles before you reach St. Louis; Chicago is 165 miles to the northwest. Both Indianapolis and Kansas City have NFL and NBA franchises. Neither managed to attract an airline hub. But as the table shows, both had more airline passengers enplaned than Columbus, and Kansas City by a very significant margin: testimony to their larger hinterlands. The same story applies to Nashville.

Being a "younger" city, though, has had its advantages. The "older" cities have a legacy that can be an impediment to their further development, and cities like Columbus, with a later pedigree, have learned how to take advantage of it. The most obvious instance of this is that it has not had to deal with deindustrialization on the scale of most other cities in the region, and this has facilitated the transition to a postindustrial character. Columbus had and has industry and it has experienced plant closures, but their implications have been more confined to particular neighborhoods and without the citywide impact experienced elsewhere.

Less obvious but of huge importance for understanding its particularity, is that Columbus as a municipality has been able to expand through annexation. In the immediate postwar period, when suburbanization took off with a vengeance, annexation for cities like Cleveland, Chicago, Cincinnati, Boston, Pittsburgh, and many others, was precluded by the fact that they were already surrounded by independent suburbs: incorporated places, in other words, that could not be annexed by another city. As a result, suburbanization meant a drain on their tax bases as central city retailing was undercut by the emergence of suburban malls and as industries in search of areas in which to expand chose sites on the urban periphery; all meanwhile helped along by the property companies keen on developing those "new" real estate products that demand large areas of undeveloped land. Meanwhile, the older housing vacated in the central city was increasingly occupied by poor, relatively unskilled African Americans from the South and in some cases, Appalachians. This was the making of what would come to be known in the 1960s as the fiscal disparities problem: a central city—suburban difference in per capita property tax bases working to the advantage of most of the suburbs, and a demand for public spending that tended to place the central cities at a further disadvantage. But Columbus—like Indianapolis, Kansas City,[14] and Western cities—was relatively insulated from this. The major shopping malls have always been built within city limits, and as more ambitious models of the same, demanding ever bigger acreages, have emerged, so the city boundaries have expanded in tandem, lassoing the tax base, including the juicy sales taxes, and the expensive housing, and bringing the money back into the city. This is not simply a matter of historical advantage. Rather, it is one that the city, from the 1950s onwards, took advantage of, mainly through a quasi-monopoly of water and sewage disposal, demanding annexation in return for those services, or limits on the expansion of that vast majority of suburbs in the metro area that decided to purchase water and sewage disposal from it. Indeed, the continuing pursuit of annexation has been a major cornerstone of city policy and an equally important aspect of what makes it different from other cities of the old Manufacturing Belt, more like Western cities and therefore, "out of place." It is with an examination of the annexation policy that we start in the chapter to follow.

14. The city is hemmed in on the east and south by independent municipalities. Annexation is still possible to the north. However, the current boundaries of the city have changed very little since 1963.

CHAPTER 2

The Annexation Policy and Its Dilemmas

Introduction

The annexation policy of the city of Columbus is absolutely crucial to understanding development and its politics, both in the city itself and in the wider metropolitan area.[1] Not least it has meant that the city has been able to keep up, geographically speaking, with the onward advance of suburbanization, incorporating successive vintages of shopping center and major office developments. The city's population has continued to grow, and its income balance relative to the suburbs preserved. All in all, the city's tax revenues have expanded on a regular year-in, year-out basis, and this in turn has allowed it to maintain high bond ratings. This has been the case even while the resultant favorable interest rates would license expenditures on what would turn out to be dubious projects, most notably the trash-burning power plant. But the overall development patterns that it underwrote would turn out to be quite unequal in their social implications—good for developers and also for those with money, but if you're poor, you could be on the tail end. This would eventually factor into struggles over schools and feed back to change the annexation policy in some of its details. In par-

1. In this, and in subsequent chapters, I make copious use of citations from newspapers. Where the material is available on the web, I have not included the page number. Where it is *not* available on the web, the page number has been included.

ticular, the balance of forces between the city and the suburbs would change and not to the advantage of the former. Again, the wealthy and the developers would get the upper hand.

The initial move would be a decision on the part of the city to make its water and sewer services available only to those properties that were within the city boundaries—in effect, those that had been annexed. This would quickly be broadened out in the form of water and sewer contracts with independent suburbs, which, in exchange for cheaper services, allowed Columbus to preserve contact between its boundary and unincorporated land and so the prospect of further rounds of annexation. What made this all possible was that until quite late in its history, and in contrast to most other cities of the old Manufacturing Belt, Columbus was not hemmed in by independent municipalities. Annexation is only legally feasible where a city is contiguous with the land to be annexed, and Columbus, in the immediate postwar period, was in exactly that situation. It took advantage of it, and it has been of huge significance to the development of the area and its politics. But the consequences, the struggles around it, could not possibly in their concrete forms have been foreseen.

The Essential Elements

The annexation policy actually consisted of two quite independent elements, though the effectiveness of both was a result of an emerging city monopoly in the provision of water and sewage treatment. The curtain went up on the first of these in 1954. Henceforth, any property owner requesting water and sewage treatment from the city would first have to annex to it. Prior to that, the city had entered into agreements with the county to provide these services to certain designated areas. This had been the way in which the Chevrolet body plant (Fisher Body), later the site of Delphi and still later that of the casino, had got its water and sewerage provision when it opened in 1946. That sort of arrangement would now cease.

One initial problem encountered was the resistance of some of the suburban school districts. At that time, schools' annexation followed municipal or city annexation. This, however, created issues for some of the suburban school districts. Still relatively small, the transfer of some of their area to Columbus City School District threatened not only their tax base but also the number of pupils that they needed to remain viable—important at a time when enrollments in school districts like that of Worthington were modest, to say the least. The upshot would be pressure on the state to do something about it. Legislation was passed severing the link between schools and municipal annexation and making the schools' bit contingent on decisions of a new entity, the State Board of Education. Subsequent to city annexation, Columbus would now have to request schools' annexation, and it would not necessarily be automatic. Rather, rules were devised to determine what should be done, the most important of which was that there should be no so-called tax grabs. This meant that if, in the area to be annexed, the assessed property valuation per pupil was greater than that in the Columbus City School District, then the school's annexation bit would be disallowed. In brief, no Robin Hood-ism!

But there was an unintended consequence of rich significance. For, given that the areas in question typically had very sparse populations—why would they not, given that the initiative for annexation was coming, usually, from a developer—the property tax valuation per pupil was almost always higher in the suburban school district. This meant that from then on, the city of Columbus would grow, and as it grew, it would incorporate increasingly large parts of the suburban school districts, but they would not be transferred to Columbus city schools. Schools' annexation had now been uncoupled from city annexation, and this was storing up trouble for a future that could not have been anticipated.

But it meant that this particular roadblock to expanding the geographic area of Columbus had been cleared away. There would be others, though, and these would lead to the second aspect of the annexation policy. For the independent suburbs and villages also had aspirations to develop and to expand geographically for that purpose. A feature of the postwar period had been a massive diversion of resources away from wartime purposes and the release of pent-up consumer aspirations. Suburban development became the flavor of the day; the golden age of suburbanization was at hand, and local governments on the edge of urban areas, as well as the developers, wanted to take advantage of it. That included cities to the north of Columbus, including Upper Arlington, Hilliard, Dublin (then a village), Worthington, and Westerville. But the problem was sewage treatment. Sewage treatment plants needed expanding, and that was expensive. On the other hand, there was also a practice of emptying semi-treated, or even untreated, effluent into the rivers of the area. Since two of these rivers, the Scioto and the Olentangy, were drawn on for Columbus's drinking water, this attracted the attention of the state Board of Health, albeit nudged into action by the city of Columbus, which smelled, to use an ironic turn of phrase, pay dirt. The Board of Health wanted a solution, and the city of Columbus was happy to help.

Suburban governments wanted sewage treatment. Columbus would provide it and also water if it was needed. Given the economies of scale available in water and sewage treatment, it could provide them at a much lower cost than they could ever hope to achieve themselves, and without getting the state Board of Health in their hair. But there would be a quid pro quo crucial to the realization of Columbus's annexation ambitions. For the second component of the annexation policy would be the water-sewer, or simply sewer, contract. This would be with a contracting suburb and, crucially, it would specify the areas that the said suburb could serve with water and sewer provision courtesy of Columbus (figure 2.1). Obviously they could serve their existing jurisdictional area. Given that they had their own development ambitions, they would be allowed to serve, in the case of annexation to themselves, a contiguous area. But here was the rub: That area—the so-called expansion area—would be limited. What Columbus officials had in mind was preventing encirclement by the independent suburbs. Growth corridors had to be preserved. Columbus refused to be encircled; rather, it would do the encircling itself, and it did as it successively cut off Worthington and then Upper Arlington and Whitehall from unincorporated land that might otherwise have been annexed by them.

This could occur in devastating pincer movements redolent of military campaigns. One of the most notable was a single annexation that brought together a mere thirteen landowners to the east and north of Worthington[2] (see figure 2.2) in the late '60s in a request for annexation by the city. The protests from the Worthington side were bitter, but they could do nothing about it in law as the tracts of land in question were not in its expansion area. Bingo. And so it would happen elsewhere. What Columbus acquired in this way was more than just land; it was relatively empty land of the sort increasingly attractive to developers. A major feature of the postwar period was a succession of real estate development forms requiring seemingly ever larger areas of

2. Who smelled their own pay dirt as their combined area happened to coincide nicely with the planned route of what would be the northern freeway, part of the city's Outerbelt interstate.

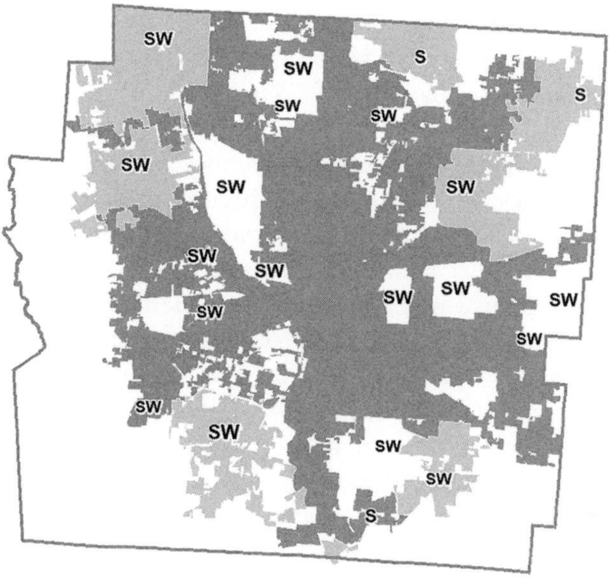

FIGURE 2.1. Water and sewer contracts between Columbus and independent suburbs, 1993. Map by Jamie Valdinger. *S* indicates a sewer contract and *W* a water contract.

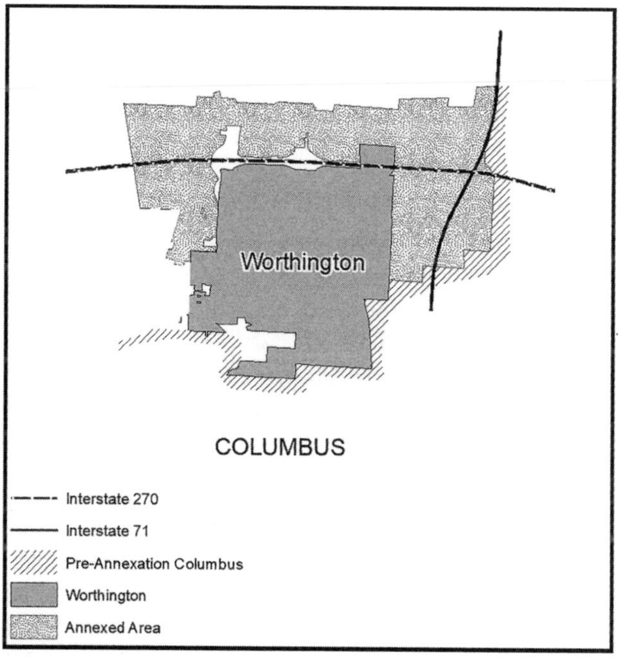

FIGURE 2.2. Blitzkrieg on the Northern Front: How the annexation policy worked to Columbus's advantage. Map by Jamie Valdinger.

contiguous land: land for shopping centers, for industrial and office parks, then for the new residential developments around golf courses and (typically artificially created) lakes, and ultimately for very large mixed-use developments, each designed to extract an increasing flow of rents. These required large areas of undeveloped land. Through its annexation policy, Columbus assured itself of a continuing stream of potential sites of the requisite magnitude. As a result, all the major regional shopping centers and then mixed-use developments like Polaris and Easton would lie within the boundaries of the city, providing it with the increasing property tax and sales tax revenues that would at the very least offset the losses as the city started to empty out from its center. From the standpoint of the city of Columbus, the annexation policy, in both of its components, worked, and often in complementary fashion. A water-sewer contract would be entered into with a suburb, along with an expansion area. The city would progressively annex through the growth corridors it had managed to secure through the way the expansion areas were designed. Brilliant! And the state had helped in all this by, first of all, clearing the way for the doubts of suburban school districts to be alleviated, and then bringing some pressure on northern suburbs to enter into sewer contracts. The story, though, would be far from over.

Successes

From some standpoints, the policy has been a major success, and certainly the envy of many of the big (central) cities of the Rustbelt. As the independent suburbs entered into contracts for the provision of water and sewer, Columbus became a quasi-monopoly supplier. Major developments just over the city boundary needed to annex to get water and sewer because there were no alternatives. Prior to the 1954 decision to insist on annexation in exchange for services, some major fish had got away, most notably the GM plant whose site would eventually be occupied by the casino. The casino developers would do their utmost to preserve the grandfathered status of the site, but Columbus insisted on snagging them, as we will see later in what was a highly questionable sequence of events.

Another recent, and less controversial, case has been the annexation of the Rickenbacker Air Industrial Park in the southern part of the county. This is a county project making use of a former US Air Force base for commercial development, including the creation of a multimodal hub. It has obvious tax revenue attractions but initially was separated from the city by a large swathe of private properties, which meant that the contiguity rule governing annexations would be hard to achieve without a lot of negotiation with the owners. So in 1991, the city allowed the county to tap into its water and sewer systems in return for allowing annexation once city boundaries reached it, which is what happened in 1995.

In other cases, like the major shopping centers at Tuttle Mall and Easton and the interlinked shopping centers at Sawmill Road, the land had already been annexed. This is not to mention the large areas of middle-class housing that have found themselves in the city as a result of the policy—all of which reflects back on the point made in the first chapter, about the way in which the city has been able to maintain a favorable revenue status and a bond rating that has permitted borrowing for public works at a relatively low interest rate.

To Annex? Or Not to Annex?

But despite the seeming success of the annexation policy, and something that many other central cities in the Northeast and Midwest would love to have available to them, the sailing has not always been smooth. For a start, there has been friction between the city and the townships that, as a result of annexation, stand to lose tax revenues. Annexation has brought peripheral development in its wake, which of course is the whole point, and as the city has had to provide the complementary infrastructure, this has set up tensions with older neighborhoods, which see themselves going without improved lighting, highway repairs, and the like. And while it is the city of Columbus that has done the annexing, not all in city government have been at one with it; there have been interdepartmental squabbles, notably between the public safety officials who get additional responsibilities but without the resources to carry them out, and those who push the glories of development, notably the Department of Development and the water and sewer people. Finally, the suburbs have contested certain aspects of a policy that has found them in a supplicant role in various ways; they pay more for water and sewer than those who live in Columbus itself and, most significantly, busing for racial balance in Columbus challenged their school districts, to put it mildly. These tensions have often overlapped and reinforced one another, and if anything, as the city has continued to expand, they have become more aggravated.

COLUMBUS AND THE TOWNSHIPS

The initiative for annexation to Columbus typically comes from developers. Townships stand to lose tax revenues. They also stand to lose control of the sort of development that occurs. A vivid example of what can be at stake played itself out in Plain Township in the mid- to late '70s. In 1974, the county had managed to mediate an agreement for the city to provide water and sewer to New Albany and Plain Township but without city annexation. Before that, people living there had relied on private wells and septic tanks. The proposal, though, was intensely contested by residents on the grounds of the costs that they would incur. This was not the only reason since the water and sewer lines were also seen as a Trojan horse for the developers, and there was good reason for their suspicions.[3] As the county proceeded to go ahead purchasing easements for the lines, there was talk of forestalling the imminent development by a proposal for New Albany, then a village, to annex the rest of the township. This was actually voted on and narrowly lost.[4]

Columbus has recently encountered other challenges. Pushing through its annexation goals has depended on its virtual monopoly in water and sewer provision and a state law that has tended to work in favor of the cities. As far as the first of these is concerned, a major threat emerged in the late '90s in the form of so-called alternate sewage

3. Opposition was quickly met with a vigorous riposte from Ben Hale, a development lawyer, who "represents about 15 individuals and development companies which own about 1,600 acres of Plain Township land, (and who) said 'the fighting isn't going to stop us' otherwise, he said, 'We will have to go to private systems . . . and we don't want private treatment plants.'" ("Improvements? No! Even at Half Price," *Columbus Dispatch,* February 16, 1975, p. B5). Angst among the locals got a further uptick with the news that the sewer line of thirty-six inches would be far more than sufficient to service current needs. The county engineer gave the game away when he noted, "We wanted to put in a sewer that will service the area, what it is now and might be later" ("Plain Township Sewer Line Dispute Heats Up Again," *Columbus Dispatch,* May 23, 1976, p. B5). So "might be later"? Read between the lines here.

4. Meanwhile, and conveniently, almost to the point of suspicion, a pollution issue had emerged at a school that put wind behind the county's sails and that of the developers.

disposal systems. These are sewage treatment plants designed for particular subdivisions. They typically spray treated wastewater on farm land, golf courses, parks, and other open space. Solid waste has to be removed and leftover water treated with ultraviolet light, chlorine, and other chemicals to remove contaminants. The Ohio Environmental Protection Agency (EPA) issued the first permit for such an alternative system in 1998. Subsequent to development, the county would take control of their operation. In other words: Who needed Columbus sewers and sewage disposal?[5]

So—surprise, surprise—this emerged as a serious issue between the county (commissioners and townships both) and Columbus, Columbus arguing for a centralized sewage system for the whole region, with itself as the provider, of course, and for a ban on spraying waste in Columbus metro area. The city was in a position of some power in this since under the federal Clean Water Act it was the designated agent for revising a 1974 sewage-facilities plan originally put together for the Ohio EPA.[6] The revised (Columbus) plan would rule out land application systems on grounds of health concerns,[7] the absence of supporting public facilities for stand-alone developments like wider highways and public safety, and sprawl. Given Columbus's record in all this, as we will see further, this sounds like a bad joke.[8] And in fact there was also a suspicion that a major concern was not so much sprawl or health but the large investment it had made in its sewage system, something

5. Water is much less of a problem: There are copious subterranean water resources in the county and treatment is far less costly than in the case of sewage.

6. How this position of advantage was achieved would make for some interesting research!

7. The problem supposedly was that some of the planned private sewer systems would be upstream of some of Columbus's drinking-water sources, though given that so are animal pasture lands, this seems a little disingenuous and even self-serving. See "Concerns Raised over Alternative Sewage Systems," *Columbus Dispatch,* October 23, 1999, p. 1B.

8. Developers, or at least some of them, were actually supportive of the alternate systems since they were cheaper, and the lobbying group Building Industries Association of Central Ohio also gave its blessing. See "Criticism Prompts State EPA to Revise County Sewer Plan," *Columbus Dispatch,* January 16, 2002, p. B3. I say "at least some of them" since I can hardly imagine something as big as the Columbus casino using a package plant to resist annexation as it would fall far short of its needs. In fact, as we will see later, its line of resistance was different: the threat to transport sewage by truck to a treatment plant in Marysville some twenty miles away.

for which it was able to gain support from the Ohio EPA.[9] So in a provisional resolution in May 2002, the Ohio EPA banned spray systems until new regulations were developed for them, but it allowed the continued use of small sewage plants that released treated water into streams.

All this, of course, reflected the fact that the township—township officials and many of their residents—had for a long time deeply resented the way in which territory was being transferred to Columbus, a feeling that was shared elsewhere in the state, where it was not necessarily big central cities like Columbus that were doing the annexing. In 1994 there had been an attempt to change the law governing the process, pushed by the Ohio Township Association and opposed by the municipalities, or at least those in a position to annex by virtue of contiguous unincorporated land. Among other provisions, the townships sought to inhibit the annexing of narrow corridors into outlying areas—such as those that Columbus had sought to create—by requiring that a city share a boundary with at least 10 percent of the perimeter of the territory to be annexed. This would have been relatively foolproof—certainly more so than the provision that in deciding on an annexation commissioners would have to consider "the good of the whole community." This particular initiative failed but the issue was back on the agenda in 2000, where, from a township viewpoint at least, it was able to bear some fruit. Under the previous set of rules, county commissioners had only to have the approval of a majority of the property owners in the area for which annexation was being requested. Now, in the new annexation law, enacted in 2001, they would have to consider the "general good" of land owners within a half-mile of the property to be annexed. There was also a provision for compensation of the township by the annexing city for lost tax revenues.[10]

9. As in a news release from the Ohio EPA's Public Interest Center, January 24, 2003, in which the EPA defends its water quality plan for central Ohio by acknowledging that "the plan recognizes and protects the extensive financial investment existing service providers have made in their wastewater treatment plants. To allow other providers to take customers away from these providers could threaten their financial stability and their ability to provide safe, affordable wastewater treatment to area residents." Indeed, but it also serves to preserve a monopoly.

10. This was on a sliding scale starting at 100 percent for taxes on industrial and commercial properties and 85 percent of lost residential and retail property tax revenues for the first three years and concluding in the eleventh and twelfth years at 27½ percent.

The matter of altering the balance of power over annexations between the cities and the townships was bitterly contested. The cities themselves, of course, were not the ones thus concerned. Rather, they were the mouthpiece for their developer friends organized under various banners like 'The Ohio Committee for Equitable Annexation' and a political action committee No on State Control of Property Rights, which pushed for a referendum on the eventually successful legislation. Crocodile tears were shed on what it would mean for the provision of housing for the poor and racial minorities, as if they cared. More serious was the supposed sanctity of private property rights, though only as a means of creating the conditions for the property and development companies to go on developing and extracting their rents. Meanwhile the *Dispatch* added its voice to the tumult, though without any acknowledgment of its own development interests. In opposing earlier, failed legislation it argued that while "the proponents of this bill, indeed, may want to establish a 'level playing field' between cities and townships, (but) to do so would be bad public policy,"[11] though this seemed to be contrary to the label adopted by the Ohio Committee for Equitable Annexation. As ever, as we will see, expedience rules.

But in fact it turned out to be a storm in a teacup. For four years later there was little evidence that annexation activity had slowed down.[12] The reason was that part of the new legislation that was supposed to protect residents from unwanted annexations also allowed expedited annexations. County commissioners *had* to rubber stamp requests that were smaller than five hundred acres, had the backing of all property owners, and where there were assurances that municipalities could provide essential services. This also stripped township officials and unannexed neighbors of powers to oppose. So what had been the original intent of the legislation? To throw a bone to the vast majority of township residents while protecting the rights of the few there who had large tracts of land that they wanted to see developed?

PERIPHERY VS. "THE NEIGHBORHOODS"

Significantly, the large sums of money that Columbus was willing to offer the developers of a major development on the far northeast side,

11. "Annexation Vexation," *Columbus Dispatch,* December 7, 2000, p. A10.

12. "Law Hasn't Slowed Annexations," *Columbus Dispatch,* January 16, 2005, p. C1.

Polaris, in order to induce them into annexation, generated some concern on city council.[13] The view was that diverting money to highways in that area when money was needed in the rest of the city was questionable policy. On the South Side, onetime center of heavy industry, and burdened by a sense of neglect by the city, the irritation was expressed by the president of the South Side Business and Industrial Association: "I'd like someone to care about the people for a change instead of the developers . . . We don't need any more shopping centers for the rich." This was followed by a suggestion that the money be used to improve health facilities on the South Side instead.[14]

Whether this was a turning point in how the annexation policy and its effects were imagined or not, a year later, in March 2001, it was given concrete expression by an announcement that the city was considering a blueprint for the geographic scope of development in the city, including where the suburbs should grow. By July, this had taken shape in the form of a map indicating an area in which development would be allowed to occur over the next twenty years, and significantly defined by a boundary. This was justified as enclosing the area the centralized sewer system was designed to serve. Growth was to be encouraged within the line and in areas with room for it and that were already annexed. This totally put the cat among the pigeons. Developers were happy to suck off Columbus utilities, but any indication that a blind faith in market forces might be challenged by a serious attempt at land-use planning quickly brought them squawking. Smith and Hale, the development attorneys, had already sounded the alarm by talking about the unpredictability of development, and how any limit to growth would simply push it in the direction of communities that were outside the water-sewer contract system, like Canal Winchester, Delaware, and Plain City.[15] Well, maybe Canal Winchester and its numerous attractions, but Delaware? And Plain City?

The *Dispatch* added its weight to the issue in an editorial entitled "Handle with Care" and the telling subtitle "Don't Let New City Laws Stifle Development." The general drift was that development of the Comprehensive Plan had relied too much on community groups and

13. "City Weighs Leap to Next County, Council Members See Pros, Cons to Annexing Development," *Columbus Dispatch,* April 18, 1990, p. 1E.

14. "Columbus Neighborhoods at Odds over Polaris," *Columbus Dispatch,* August 10, 1990, p. 6C.

15. "Smith and Hale: Growth Not Dependent on City," *Worthington Suburbia News,* June 19, 1991, p. 11A.

implying that they had a "narrow agenda . . . [that] would erect so many roadblocks to development that companies would look to the suburbs and other cities that are more accommodating." "It is the economy—not a planning official or body—that drives development," it opined, along with making other choice claims like "Communities mortgage their futures when dogmatic regulations are imposed on development over extended periods" and "Any changes in zoning and other regulations should not allow the interests of the few to take precedence over the needs of the many." The rhetoric is exquisite: "roadblocks," "dogmatic," and "mortgaging futures." The implication, of course, was that the *Dispatch*'s "agenda" was the very antithesis of "narrow" and that the "few" being referred to were certainly not the developers. No comment.

But what was pushing Columbus in this direction of growth limits were serious financial constraints: finding the money for parks, for expanding and upgrading erstwhile rural highways, and for new police and fire substations.[16] The city would retreat for a while, but the issue refused to go away and it came back, this time with a proposal that the developers, for obvious reasons, would find more to their taste. This would be mayor Michael Coleman's "Pay as we grow" or "The 21st Century Responsibility Growth Plan" (one weeps at the pomposity of it all). This, the product of a panel that included "a large contingent of developers" along with the Columbus Board of Realtors and the Building Industries Association of Central Ohio,[17] sidestepped the question of geographic limits to growth and concentrated on the public costs of new development wherever it might be.

The basic principle was that developers should shoulder more of the costs that had hitherto been pushed on to the public; the unasked question, of course, was exactly how much they would "shoulder." Quite how it would work became clearer in city plans for what was known as the Hayden Run corridor on the northwest side[18] and

16. Hence Clark, the Comprehensive Plan supervisor: "We have started to look at the costs of past growth and the numbers are mounting. . . . Even if we don't add another acre, the dollars needed to getting what we already have up to par are significant" ("Developers Differ on Columbus Growth Plan," *Business First of Greater Columbus,* July 15, 1991, p. 8).

17. "Mayoral Panel to Develop 30-Year Outline for Growth," *Columbus Dispatch,* February 19, 2004, p. C5.

18. "Development Plan Unveiled," *Columbus Dispatch,* May 27, 2004, p. A1.

burgeoning areas to the southeast of the city.[19] Developers would contribute to road improvements; those owning the new homes would pay a yearly fee added on to their property taxes to cover expanded city services police coverage, and tax increment financing districts would be put together to provide additional money for the highways. So now we knew. Developers were intent on shifting the costs.

This is interesting because it sheds additional light on a subject to be taken up at greater length in the book; this is the resistance of developers in the Columbus area to impact fees. In some parts of the US developers contribute to the public costs of development by paying what is called an impact fee: a fee levied on each house sold. This is common practice in Southern California, the Bay Area, and parts of the Northeast. But in the Columbus area, developers have dug in their heels. Their claim is that they would have to pass it on to the final buyer, as if they cared. But there are good reasons having to do with the quite extraordinary elasticity of housing supply in the Columbus area[20] that this would not be easy and that it would come out of their profits. And indeed in the case of "Pay as you grow," they seem to have been quite happy to push the cost on to the home buyer, albeit and importantly, in a form that would not give them serious sticker shock.

The big sleeper in the room when it comes to who pays the cost of new development located toward the edge of the city is the cost of an expanded water and sewer infrastructure. The water and sewer department, now the Department of Public Utilities, has always been rather defensive about this. Increases in water and sewer rates or new bond levies, both of which have been used to raise money for expansion, have been defended by claiming that the vast bulk of the money will go into upgrades of existing systems, some of which have been mandated by the federal government. A bond issue in 1975 to be retired by increases in rates is exemplary. Service Director Robert Parkinson had said in the February of that year[21] that "the projects would provide a base for expansion of the systems but added that items put in the package only for expansion purposes make up only a very small part of the package."[22] Furthermore, failure to keep pace with federal standards would mean the federal government would no longer pitch in to help

19. "Growth May Come with Added Fees," *Columbus Dispatch,* November 20, 2004, p. B1.

20. Saiz 2010, 1284.

21. "City Faces Selling Job," *Columbus Dispatch,* February 2, 1975, p. B3.

22. The figures mentioned (*Columbus Dispatch,* February 9, 1975) were 7.7 percent for new sewer lines and 5 percent for new water lines.

pay for the projects. That the defensiveness was justified was apparent in a challenge from Herbert Pfeifer, a Democratic candidate for mayor "who recently claimed most of the city's sewer and water revenues are going for expansion of a system that benefits only certain land speculators. He has said there is no need for increases in water and sewer rates if expansion is frozen. He said new customers currently do not have to pay for the new burden they put on the system."[23] His claims were rebuffed in short order, but they resurfaced again a year later, even while in the meantime the council had had the sense to increase hookup fees for new homes.

The council president of the time, M. Portman, "said the capacity charges are being increased to insure that developers will pay a fair share of the cost to expand city services."[24] But the issue remained. The city council tabled the proposed capital improvements budget for 1978–80: "Hammond [city councilor] said it appears several projects are scheduled to expand water and sewer services into undeveloped areas. 'We have enough trouble providing services. These projects would excite new development,' Hammond said."[25] The response from Service Director Robert Parkinson was that all the proposed projects have been promised and are in areas already annexed to the city. Promised? By whom? On what authority? And most significantly, *to whom*?

Interestingly, this was also at a time when the federal EPA was beginning to flex its muscles, emboldened by the anti-sprawl rhetoric of Carter's presidency. Environmental impact statements for expansion projects expecting federal financial support were now necessary and could incite federal recommendations that would meet local hostility from a city water and sewer department bent on expansion. According to a report in the *Dispatch* for March 31, 1977, Public Service Director Parkinson denounced federal recommendations as "ill-conceived attempts to curb population sprawl." He argued that developers would simply introduce package sewage plants and septic tanks while warning of court proceedings. A year later a *Dispatch* editorial would, not surprisingly for a paper that has always prided itself on its boosterism, support his position.[26] Carter would fail in his bid for a second term

23. "Water, Sewer Rate Fight Brewing," *Columbus Dispatch,* May 18, 1975, p. C6.

24. "Sewer, Water Rates to Jump Jan 1," *Columbus Dispatch,* September 9, 1975, p. A1.

25. "Planning Study Produces Battle," *Columbus Dispatch,* July 20, 1976, p. B1.

26. "Something is ominously amiss when a federal agency's demands are so oppressive that a major city's growth is jeopardized and its officials ready to throw in the towel" ("Federal EPA Clamp Gripping Columbus," *Columbus Dispatch,* April

and the sprawl issue would lose its urgency, but the question of water and sewer expansion has been taken up by others, notably the Sierra Club, whose response to Mayor Coleman's call for "pay as we grow" in 2003 was a counter-call for developers to pay the full cost of extending sewer lines—and quite right, too.

CITY GOVERNMENT AT ODDS

In 1981 there were several house fires in northeast Columbus in a condominium development known as Little Turtle. The damage amounted to almost $1.5 million (or over $4 million in today's money). Its significance here is that it drew attention to a seeming inability of Columbus to keep up with the pace of annexation and subsequent development, as it then was; the nearest fire station was six miles away. The city had been aware of the underprovision. But given scarce resources, the city's Fire Service had decided to build a fire station in 1978 in the northwest at Smokey Row, since it would serve more people.[27] These issues were underlined five years later, in 1986, following a fire in The Glen on the west-northwest side. Residents of the area were reported to be concerned about their distance from the nearest fire station: ten miles, as it turned out.[28] This would shed light on the degree to which Columbus was able to take advantage—or not—of help from township fire services. In that instance, the closest fire station was in Norwich Township, but there was no mutual aid agreement since Columbus had no fire station in the area.[29]

4, 1978, p. B2). "Throw in the towel"? This is something the city will *never* do; the developers won't let them.

27. "Motif of Condominiums Contributes to Fire Woes," *Columbus Dispatch,* February 22, 1981, p. B1; "Little Turtle Plods on Despite Fire Perils," *Columbus Dispatch,* October 25, 1981, p. B1.

28. "The Glen Residents Worry about Fire Response Time," *Columbus Dispatch,* May 30, 1986, p. 3D.

29. "In answer to a request from Columbus Mayor Dana G. Rinehart for an automatic response agreement in The Glen, Norwich trustees wrote, 'We cannot in good conscience take fire and emergency protection from our residents . . . we feel this is on the shoulders of the county commissioners who just keep giving township land away without regard for the consequences" —though in practice, most townships did have mutual aid agreements at that time ("Growth Strains Rescue Services," *Neighborhood News Northwest,* June 25, 1986, p. 1).

It was more than a matter of the fire service. There were also issues about highways and police, ones that the county commissioners were more than willing to brandish in the city's face in its attempt to gain some advantage over annexation questions. There was a shot across the bow in 1984 about their hesitation to agree to annexation of land that in their view Columbus could only imperfectly service; reference was made to police, fire, water, and sewer. A major highway issue was that Columbus, rather than widening highways to accommodate development, was anticipating the problem by leaving them out of its annexation requests. Very crafty. This led to a decision on the part of the county commissioners that in considering annexation requests, roads would in future have to be in the package.[30]

But police and fire service were also a concern, and this would later cause rifts in the city administration. It started in 1999 with the Columbus police chief going public in his objections to five new annexation requests. The police, he claimed, were unable to cope with the added responsibilities.[31] The response of the city trade and development director was that "the chief is unilaterally trying to reverse an annexation policy that has helped the city prosper and grow." The city safety director added to the chorus of disapproval by calling the police chief's position "asinine" (!) and claiming that the chief was in effect "holding the city's growth hostage."[32] These retorts were utter red herrings, in fact remarkable only for their impertinence, for nothing was said about how the police might be given the resources that would allay the concerns. After all, it was not the case that the police chief was trying to halt annexation and growth; he just wanted to see some proportion in the way the city dealt with its subsequent responsibilities. In fact, rather than confront the issues, the city safety director, to whom the police chief was responsible, relieved him of his authority to decide whether or not the police could provide services to areas where property owners were requesting annexation.[33] So there. There is a limit to what you can take when growth and keeping the developers happy is at stake.

---

30. "Annexation Package Must Include Roads," *Worthington Suburbia News,* December 18, 1985, p. 31A.

31. "Police Chief Opposes 5 New Annexation Bids," *Columbus Dispatch,* September 13, 1999, p. 1A.

32. Ibid.

33. "Chief Loses Annexation Authority," *Columbus Dispatch,* September 25, 1999, p. 1D.

The Difference That Busing Made, or: Who Actually Won?

Until the late '70s, everything seemed to work. Columbus grew and maintained its fiscal health. The independent suburbs got cheaper water and sewage treatment than they could have imagined on their own and they managed to grow some too. It seemed like the annexation policy was a win-win all round. But all of a sudden things changed and the search was on for a new institutional fix. This one would be the "Win-Win" that the Columbus media now refer to, though who won aside from the more affluent suburban residents (a bit); the Columbus Public Utility Department (a bit more), which continued to provide water and sewage treatment to a widening area; and the developers (hugely) is far from clear.

The watershed came in the wake of the civil rights movement and efforts to undo racial segregation, including in the schools. Columbus City School District had been the object of a desegregation suit in the 1970s and the judge found for the plaintiffs; this was in 1977. It was not a matter of *de jure* racial segregation, as in the South; rather, it was *de facto*—as residential patterns in the district changed, so the school district had been altering the boundaries of school catchment areas so as to maintain the status quo ante: the racial one, that is.[34] It had to be undone, it would be undone, and in 1979 the undoing commenced through a policy of busing students in order to achieve racial balance among the schools in the district.

This would be the moment when Columbus experienced what the pundits of the time referred to as "white flight," even though it was scarcely just white, for there was a significant African American component too, and even though "flight" is a bit of a misnomer—people moving to Columbus simply looked at what was happening or took their cue from a friendly realtor, and decided accordingly. And it was the parents, either actual or would-be, who were the ones most affected. For in the real estate market it was the values of houses with three or more bedrooms that tended to diverge between Columbus

34. What had actually brought the matter to a boil was a school building program dating back to 1972. African American board members—the fact that they were there was progress of a sort—saw it as an opportunity to build on sites that would result in multiracial enrollments, but this was opposed by the white board members. African American opposition in Columbus would subsequently be shown to lack the teeth it had elsewhere in the country, but in this instance it was seriously underestimated.

school district and its suburban counterparts—down in the former and up in the suburbs.[35]

As Jonas has shown, there had been some anticipatory movement.[36] The 3,415 transfers out of the district in 1972–73 increased to almost 12,000 just before the busing decision was handed down. Then between 1977 and 1980, the district lost 15,500 white students. Accordingly, and given the fact that most of the "flight" was in fact white, the racial composition of enrolments in Columbus public schools started to be increasingly African American: From a share of total enrolment of just over one third in 1977, by 1991 it was over half. To some degree, it seemed, what had been racial segregation of schools within the city school district was being superseded by racial segregation between the suburban districts on the one hand and Columbus city schools on the other. Racial segregation had not been undone; it had simply changed its geographic shape. The Columbus Board of Education was unhappy about it. It was more than just a matter of principle; in fact, that may have been the least of the worries for them. Rather, the school district was losing those parents who, by virtue of their higher incomes, were most likely to vote for the district's operating levies. And it is here that the Columbus annexation policy reenters the story.

For among the areas that tended to be favored by the movement of anxious parents were those that were in suburban school districts but also in the City of Columbus: the discrepant areas that resulted from the decoupling of schools and city annexation dating back to 1955 and the refusal of the state Board of Education to play Robin Hood (figure 2.3). They had the city services since they had been annexed to the city, and they had what was now seen as the advantage of not being subject to court-ordered busing and all the horrors believed to follow in its wake. And the developers were making hay of it. For them it was a total bonanza, a once-in-a-lifetime opportunity, and they were not about to let go of it, as we will see.

So starting in 1980, the future of the discrepant areas was on the school board's agenda. It would be, for them, a matter of retroactive annexation: The areas that, in accordance with the state Board of Education's rulings, had stayed in suburban school districts, even while the City of Columbus annexed them, had to be brought into the city school district. Result: Uproar.

35. Gill 1983.

36. Jonas 1998.

The areas in question were significant from multiple points of view (see table 2.1). There were issues of tax revenues and pupil enrolments, both. The effects were very uneven. Some of the suburban school districts were far more affected than others: the very middle-class to affluent areas of Dublin, Westerville, and Worthington and the somewhat less well-to-do Southwest City schools and Groveport-Madison. Citizen groups emerged virtually everywhere. School boards also got involved as a result of anxieties about loss of revenues and downsizing. Local teacher unions, or education associations as they are called, were anxious about the teacher transfer and disruption of career lines that reversion to Columbus city schools might entail. The result was a loose coalition, the Coalition for Local Administration of School Systems (CLASS),[37] which brought together school boards, parents, and school superintendents from suburban districts across the county. It was also, though, an issue for developers, and from more than one angle.

TABLE 2.1. Suburban school district property and pupils in the city of Columbus

SCHOOL DISTRICT	COLUMBUS PROPERTY VALUE IN $ MILLIONS	PERCENTAGE OF PROPERTY IN COLUMBUS	AREA IN SQUARE MILES	STUDENTS FROM COLUMBUS	PERCENTAGE OF COLUMBUS STUDENTS
Dublin	124.0	34.3	7.4	2,023	48.8
Gahanna–Jefferson*	105.0	35.8	2.5	320	6.2
Groveport–Madison*	70.0	34.0	14.0	2,877	48.9
Hamilton	8.0	9.3	3.8	381	18.7
Hilliard*	145.0	43.6	12.0	915	22.1
Olentangy	0.03	0.02	n/a	0	0
Pickerington	1.5	1.2	1.9	0	0
Plain	2.3	4.9	2.6	0	0
Reynoldsburg	15.0	8.2	0.64	233	5.3
Southwestern	213.0	29.7	n/a	4,200	26.5
Upper Arlington	0.91	0.2	0.48	2	0
Westerville	128.0	26.1	n/a	2,779	25.9
Worthington*	271.0	44.3	10.0	2,856	37.3
Total	1.1 billion			16,586	

Source: Ohio Department of Education, November 1985.

*Active anti-annexation citizens' group.

37. From some viewpoints, at least, a provocative, even malicious, acronym. On the other hand, that it was indeed about class rather than race is probably correct.

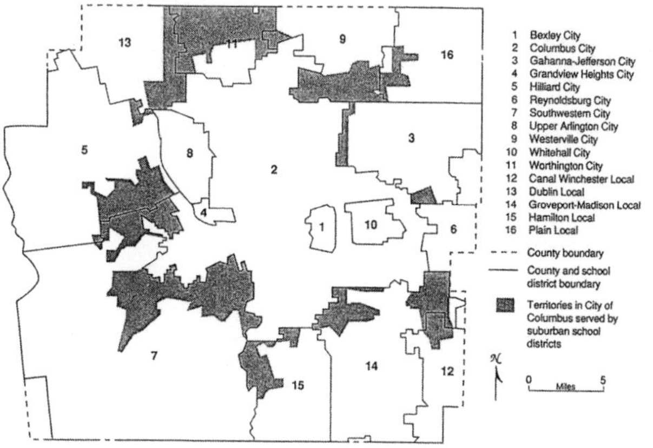

FIGURE 2.3. School districts in Franklin County, 1989. Source: Ohio Department of Education.

The threat to the developers took two distinct forms, the first one of which was easily seen off. This was the collateral damage for long-time resident homeowners in the school districts affected. Their children were not the ones who were at risk, for typically they did not live in the discrepant areas. Rather, they were in those parts of the school district within municipal boundaries. The problem for them was that the sudden inflow of those who saw themselves as refugees from busing meant that new schools had to be built, and that would be at everyone's expense. This would include those who no longer had children in schools, for there was a demographic difference from the predominantly younger population with children moving into the area. And the growth *was* sudden and major in magnitude (see table 2.2). Growth was especially rapid in an arc of suburban school districts stretching from Hilliard in the west, through Dublin, and Worthington to Westerville in the northeast. Dublin was massively affected—a growth in enrolments of almost 350 percent over a fourteen-year period between 1977 and 1991—while Hilliard and Worthington also recorded big gains.

There were tensions to the point at which those who were insulated from the threat of retroactive annexation since they were not in Columbus, wanted respective suburban school districts to accept Columbus's demands for it and be rid of the problem posed by the newcomers. This did not happen. What did happen, though, was an attempt to shift the cost of the new facilities on to the new residents through impact fees.[38]

38. Jonas 1998.

TABLE 2.2. Changes in school enrollment in Franklin County school districts, 1977–1991 (%)

SCHOOL DISTRICT	% CHANGE
Bexley	–3
Canal Winchester	–12
Columbus	–28
Dublin Local	+344
Gahanna–Jefferson	+4
Grandview Heights	–9
Groveport–Madison	–10
Hamilton Local	–23
Hilliard	+73
Plain Local	–32
Reynoldsburg	–4
Southwestern	–2
Upper Arlington	–27
Westerville	+24
Whitehall	–16
Worthington	+60

Source: Data from the Franklin County Board of Education.

Some mitigation might have come about through requiring developers to donate land in exchange for zoning approvals. This had been the practice in Worthington. But the city had no control over practice in the discrepant areas since this was a matter for the city of Columbus and it refused to make the same demands.[39] There were similar problems in Dublin.[40]

Attention then turned to the state and a request from officials in the impacted school districts to allow them to levy impact fees. According to Ohio Senate Bill 303, school districts where enrolment growth per year was at least 3 percent per annum for two consecutive years would have been empowered to ask voters to approve fees per new house constructed that could be dedicated to the construction of new schools and renovations of older ones.[41] Hilliard, Dublin, and Worthington would all have qualified. But this threatened the development industry

39. *Worthington Suburbia News,* February 18, 1987, p. 1; *Worthington Suburbia News,* October 17, 1987, p. 1.

40. *Neighborhood News Northwest,* July 9, 1986, p. 11.

41. *Worthington Suburbia News,* March 18, 1992, p. 8.

that was making a lot of money out of home construction and under their pressure, including that of the Ohio Home Builders Association, the initiative failed.[42]

The major action, though, was elsewhere. The request for impact fees in a sense accepted existing school boundaries. The demands had started before the resolution of that issue and continued after. For the developers, the drying up of demand altogether for housing in the suburban school districts should retroactive annexation occur was the big issue. In short, they risked getting caught with their proverbial pants down. The trend had been set: a continuing growth of demand for housing, most notably in the discrepant areas. Land had been purchased with a view to more house building; in other cases, the development process was further along. What had seemed like a pretty safe bet risked turning into a bust. The Building Industry Association of Central Ohio (the BIA), the home developers' lobby, moved into pole position, sponsoring a bill in the Ohio House that would have frozen existing school boundaries and so prevented retroactive annexation. Financial support was then directed by the BIA and the Columbus Board of Realtors to those legislators supporting the bill.

They would not get their total way. There was a standoff. The Columbus Board of Education had its supporters, or more accurately those who saw that its resolve needed some stiffening. One of the strategies of the opposition to retroactive annexation had been to make it dependent on a vote of the people in the areas affected. Very obvious: how to act democratic but to achieve goals entirely to the contrary. But bills were introduced to that effect in the Ohio House by Republican representatives of the areas affected only to be beaten back by a mix of African American groups, city schools teacher unions, and Democratic representatives not just in Columbus but elsewhere in the state.[43] There was also something called the Apple Alliance, which would also feature later on in the saga. From 1985 on, it kept up the pressure on the Columbus school board not to give way on the issue, arguing that to do so would deprive the poor and minority students of educational resources.[44] They had some support from the Columbus educational association, from Black politicians in Columbus and civic associations representing African American neighborhoods.[45] A particular target

42. "Schools Embrace Housing Fee," *Columbus Dispatch*, April 19, 1992, p. B1.

43. Cox and Jonas 1993, 22.

44. *Columbus Citizen Journal*, October 5, 1985, p. 10.

45. Cox and Jonas 1993, 22.

of their criticism were the developers and realtors who were taking advantage of the situation, not least in their advertising strategies that emphasized what school district a particular house for sale was located in: not immoral, just amoral.[46]

So there could be no movement between two seemingly implacable forces: on the one hand, a coalition of "refugees" from Columbus city schools, suburban school boards who were evidently less swayed by concerns about funding new schools than they were about losing pupils and tax base, teachers unions there, and above all the developers, and on the other, African American pressure groups of various sorts, the Columbus teachers union, the Apple Alliance, and the Columbus school board. State legislation had failed, so what to do? Answer: Call in those who define themselves as experts in what is antiseptically called "conflict resolution." The search for a so-called Win-Win solution was on.

The result would be a compromise of sorts. There were three major critical points:

1. There would be no retroactive annexation of suburban school district property already annexed by the City of Columbus. So the "refugees" were safe, and so too were the investments of the property developers. The refugees had powerful allies who, one would guess, made all the difference.
2. Tax revenues from future nonresidential uses like those from shopping centers would be split fifty-fifty between the respective suburban school district and Columbus school district.
3. In future, schools and municipal annexation would proceed, as they had prior to 1955, in tandem. They had been uncoupled and the consequences had not been pretty. Now they would be recoupled. But as we will see, the devil would be in the detail.

46. Meanwhile the *Dispatch* put in its oar, trying to stifle debate about the issue. In an editorial pompously entitled "Board Acts Wisely" for February 22, 1985, it praised the Board of Education for rejecting the request of one of its members for a public hearing on the possible annexation by the school district of the areas about which feelings had been so intense. The reasoning for support of the Board's position was the entirely spurious one that with the desegregation process underway, the Board had its hands full anyway. And with respect to the board member in question, "We know of no organized support among those who elected him to represent them on Columbus school issues." Nice touch.

Airbrushing History Out

Some thirty years later, though, the schools annexation issue and the subsequent agreement seem to be passing into history. This is because a significant part of the Win-Win agreement dating back to 1986 has been scotched. The part at issue was that of the payments the suburban school districts had to make to the city school district. Just *exactly* what was at stake, and who thought that they might benefit from it, remains unclear. Taking the lead in the challenge was a state representative, Mike Duffey, who claimed, when inserting an amendment in the state 2015 budget bill that would have given the suburban districts a veto over Columbus annexing any of their land, to be "acting on behalf of Dublin school officials who are fed up with Win-Win." Reincorporation into the Columbus school district remained a possibility if the agreement could not be reached on renewal every sixth year. With the veto, the balance of power would shift, which would allow them to refuse to make any payments thereafter.[47] This was something that Duffey recognized and seemed to approve: "If Columbus no longer had that leverage, Duffey said, Dublin would no longer pay."[48] On the other hand, there would later be reference to the anxieties of residents in the areas affected, though over the twenty-nine years since the agreement had been in effect, this had received absolutely no publicity at all.[49] So just what was going on was and remains a mystery.

The response of Dan Good, the Columbus schools superintendent, to this news was significant: "We have to be cautious that we honor the

---

47. "Local School Districts 'Win-Win' Debate May Rekindle," *Columbus Dispatch,* May 17, 2015.

48. Ibid. This was a position from which he later retreated, in the context of legislation to freeze the school district boundaries in question that was introduced into the Ohio House in 2016: "The point isn't to kill the accord, said Rep. Mike Duffey, R-Worthington; it's to give suburban districts some negotiating leverage" ("Two Central Ohio Lawmakers' Proposal Could End School's Win-Win Agreement," *Columbus Dispatch,* May 9, 2016).

49. "The renewal of Win-Win every six years struck fear into homeowners whose neighborhoods are in the city of Columbus because of long-ago annexation. Their children attended the suburban schools, and property values and taxes are affected by the school district. Rumors would swirl until Columbus schools and the nine districts that paid to keep Columbus schools from taking their territory renewed Win-Win, which was first signed in 1986" ("Hilliard, South-Western, Westerville Districts Amending Win-Win Deals with Columbus Schools," *Columbus Dispatch,* August 16, 2016). Really? If so, these concerns got absolutely no publicity. So one still has to wonder where this issue came from and why.

history [of Win-Win] as well and what it represented."[50] The amount of money at stake was not that much. In fact, in 2016 the money that Columbus City School District received was pretty derisory—no more than half a percent of its general fund—which is interesting in itself, testifying to the shallowness of the bargain that had been struck back in 1986. But it had symbolic value: in his words, "honoring" a history. The background to the agreement had been, after all, a standoff about the rectification of racial inequalities. Those who took flight from busing by moving to what I called earlier the discrepant areas—in suburban school districts but in the city of Columbus—were on morally questionable ground. Furthermore, the suburban school districts themselves had connived in this by building additional school space to accommodate their children and making everyone in their districts, regardless of whether or not they were in the discrepant areas, pay the bill. They were, in short, more than happy to go along with this morally dubious enterprise and raise no objection. The fact is, they benefited from people trying to escape policies designed to rectify decades of wrongs heaped on the most vulnerable sections of the population. It is well established that children from less privileged backgrounds—African American or white—benefit from social mix. But that was out of the question. The affluent can congratulate themselves by saying that they earned their privilege, but in a world where wealth and cultural advantage is conveyed down the generations, this is little more than self-serving fantasy.

History evidently had been forgotten, something clearly on display in an editorial about rescinding this aspect of Win-Win in the *Columbus Dispatch*:

> Their predicament results from the city of Columbus having annexed, over decades, unincorporated areas of the county historically served by suburban school districts. In the mid-1980s, rumors flew that Columbus schools planned to take over those same areas. The Win-Win agreement called a truce: Suburban schools agreed to give Columbus schools a cut of commercial and industrial taxes from new construction within their areas of the city of Columbus. The payments total $5 million a year. The deal has soured as suburban schools grapple with tighter funding and poorer, needier students.[51]

50. Ibid.
51. "Win-Win Pact Lacks Teeth," *Columbus Dispatch, May 22, 2016.*

Significantly, the editorial states that for the suburban districts, "their predicament results from the city of Columbus having annexed, over decades, unincorporated areas of the county historically served by suburban school districts." This makes the city sound like an aggressor. The "predicament," though, is one in which suburban school districts at the time connived and from which the various cities whose populations they served gained immensely. As I outlined earlier, the suburbs got cheaper water and sewage disposal, and the school districts got to keep their areas intact, along with the students that went with them. Most significantly, the editorial made absolutely no mention of racial desegregation, busing, and how it would be that that would lead to a series of events culminating in Win-Win, even while it is the indispensable ingredient in the whole story. It changed everything. In the current arguments about the future of Win-Win, this history needed to be remembered and not airbrushed out. But it was forgotten, conveniently or not, and the payments will lapse after 2021.

How the Annexation Policy Continues to Work and for Whom

The annexation policy is typically touted as a "success" for the city of Columbus. Of a peer group of twelve major Midwestern cities (table 2.3), only four have managed to increase in population, and Columbus heads that particular league. It has the lowest unemployment rate of any, testifying in part to its occupational diversity with a good representation of the more secure technical, professional, and managerial positions. It has the second highest rate of retail sales per capita: All four regional shopping centers[52] are within the city boundaries, providing a healthy stream of sales taxes. All these considerations have allowed Columbus to avoid the fiscal problems common in major cities elsewhere in the Rustbelt. This in turn has been parlayed into favorable bond ratings, which allow the city to raise money for capital works on very favorable terms. How this connects to the annexation policy is indicated by the final column of the table, the proportion of the county area assumed by the central city providing a crude measure.

52. From west, through north, to east, Tuttle, Polaris, Easton, and Eastland.

TABLE 2.3. Local economic conditions and bond ratings for Midwestern cities

CITY	POPULATION GROWTH 1990–2000	UNEMPLOYMENT RATE 2000	RETAIL SALES PER CAPITA 1997	S&P BOND RATING 2005*	CITY AREA AS PERCENTAGE OF COUNTY AREA
Chicago	+4.0	5.6	4944	AA–	24.0
Cincinnati	–9.1	5.1	8871	AA+	19.1
Cleveland	–5.4	8.7	4751	A	17.0
Columbus	+11.8	2.8	12852	AAA	38.9
Dayton	–8.9	6.5	6072	**	12.1
Detroit	–7.5	6.6	3269	BBB	22.6
Indianapolis	+6.9	3.0	13751	AAA	91.0
Louisville	–5.0	3.7	8061	AA+	16.1
Milwaukee	–5.0	6.7	5785	AA	39.7
Minneapolis	+3.9	3.2	6588	AAA	9.9
Pittsburgh	–9.6	4.1	7922	BBB–	7.7
St Louis	–12.2	6.6	6856	A–	12.2

*Fourth quarter; order of rating categories: AAA, AA, A, BBB, BB, B; the addition of a plus or minus sign indicates relative standing within those major rating categories.

**Not available

Seemingly successful, therefore, but closer scrutiny suggests that the success has been felt rather unevenly. Tables such as this one highlight geographic difference, but there are other ways of looking at it. And while Columbus as a whole might seem to have benefited, within the city, indeed within the whole metropolitan area, there have been winners and losers. The big winners have been the developers and, to some degree, the land owners. The former buy land on the urban periphery for their typically land-extensive developments and then request annexation with a view to getting the water and sewer that will allow them to move ahead. And the city has been a willing participant in this game, sometimes offering big financial sweeteners in order to hook the fish. But exactly where the tax revenues gained for the city go has to be a bit of a mystery. Evidently it is only with a considerable time lag that it goes into the additional highway improvements, and police and fire stations to service the new areas. Part of the problem is the willingness of the city to offer tax abatements to new developments,[53] supposedly

53. According to a report by the District of Columbia's Office of Revenue Research, in 2014 Columbus had the highest property tax burden of any city in the country: $3.57 for every $100 in home value, though part of the reason for this is that

on the grounds that without them the development will go elsewhere, though exactly where in the metro area is hard to fathom given the stranglehold that the city has over water and sewer availability and the different politics that play out in the independent suburbs.

This is different because by virtue of their smaller size, citizen groups and initiatives can make it harder for the developers. Exclusive suburbs tend to remain exactly that: exclusive. This is partly on fiscal grounds but also something pushed by neighborhood organizations in order to protect the property values of their members. And they have weapons. Under Ohio law, rezoning ordinances can be repealed. What it takes is a petition with a number of names equivalent to 10 percent of the number of people voting in the local government jurisdiction in question at the last gubernatorial election. In a city with a population of, say, 20,000, that is not that difficult to do; the logistics of coming up with the necessary number of names is not that challenging. And given the geographic size of the jurisdiction in question, more people are likely to see themselves affected by the issue—more people than in a large area like that covered by the city of Columbus. There have been referenda around local issues in Columbus, and on at least one occasion, they met with success for the neighborhood in question, but both referenda and success are much less common.[54] So many developers, except residential developers in pursuit of the sort of the elevated rents they can gain from locating in an exclusive suburb, like New Albany, prefer the city: just easier to deal with. But nevertheless generosity in tax breaks continues.

The other big winner has been the Columbus Department of Public Utilities, but not necessarily without a struggle. As the city expands, so too do its revenues from tap-in fees, and then from user fees. So it expands its infrastructure of sewage treatment plants, water treatment facilities, reservoirs, and well fields to cope with the demand. But here

---

home values tend to be relatively low in the city. See "Top ten cities with the highest tax rates." USA Today, February 17, 2014. Available at http://www.usatoday.com/story/money/personalfinance/2014/02/16/top-10-cities-with-highest-tax-rates/5513981/ (last accessed 10/25/20).

54. This was the Glen Echo ravine case in 1978. The plan was to fill in part of a ravine adjacent to Clintonville to make way for a supermarket, restaurant, and shops. Rezoning from residential was required and was granted by the city in January of the following year. There were objections from local residents on environmental and traffic grounds. A petition for a referendum to overturn the rezoning went to the ballot in June of 1978 and was overturned on the necessarily citywide vote by a margin of almost two to one.

is the catch: In these expensive investments, the cost of which will only be recouped over a long period of time, it has to anticipate demand, and it knows it can be wrong; bad things can happen, as we will see later. The result is that it will come down on whatever side is going to opt for Columbus water and sewer and others be damned.

This is not to chastise Columbus and the developers. They use the hand that has been dealt them, and it is not that much different from other cities in the US. For regardless of the ability of cities to annex or not, all metro areas are characterized by an extraordinary local government fragmentation of powers and responsibilities. The responsibility bit is the need to find the money for local highways, public safety, city parks, libraries, and community centers. The power bit is the ability to annex and to rezone land. No wonder, therefore, that the developers become expert at being friends with local officials, elected and otherwise, and that cities engage in annexation struggles with others.

Nevertheless, from the standpoint of the city of Columbus, and referring back to the table comparing the city with Midwestern peers, the annexation policy has to be regarded a success. The city has managed to control its immediate area to its benefit. It has been able to take control of annexation activity and continued to expand to the advantage of its tax revenues and the bond ratings that help it to keep on expanding still more. Its success in the immediate geographic area, though, has not been matched by its ability to impose itself on the wider region or even the country as a whole. For a city of its size, Columbus is strangely lacking in those indicators that would allow it to boast of being a "major league city." In the next chapter, I turn to how that is apparent, why it is, and how the city has tried to counter the card that it has been dealt.

CHAPTER 3

Fighting the Image and Trying to Catch Up

FOR THE LONGEST TIME, it seems, Columbus has had an image problem. According to one critic reviewing a book on the city: "The city's main feature is its featurelessness, blandness its principal flavor. . . . Not even its mediocrity recommends it as a sort of social common denominator; the city is so average that it resembles nothing. Not even Indianapolis is so utterly devoid of idiosyncrasies,"[1] which all sounds pretty devastating. And there are lots more quotations that could have been used. Things have changed slightly. Columbus now has a major league professional sports franchise, even if it is other than the NFL or MLB. But compared to the Denvers, the Tampas, the Nashvilles, even the Portlands or Salt Lake Cities of this world, people not living in Columbus wonder why they would even want to visit. Aside from the fact that the city lacks natural attractions, everything seems rather "minor league." This can put Columbus at a serious competitive disadvantage. Columbus's bid in 1990–91 for a 450-employee operations center that the brokerage firm Salomon Brothers was relocating from New York is exemplary. Salomon Brothers was planning to relocate over one hundred key workers at considerable expense, and retaining

1. David Steigerwald, review of Gregory S. Jacobs's 1998 *Getting Around Brown: Desegregation, Development, and the Columbus Public Schools,* H-Urban, H-Net Reviews, February 1999.

those workers was an important priority.[2] The—eventually successful—competition was Tampa, Florida. As the then mayor, Dana Rinehart, ruefully commented: "We cannot out-civic-arena them, we cannot out-major-league them, and we cannot out-ocean them. That's just the way it is. Columbus has to fight twice as hard."[3] So for a city of its size, Columbus is neither attractive to more highly skilled workers, nor very visible. Aside from the way it is dogged by the "Columbus, Ohio" tag, it is known for things more likely to raise eyebrows.

The most notable of these is college sport. Remember the movie *Goodbye, Columbus*? Columbus is home to The Ohio State University—don't forget the upper-case "T"—and most notable of all, to the Ohio Buckeyes, a football team that has won the national championship on more than one occasion, most recently in the 2014–15 season.[4] Aside from the way its sport success has been a distraction and a very popular one too locally, the university has also been a problem in developing the infrastructure for a national visibility in professional sports, as we will see.[5] Alas, the football team has been pandered to by the local media, most prominently of all by the *Columbus Dispatch*: Where else in a city of close to 800,000 people is the headline of the local newspaper going to blare forth about a university team's

2. "Salomon Picks Sunny Tampa," *Columbus Dispatch,* February 20, 1991, p. 1G.

3. This is a more general problem for the city. Ohio State University (OSU) would almost certainly be somewhere else in the rankings, other than its rather middling position, if it were on one of the coasts; it just makes faculty recruitment that much harder, and as a former faculty member called on to try to generate interest, I speak with some experience of this.

4. "Ask CEOs nationwide about Columbus' image and most of them draw a blank. But ask them where the Ohio State University football team plays and—no surprise—it's 'Columbus.' In its second survey of chief executives both here and across the country, the Greater Columbus chamber of commerce found the city still has an image problem. Sixty-four percent of national CEOs said they had no top-of-mind image of Columbus" ("City Image Still Draws Blanks, Survey Finds," *Columbus Dispatch,* November 24, 1998). Admittedly, this quote is almost twenty years old, but my guess is the distraction of OSU football is still a problem, even after the arrival of NHL and MLS franchises.

5. Though in 1987, a major league franchise had not seemed out of the question. Interest was shown by the then St. Louis Cardinals of the National Football League. The owner, not getting his way for the sort of new domed stadium that he wanted St. Louis County to build, was looking for a new location ("Cardinals Owner Looks over City, OSU," *Columbus Dispatch,* December 2, 1987, p. 1A). Ohio Stadium would serve an interim purpose while the domed stadium was being constructed. From the start, it was admitted that Columbus was a long shot and, indeed, nine days later it was all over ("Columbus Cards Not in the Cards," *Columbus Dispatch,* December 11, 1987, p. 1A).

Buckeye Fever

And it is not just the *Dispatch* that grovels before "the team." The media in general bow and scrape. Where else in the country, on the evening prior to a college game, do the local newscasters don varsity garb to present the news? And where else is Sunday morning newspaper delivery delayed because the football team had an evening game the night before and the reports are not yet in? Things might—just might—have been different. The major watershed came in 1962. The university football team won the Big Ten championship and was invited to play in the Rose Bowl. But at that time, university faculty councils had to agree. At Ohio State, there had long been anxieties about college sports encroaching on the university's academic mission, and the council rejected the invitation by a vote of 28 to 25. All hell broke loose. Students marched on the Statehouse and there was minor rioting on campus, but, and most heinous of all, the *Columbus Dispatch* poured fuel on the fire by publishing in its pages the names and addresses of all those voting against, along with the amount of university travel that they had engaged in and the money that paid for it. This would never happen again because the rules would be changed so that the faculty council would not get the chance to express its concern. And despite the fact that Columbus now has a major league ice hockey franchise, a second-tier baseball farm team, and a soccer team in the MLS, enthusiasm for the university football team continues at little less than fever pitch. As Odenkirk remarked, "In 1961, not counting the Buckeyes, Columbus was home to one professional franchise, a Triple A baseball team. In 2007 Columbus supports three major professional sport franchises. This increase in number of professional teams in Columbus has had little impact, financial or otherwise, upon the athletic program at Ohio State. The Buckeyes are the number one show in Columbus. The frenzy and insanity associated with collegiate football, and especially at Ohio State, has intensified over the last forty-five years."[1]

1. Odenkirk, J. 2007. "The Eighth Wonder of the World: Ohio State University's Rejection of a Rose Bowl Bid in 1961." *Journal of Sport History* 34(3): 389–85. Quote from p. 394.

latest success, or will the sports pages be filled with anxious whisperings about who the team might recruit, who eluded them, and so on? (See "Buckeye Fever.") And after all, these are just kids, just out of high school.[6]

6. The search for national visibility continues. The most recent marker is the decision to rename the airport, formerly Port Columbus International, the John Glenn Columbus International Airport. Well, maybe, and assuming that John Glenn is a native son—a stretch since he is from Wapokeneta, almost ninety miles away—it certainly beats renaming it after that more authentic one, Curtis "Nuke-'Em" LeMay.

While the college town image has been a problem in attracting the attention of those who locate the corporate headquarters and choose convention sites—as in, "Why would we want to go there?"—it is far from being the only issue and in fact may not be that crucial: What, after all, is the image of Charlotte, North Carolina, or Austin, Texas, both peer group cities and more successful along certain dimensions? For there is also the question of "How would we get there, even if we wanted to?" As discussed in chapter 1, Columbus has also had national, not to mention international, accessibility issues. The Chamber of Commerce has long agonized over the relative weakness of connections to major US cities, particularly those on the West Coast. Columbus now has direct service to Los Angeles and service to San Francisco and Seattle started, but it has been a struggle.[7] And unlike cities that are in the same rough population bracket, like Charlotte, Austin, Indianapolis, and, not so long ago, Nashville, it lacks any service to Western Europe and, most cherished of all, London. At one time the hope was that the airport would become a hub for a major airline and that this would provide the direct services so longed for. The consolation prize for failure was relatively cheap airline tickets as, in the absence of a hub, numerous airlines meant more price competition. Consolidation of airlines and subsequent reduction in the number of hubs that they operate, including their abandonment of local rivals Cincinnati and Cleveland, means that hub status is now rarely discussed; the decisions of the airlines about adding or subtracting flights or even serving the city at all are still anxiously monitored, but a hub has become just too remote a possibility. There was a time when it was a serious focus of attention and, of course, it was connected to the question of Columbus as a site for conventions as well as its ability to attract corporate headquarters.

Longing for a Hub

Prior to the late '70s, the language of "hub-and-spoke" would have been foreign to the American commercial airline industry. Something called the Civil Aeronautics Board, or CAB, regulated airline fares. As

But why name it after anybody unless to underline your provinciality? Los Angeles doesn't need it, San Francisco and Denver don't, and nor do Dallas-Fort Worth or Atlanta. And who remembers O'Hare or La Guardia? They have become as much part of the accepted language as Xeroxing and Googling. But John Glenn?

7. And still no service to Portland or San Diego.

a result, competition was minimal and restricted to the service that an airline could offer. It was also difficult for airlines, and that included new ones, to enter new markets. After 1978 and the Airline Deregulation Act, this would change drastically. Airlines would now be free to set their own fares. But "freedom" was hardly the appropriate word. For the problem for them then was how to establish some control over fares rather than face undercutting from rivals and a mutual cannibalization of the market. One of the solutions hit on was a reorganization of airline routing. Without any evident coordination, airlines decided that the best approach would be to try to establish a monopoly of flights at a few airports: This would be the hub bit. Traffic would then be concentrated at those points by creating a spoke-like pattern with smaller, surrounding airports at the end of the spokes, and once at the hub, it would be sorted according to long-distance connections to—hopefully—another hub of the same airline.

Nice work if you can get it, and from numerous standpoints, and not just that of the airlines. For local growth promoters recognized that hub status would enhance a city's accessibility and its attractiveness for businesses in a number of different ways. Corporate headquarters prefer hub cities since they facilitate access to the numerous places where they have or do business. It is also an important adjunct of a city's convention business and therefore of its hotels.[8] It can be a big earner for a city's airport: more gate fees, and the through-flow of passengers changing planes irrigating the concourse businesses and hence the rents that they can afford.

But among Ohio cities, Columbus got left out. It was surrounded by airline hubs at other major cities—Delta at Cincinnati, Northwest at Detroit, Continental at Cleveland, Allegheny (later to become US Air) at Pittsburgh; even smaller Dayton was a hub for Piedmont Airlines (later absorbed by Allegheny) and Emery Air Freight. Just why it got left out is not entirely clear. Historically it was not so attractive as Cincinnati and Cleveland since over thirty years ago the local market was smaller: a consequence of Columbus's latecomer status. It was also a matter of spacing. Once Continental had chosen Cleveland and Delta Cincinnati, the likelihood of an airline choosing Columbus was

---

8. Just how important has been underlined recently by the fallout from loss of hub status on the part of other Ohio cities, notably Cincinnati and Dayton. Chiquita abandoned Cincinnati in favor of Charlotte, a hub for American airlines; Dayton, once a hub for the now defunct Piedmont and then Allegheny Airlines lost National Cash Register to Atlanta. In both cases, airline service was cited as a major reason for the move.

quite low since it would be encroaching on the hinterlands of those other hubs and intensifying the competitive pressures to which the new hub would be subject. Columbus became a center, but a center for feeder routes to hub cities like Atlanta, Chicago, Cincinnati, Cleveland, Detroit, and Pittsburgh.

So from the early '80s on, anxiety set in in Columbus development circles. Criticism of airline service on the part of larger businesses was an ongoing issue, a repeated focus of attention for the *Dispatch*. A report in the paper July 19, 1990, laid out some of the salient facts:

Columbus was holding up the rest of the league, and its peers were ahead by very, very considerable margins; Dayton had almost four times as many nonstop destinations (see table 3.1)!

TABLE 3.1. Comparative airline statistics for Columbus and some peer cities, 1990

CITY	METRO POPULATION IN '000,000	HUB	NONSTOP DESTINATIONS	TOTAL DAILY DEPARTURES	OVERSEAS FLIGHTS
Columbus	1.3	No	24	130	0
Cincinnati	1.4	Delta	73	370	Frankfurt, London, Paris
Dayton	0.95	USAir	88	225	0
Cleveland	1.8	Continental USAir	61	494	0
Indianapolis	1.2	USAir	44	194	0
Charlotte	1.1	USAir	96	466	Frankfurt, London

Source: "Air Race Leaves Business Grounded," *Columbus Dispatch*, July 15, 1990, p. 1G. (with permission of the *Columbus Dispatch*)

What to do? Hopes had been raised by the idea of a minihub—something halfway between a hub and relegation to feeder status. The initial attempt failed; later there would be America West, but it would last barely ten years. In May 1987, TWA—remember them?—announced that they were considering establishing a mini-hub at Columbus. The prox`posal was to add eighty flights a day: a significant 60 percent boost of total flights out of the airport. This was followed five months later by an informal agreement among city and county officials to offer TWA $50 million in incentives in addition to a terminal expansion costing $21.5 million: $2 million per year from Columbus and $3 million from the county for ten years. Less than a year later, hopes were dashed when TWA announced that it had postponed a decision indefinitely.

The story did not end there. Dreams were seemingly realized some three years later when America West established a mini-hub at the airport as part of an expansion to the east away from its existing hubs in Phoenix and Las Vegas. The idea certainly had something going for it. America West would channel passengers from smaller airports in the northeast through Columbus, avoiding the competition of hub cities in the wider area, and on their way to Phoenix and Las Vegas and possibly beyond. Alas, it got off to a less than auspicious start, particularly for an airline still in bankruptcy proceedings, low ridership resulting in the withdrawal of six flights and postponement of achieving the goal of sixty daily departures in toto to the end of the year.[9] The fact that existing airlines at Port Columbus matched America West's fares in an effort to retain passengers did not help either. The competition of US Airways was a particular problem as America West's spokes to the east were to points already served. The overlap was a serious difficulty.[10]

It would, however, be another ten years before it was all over, as the airline rode the boom of the Clinton years. But in February 2003 and subsequent to, first, the dot-com bust and then 9/11, came the announcement that America West would eliminate its mini-hub and cut its destinations to just two, eliminating all but four of its forty-nine daily departures: almost as drastic as it comes, in other words. The mini-hub experiment had ultimately been a failure, even while America West had become the largest carrier at the airport. According to the *Wall Street Journal,* Columbus had always been the weakest of the airline's three hubs, accounting for just 7 percent of annual revenue but reflecting a much larger percentage of total losses.[11]

In retrospect, the failure to land a hub might not have been such a bad thing after all. In the absence of a hub, there was greater competition among airlines, with the result that Columbus benefited from much lower airfares than hub cities, including Cincinnati, which, as a Delta hub, was one of the most notoriously expensive cities to fly out of. The absence of a hub airline also made the city more attractive to the low-cost airlines, which otherwise feared devastating competition

---

9. "Airline's Plan for Local Hub Stalled at Gate," *Columbus Dispatch,* September 19, 1992.

10. "America West Airlines Rebounds: Carrier Faces Uncertain Future in Columbus," *Columbus Dispatch,* December 12, 1993, p. H1.

11. "America West to Shut Hub in Attempt to Staunch Losses," *Wall Street Journal,* February 11, 2003, p. D4.

as the hub airline defended its turf. So Columbus was an early beneficiary of the rise of Southwest, which provided some of the point-to-point service that the local boosters had craved.[12] Likewise, with airline consolidation in the years after 2000, airlines would also reduce the number of hubs, and this meant closure. A very early victim of this was Dayton, but St. Louis, Cincinnati, Cleveland, Memphis, and Pittsburgh all followed, resulting in quite dramatic reductions in flights and unused capacity, sometimes capacity with considerable remaining debt.

But having said all that, airline connections remain a serious problem.[13] As table 3.2 demonstrates, when compared with a peer group, Columbus does not fare well for an urban area of its size. Austin is barely larger, but has over 50 percent more flights, including a direct flight to London. So in an age when major hubs at Pittsburgh, Cincinnati, and Cleveland have disappeared, Columbus apparently still underperforms.

TABLE 3.2. Comparative airline connections for Columbus and a peer group of urban areas

	SMSA POPULATION 2018 (EST.)	DIRECT AIRLINE DESTINATIONS 2019
Austin	2.17m	63
Cincinnati	2.19m	53
Cleveland	2.06m	54
Columbus	**2.11m**	**41**
Indianapolis	2.05m	50
Kansas City	2.14m	54
Pittsburgh	2.32m	59

12. The other "low-cost" airline venture that bears mention here is that of Skybus. This was more than just low-cost; it was *ultra* low-cost. Funded by local investors, including Huntington Bank, Nationwide, and Wolfe Enterprises (then owner of the *Dispatch*), and some developers, it entered the market at an unfortunate time: Dramatic oil price increases intervened along with the recession ignited by the subprime crisis. For a brief while—just less than a year and starting in 2007—it seemed to hold some promise, but its collapse came very quickly.

13. The perception that airline service is distinctly minor league seems to be widespread. A recent article in the *New York Times* on the fate of the airport at Memphis, where downsizing, in the wake of the closure of the old Northwest hub, has been dramatic, opines that it is now "a lesser passenger magnet these days than Omaha or Columbus, Ohio." Aside from the "Ohio" tagline, Omaha? ("The Trouble with the Memphis Airport: No Crowds," *New York Times,* May 23, 2018).

Building a Convention Center

Since 1999, Columbus has had a halfway competitive convention center. It originally opened in 1993, but there was a major expansion from 212,000 to 512,000 square feet in 2001, and according to one source, in terms of size it is now ranked eleventh in the country:[14] quite a turnaround, in other words. The emergence of the adjacent Arena District and then the Short North just a step away has also helped mitigate the absence of after-hours activities for conventioneers that was long lamented. Even so, the city is missing from a list of the top twenty-five convention centers put together by the Travel Industry Association of America (TIA), the National Business Travel Association (NBTA), and the Institute of Business Travel Management,[15] suggesting that long-term problems of airline service and image continue to dog it. And to get even to where it is, it has been a long and hard road.

The story began in 1971, when Columbus voters approved a $6 million bond issue to buy land and build a convention center, but land costs consumed all the money.[16] The additional financing was a windfall released by the resolution of a legal dispute with the Battelle Memorial Institute, a private research organization in the city. Its founder, Gordon Battelle, had specified that the Institute had to make donations of a certain amount to charities, and this had not occurred. Whether or not a convention center amounted to a "charity" was questionable, but nevertheless in 1974, in resolution of the issue, the Institute agreed to put up the money for construction. A five-story structure duly emerged, to be dubbed the Ohio Center, but it was quickly determined that the exhibit hall was too small. From then on it was all uphill. In both 1986 and 1987, issues were presented to the voters requesting money for a more appropriately sized convention center: Both failed. Only in 1989 would the funding be put together, and then for a scaled-down project that would not be financed by the voter, but

14. "Which US convention center is biggest?" *The Beat,* April 30, 2012. Available at http://www.comicsbeat.com/which-us-convention-center-is-biggest/ (last accessed 10/25/20).

15. *MeetingSource.com* October 20, 2020. Available at http://www.meetingsource.com/convention_centers.htm.

16. An ironic but common situation. The city, through its public expenditures, makes land within its limits more attractive. That ups the value for the lucky owner, who is then not about to share his or her luck with his or her benefactor.

in a sense externalized to a nonvoting public through hotel and motel taxes.

The first attempt to gain funding was highly ambitious. This was the so-called New World Center. The idea was to kill two birds with one stone. In 1978 and then in 1981, there had been proposals to fund an arena seating 22,000 people with an increase in the city property tax, and both had been defeated and by hefty margins.[17] But optimism sprang eternal. So the proposal in 1986 was for a 300,000-square-foot convention center and a 65,000-seat arena, despite the fact that much smaller arenas had already been rejected, to be funded by a countywide 0.5 percent increase in the sales tax to be levied over a ten-year period.[18] It got business endorsements, but the big story was the opposition. Some of this was fairly minor: anxieties about parking from gentrifying areas in the vicinity, notably in Italian and Victorian Villages. There were also union anxieties. The management of the Ohio Center had stymied organization efforts, and the local AFL-CIO wanted assurances in the form of a neutrality pact that this was not going to be repeated, given the fact that the same management would take over the New World Center.

What made the headlines, though, was more city-, even countywide. This was the group going under the name Citizens for Private Development, led by one Richard Sheir. The argument in brief was that the proposal was a matter of welfare for the well-to-do—"a handful of wealthy hotel and restaurant owners"[19]—so why shouldn't they fund it themselves: a question that would be repeated throughout subsequent campaigns to stiff the taxpayer for convention centers and

17. By 65 to 35 percent in 1978 and then, to drive home the message, a whopping 79 to 21 percent for the 1981 proposal.

18. The logic was laid out by John Christie, president of the Columbus Area Chamber of Commerce, who pointed out that "voters in the mid-1970s rejected two efforts by the late educator Jack Gibbs to pass a property tax to build a 22,000-seat arena. 'Ten years ago, Franklin County voters didn't have the guts to approve the tax,' he said. 'In the meantime, similar or larger facilities were built in Indianapolis, Cleveland, Minneapolis and Cincinnati. Everything concerning sports that you watch on television comes from facilities built in the last 10 years. We need the New World Center to catch up on the entertainment and convention dollars'" ("Suburban Leaders Back World Center," *Columbus Dispatch*, April 18, 1986, p. 1A). He has his details wrong: The earlier efforts were in 1978 and 1981, and they were city rather than county issues; in fact, the decision to make the New World Center a county issue was probably strategic, as it meant diluting the impact on the voter.

19. "Chamber Plans Big Push for Center Tax Approval," *Columbus Dispatch*, March 9, 1986, p. 7D.

arenas.[20] And furthermore, to promote it, the protagonists were indulging in projections that did not hold water.[21] So, and not surprisingly, the issue went down to defeat.

Undaunted, and remarkably, six months later, the convention center advocates came back with a new proposal, this time for what would be called the Columbus Arena and Convention Center Complex. Some lessons had clearly been learned. The arena had been downsized from 65,000 to 20,000 seats, indicating that landing an NFL franchise was no longer on the agenda. Appropriately, the bill had also gone down: a 0.25 percent sales tax increase for eight years, as opposed to the previous 0.5 percent over ten years. Another reason for this was that this time around, for three years the cost would be subsidized by the motel-hotel tax, even while this would mean a transfer of that money from other public uses. Aside from African American concerns about jobs and contracts, the opposition was familiar: the same anxieties about parking and traffic in the area and drawing on public money, and Citizens for Private Development were once more to the fore. Union concerns about a neutrality pact were voiced once again. And the result would be the same: rejection at the polls, and by a slightly larger margin.[22]

So it was back to the drawing board. Again, lessons had been learned—it was just that in the past, they had not been learned fast

20. This was a concern that would be deepened with the news of two prominent advocates of the center, John Kessler and Dan Galbreath, planning hotels, though Kessler said that his hotel would be built regardless. Kessler's plan called for a hotel plus a parking garage just to the south of the center site, along with Nationwide as a partner: "Downtown will get hotel, garage," *Columbus Dispatch,* April 8, 1986, p. 2D. But the idea of welfare for the rich continued to echo in letters to the editor.

21. A hard-hitting statement from Richard Sheir of the Citizens for Private Development in a Con/Pro Forum in the *Dispatch* ("Should Voters OK Center-COTA Issue?," April 18, 1986, p. 13A), raised issues first of the highly speculative nature of the project: "We are being asked to invest our sales tax in a dream that, if we are lucky, might steal convention business from neighboring cities that we presume are going to play dead. This is a high-stakes gamble. If we lose, the result will be deficits on the 65,000-seat facility that will dwarf those of the trash burning power plant." He then attacked the jobs claims: "The so-called 6,000 jobs to be gained is nothing but a misleading campaign slogan. None of the studies have ever pointed to 6,000 permanent jobs for Franklin County residents. The jobs that will result are 2,000 construction and construction-related jobs. . . . The remaining jobs are the part-time, no-benefits jobs for $4 an hour and under in restaurants and hotels. These aren't the kinds of jobs that you build families on."

22. The figures were 56 percent to 44 percent, as opposed to 53 percent to 47 percent for the New World Center.

enough. This time they would get it right—almost—and they would have a convention center. It would be drastically scaled down. And it would not, directly at least, be at the cost of the county taxpayer. There would be no arena—that would be postponed into the future, and an interesting future it would turn out to be. Instead of the 300,000 square feet previously planned, it would be 212,000 square feet. And the finance would be through a 4 percent tax on motels and hotels, a tax that, given their willingness to accept it, suggests that they anticipated being able to pass it on to the customer. It would also, though, give them—the Greater Columbus Hotel and Motel Association, that is—the leverage to request a transfer of funds from the 6 percent bed tax that they paid to the Greater Columbus Convention and Visitors Bureau. This was not uncontroversial, since those monies were already spoken for. So how to make up the difference other than a transfer of money from elsewhere in the city budget? In other words, taxation through the back door and setting an interesting precedent for the future.[23] But Columbus would finally have a convention center worthy of the name.

Spinning Wheels

Meanwhile there was some spinning of wheels. The view was that one road to the much desired enhanced visibility would come from a series of major events. The so-called Son of Heaven Chinese art collection and then the AmeriFlora exposition were hyped to the nth degree but turned out to be damp squibs. The vast crowds anticipated just did not show up. And prior to Son of Heaven and AmeriFlora, there had been the Columbus Ford Dealers 500, a street car race that ran for four consecutive years, from 1986 on, before foundering on a mix of poor attendances and the refusal of the city council to help bail the organizers out of their debts. But simply because of their lengthy runs, Son of

23. Sally Bloomfield, chair of the Franklin County Convention Facilities Authority, raised the possible need for an operating subsidy to make good the transfer of funds from the Greater Columbus Convention and Visitors Bureau in no uncertain terms: "A shameless trial balloon has been floated. Hotel and motel executives have started whining that the center won't be big enough, given the amount of money to build it. To get the money they want an increase in the share of the hotel and motel tax to be set aside to build the center. That share of the tax would drain money from the general fund, the arts and human services. That means you and I, the voters, would either have to do without some services or—guess what?" ("A Back-Door Convention Center Tax?" *Worthington Suburbia News,* February 22, 1989).

Heaven and AmeriFlora had stoked more optimism among the local ruling class; both were supposed to help put Columbus on the map as well as boosting the local hospitality industries.

Son of Heaven was an exhibition of twenty-six centuries of Chinese art, held in 1989, that was promoted by a Seattle organization going under the same name, but it left uproar in its wake. Whether or not attendance figures were overestimated by the planners, it ran at a loss. Revenue amounted to $7.7 million but fell short of expenses by $1.67 million. In the original planning, shortfalls were to be covered by $1 million from the state and the remainder from the city, but amounts that were pledged originally as "guarantees" amidst suspicions, first, that exhibition organizers knew ahead of time that the guarantees would have to be called on,[24] and second, that insiders had been advantaged in appointments and the granting of contracts.[25] It left a bad taste in the mouth.

AmeriFlora was a floral exhibition held in 1992 and designed to celebrate the five-hundred-year centenary of Columbus's voyage to the Americas. From the start, it was dogged by controversy. Corporate sponsors failed to pony up to fund the event, which meant that the original plans had to be scaled down. To save money, the organizers rejected the idea of investing money in rehabbing an existing city wasteland like the old state penitentiary site and opted instead to hold it in an existing park, without realizing the significance of the park for the social life of the African Americans who lived in its vicinity. And to cap it all off, attendance fell some 1.8 million visitors short of the anticipated 4 million.

In short, none of these different attempts to put Columbus on the national map can be regarded as massive successes.[26] There were attendance problems and problems in raising the necessary money. Finance would also be a stumbling block, at least initially, in bringing the long-sought-after "major league" franchise to the city.

---

24. "City Jumps into 'Son of Heaven' Controversy," *Columbus Dispatch,* January 30, 1990, p. 1B; "State Knew 'Son' Loss Was Likely, Firm Says," *Columbus Dispatch,* February 1, 1990, p. 3C.

25. "Locally, the uproar is about the public debt. It's about whether that debt is legitimate and about who got paid what while racking it up. It's about hints of cronyism and nepotism, about at least an appearance of club-like management, with insiders deciding staff, salary, contracts and loans to each others' mutual benefit. Finally, it's about exaggerated claims, exaggerated promises and a wildly exaggerated economic report" (Margaret Newkirk, "Why There's an Outcry over Heaven's Debt," *Worthington Suburbia News,* February 7, 1990, p. 4).

26. See also Hunker 2000, 161.

A National Franchise, but Major League? And Privately Funded?[27]

DOUBTS, BUT THE DEVELOPERS TAKE A GAMBLE

What was still missing, of course, was a sports arena and a major league franchise to use it. Four times, twice in connection with convention center plans, increases in taxation to fund an indoor arena had been voted down. The problem for the boosters would not go away. As an article in *Business First of Greater Columbus* pointed out, with the exception of the Norfolk–Virginia Beach–Newport News metropolitan area area, Columbus was the largest city in the US without a major league sports franchise; nine smaller ones, including Charlotte, North Carolina, Indianapolis, Salt Lake, Portland, and Orlando had one—but not Columbus.[28] It also lacked a multipurpose arena to house concerts or major entertainment events. But how to fund it, that was the question.

Already by 1988, what was emerging was the idea of an arena to be shared with Ohio State University. It was more than the advantage of joint funding. It was also the doubt attending building an arena without a franchise; no necessary happy ending to this particular field of dreams. At least with the Ohio State basketball team playing there, there would be some revenue to defray the expenses. But significantly, the university had raised a warning signal about siting.[29] It was certainly interested in a new basketball arena since its own facility, St. Johns Arena, was judged outdated: Not least, it lacked sky boxes—an important consideration in the context of the ongoing corporatization of universities. Furthermore, jointly funding an arena with Columbus was OK, but from the university standpoint it had to be on campus, and campus was some two to three miles north of downtown.

---

27. For a different slant on this saga, more from the position of whether, from the development standpoint, major league franchises are worth the candle, see Curry, Schwirian, and Woldoff 2004.

28. *Business First,* October 30, 1989, p. 6.

29. It has also been suggested that the university did not want competition for a market in spectator sports that it had come to dominate in Columbus. In hindsight, Gee, then president of the university, said, "Any university president would honestly admit that the notion of a sports franchise coming in, you aren't going to greet with enthusiasm" ("A Long Time Coming," *Columbus Dispatch,* August 15, 2011).

By 1994, the split had widened. The university was clearly bent on building its own facility. The university had lobbied state legislators for help in building a new sports arena on campus. It asked for $15 million at the same time as the city asked for $1 million in planning money. The fact that the university had made its request was seen by the then mayor, Greg Lashutka, as a breach of trust. The assumption had been that the university president, the flamboyant Gordon Gee, had promised not to seek construction funds for a new arena unless the mayor's capital budget request of the state was met in full. Worse was to follow. In May of 1994, the university got its $15 million and the city, with its very modest request, got nothing: a symbolic slap in the face, even while the grant to the university came with a request that the city and university negotiate on a site.

The university was now off and running. Aside from the $15 million from the state, it would fund the arena with tax-free bonds worth $35 million and with donations from alumni and other supporters that were projected to amount to $25 million. The city's reply was a decision in September of that year to go ahead with its own arena. The university, in a peace-making move, also made some concessions: It would not put skyboxes in its new arena, and it would not compete for major concerts. For various reasons, neither of these commitments would endure. A warning from a Peat Marwick report,[30] that "a scenario where two arenas are built, if both compete for the same commercial market, would be financially disastrous for both facilities," would come eventually to have some validity. For two arenas would indeed be built.

The city's plan was, again, nothing if not ambitious: not just a downtown arena to seat 20,000 but also a 30,000-seat soccer stadium, all to be funded by a 0.5 percent sales tax for three years, $57.5 million from private sources, and $41.5 million in state grants. The site would be to the northwest of the central business district and include the former site of the state penitentiary, which was where the soccer stadium was supposed to go. The plan was that the arena would house an ice hockey franchise for which, by that time, Columbus was in the running. The principal owner of the teams likely to play there would be Lamar Hunt's Hunt Sports Group. Hunt already owned the franchise for a major league soccer team, the Columbus Crew, which had been

---

30. "Arena Would Need Pro-Sports Team to Succeed," *Columbus Dispatch,* June 10, 1994, p. 1A.

playing in the Ohio stadium on the Ohio State campus, but that had always been an interim arrangement.

From the start, there was anxiety about competition between two arenas. Gordon Gee, who had signed on as cochair of the referendum campaign, claimed that there was indeed room for two.[31] But in the same article, there was a word of warning from Jules Belkin, president of Cleveland-based show promoter Belkin Productions: "Belkin said the key in Columbus would be for OSU to stick to its pledge of primarily filling the Schottenstein Center with university events and booking only a handful of shows." This would be prophetic, as would be the claim from an opposition group: VAST (Voters Against Stadium Taxes), which raised the issue of not just the competition between the two arenas but a broader competitive field including the Vets Memorial, Battelle Hall at the Greater Columbus Convention Center and the Coliseum, and the Celeste Center on the state fairgrounds.

Additional opposition arguments were redolent of the earlier campaigns against convention center proposals. There were similar concerns about traffic issues in gentrifying neighborhoods to the immediate north, including Victorian Village and Harrison West. VAST talked about the danger of cost overruns and the regressivity of the sales tax. African American groups expressed concerns about deteriorating neighborhoods. The pro- campaign did not seem to be going well. A month prior to the vote in May of 1997, only 38 percent of those in an opinion poll expressed support.

So how to turn it around? In an attempt to gain the support of African American organizations, the city upped the ante. If the issue should pass, it would spend $12.1 million on neighborhood improvements. This promise, though, would drown the campaign in a sea of farce. For whatever effect it might have had on public opinion, it was thwarted in spectacular fashion by a letter to the editor of the *Dispatch* four days before the vote, from the wife of Gordon Gee, co-chair of the group promoting the downtown arena, Constance Bumgarner Gee. Arguing that the $12.1 million promise was a bribe, she not only shed doubt on the morality of the city's offer, she also undermined the work of her own husband as co-chair:

> Dangling carrots in front of citizens to garner votes is unworthy of our esteemed and well-meaning City council. The encouragement of

31. "Gee: Room for 2 Arenas," *Columbus Dispatch,* March 16, 1997, p. 1A.

public discourse and development of well-considered alternatives are more responsible courses of action for community leaders concerned about Downtown development and the needs and interests of the people of Franklin County.[32]

Goodness knows what was going on in the marital bed chamber at that time, but as a spoke in the wheel it must be without peer.

In the event, and like the numerous convention center proposals before it, the arena one would be rebuffed at the polls, and decisively: 56 percent to 44 percent. And this despite the fact that the organization responsible for the campaign, Citizens for Downtown's Future, outspent its principal antagonist, VAST, by 250 to 1.[33] In other words, the arena backers spent $13 per "yes" vote, while the opponents spent 4 cents per "no" vote.

But the saga was far from over. In the immortal words of boosterspeak, "community leaders" came to the rescue, or rather, to continue with the corny sports metaphors so beloved of that fraternity, they "stepped up," which, of course, raises the uncomfortable question of why they did not "step up" earlier instead of trying to dump the cost on the public. *They* would be Nationwide Insurance, which would develop and own the arena along with a 10 percent commitment from the Dispatch Printing Company; the inclusion of the latter would prove to be a highly strategic move on Nationwide's part. They would then lease it to another "community leader," John McConnell, CEO of a very successful local industrial firm, Worthington Steel, who would hold the franchise for a team in the National Hockey League. But the city also "stepped up," and as we will see, would continue to do so right down to the present day, almost twenty years later, and a continuing challenge to the notion that it was all a matter of private initiative; in fact, the "private" aspect would continue its great disappearing act, all the while holding on to the profitable bits and allowing the public to take over the ones losing money.

The arena would be exempt from city property taxes, though with a ticket surcharge to compensate the school district for lost revenues. The council declared the arena site a blighted area, allowing the Frank-

32. "Proposal Amounts to Bad Deal for Taxpayers," *Columbus Dispatch,* May 3, 1997, p. 11A.

33. "Arena Forces Outspending Opposition," *Columbus Dispatch,* April 25, 1997, p. 1D.

lin County Convention and Facilities Authority to acquire the land via eminent domain. The site would then be leased for ninety-nine years to the arena owners, with an ownership option at the end of the lease. The city also committed itself to highway improvements and utilities, at an estimated cost to the city of $20 million. Part of the deal was the city making available sixteen acres of the state penitentiary site. Nationwide paid $11.7 million, but the city had already absorbed $7.4 million in clean up costs ("Casino annexation starts; City Council ensures services to site," *Columbus Dispatch,* July 25, 2011).

The penitentiary land question would attract unfavorable attention, as in an article in *Columbus Alive* with the title "The Great Land Giveaway."[34] It was far more than a matter of what sale at "fair market value" might actually mean:

> The Pen site was the juicy part that may have taken this deal beyond the description of a "private" arena. Roads and infrastructures are one thing, but signing away the Pen site makes the deal a second cousin of a publicly financed arena.

The article continued along the same theme of just how "private" it all was:

> And we need to salute Nationwide. It's a pretty solid outfit. Once they start building that arena, it'll get done. Just think of all the great construction photos down the road. That's what happens when your 10 percent business partner publishes the daily newspaper. We're in for a bolt-by-bolt description. However, if there are cost overruns, we probably won't read about these. But then Mr. McFerson (CEO of Nationwide) and Mr. Wolfe (CEO of the Dispatch Printing Company) will know what a "private" arena is all about.

Indeed. Including the *Dispatch* was a clever move, whether intended as such or not. In a city where people scarcely knew the difference between a puck and a golf ball, there was a lot of work to do building up a market for ice hockey—part of the baggage of getting a major league franchise that is more of a consolation prize. But the *Dispatch* would go about its task with gusto. The Blue Jackets, as the team

---

34. June 1, 1997, p. 4.

would be called, would henceforth be regular fare on the front page of the newspaper's sports section: results, hirings, team gossip, and later, when it looked like the team might skip town and needed some financial enticement to stay, articles telling the hapless public what a great thing the team was for Columbus.

But to return to the Pen land, the twenty-three-acre site was key to the deal. As Robert Woodward, then executive vice president and chief investment officer for Nationwide, affirmed, "It's no different than any developer who would take a high risk with the idea of capitalizing on the ancillary development. That makes it a reasonable project."[35] This would be the key piece that would allow the development of what would come to be known as the Arena District: an area of office buildings, some residential, restaurants, and entertainment that would become central to the redevelopment of the central city, even while it was a little away from its historic center. But once these major rent earners were in place, you could forget about the arena, which is exactly what they would do when it threatened to become a financial incubus.[36]

And a financial incubus it would become. Part of the problem would be competition, particularly with the new Ohio State arena, dubbed "the Schott."[37] From the start, a good deal depended on the willingness of the university to limit the number of special events it

35. "Council OKs Arena Proposal," *Columbus Dispatch,* June 3, 1997, p. 1A.

36. Quoting: "To make the deal work, NRI [Nationwide Real Estate Investors] was granted control of a large, mixed-use district that it could develop and control. NRI President Brian Ellis says that the insurer was willing to accept a lower return on the arena if it could secure the land to undertake the Arena District development. Ellis says that the return on the arena has ranged between 4% and 5%, but that NRI expects to get stabilized returns from 9% to 10% on other Arena District projects. 'Once we subsidized the [arena] return, that gave us an opportunity to do a development and earn market returns'" (Michael Pramik, "Urban Hot Spot Alters Columbus," *National Real Estate Investor,* January 1, 2007, http://nreionline.com/industrynews/real_estate_urban_hot_spot).

37. A nickname. The actual name is Value City Arena. This is to recognize a large donation from Jerome Schottenstein, founder of a privately held retail company known as Value City Furniture, but "Schott" as shorthand for "Schottenstein." The shameless commercialization of these public spaces is too obvious to require extended comment.

leased out space to.[38] According to an article in the *Dispatch* in 2008,[39] both arenas ran $1 million deficits the first two years, and the Nationwide Arena was still not being used to its full potential as a result of the competition. It was putting on 125 events a year, which was judged a mere half of what was possible. The big gainers were the event promoters driving up the costs of putting something on; the two arenas simply had to pay more compared with, say, Indianapolis. But there would be worse to come as the major tenant of the Nationwide Arena started to have trouble paying its bills, as we will now see.

Chickens Come Home and the Public Be Damned

In a column in August of 2011 *Dispatch* journalist Michael Arace suggested what had really happened in the calculations behind the Arena decision when he opined about the original franchise owner, John McConnell:

> I have always believed that Mr. Mac took a calculated gamble. He had to know that the lease wasn't the best thing, business-wise, and he bet that when the issue came to a head the city and the community would find a solution. Mr. Mac wanted Columbus to be major-league, that was his main goal. Any other problem was minor by comparison.[40]

And come to a head the issue would, and indeed a "solution" would be found—a "solution" of public ownership that had been rejected soundly and repeatedly by the local taxpayer. The tenant would be the Blue Jackets, owned 80 percent by local industrialist John McConnell, aka Mr. Mac, founder and CEO of a local company, Worthington Steel. Ten percent was held by a subsidiary of the Dispatch Printing Company, and the remaining ten percent was dispersed among three

38. As Mark Rosenberg, author of *Major League Losers: The Real Cost of Sports and Who's Paying for It,* argued at the time: "There's no question the NHL wants to come into your market," he said. "The challenge is to turn the other events, to have enough dates to make it viable. . . . The two private sector entities doing this [Nationwide and Dispatch Printing Company], they must have done their research and gotten the assurance from OSU that they will have the lion's share of the dates. . . . If OSU is going to limit their shows, it will work" ("Not Many Privately Built Arenas in Medium Cities," *Columbus Dispatch,* June 5, 1997, p. 10C).

39. "Rivals to This Day" *Columbus Dispatch,* November 17, 2008.

40. "A Long Time Coming," *Columbus Dispatch,* August 15, 2011.

other local notables. Their first season was in 2000. But nine years later, they were complaining of a lack of money. In fact, over the period of 2002 to 2009, it seemed that they had lost $80 million. A major problem was that they lacked the usual sources of revenue available to major league franchises like parking, naming rights, and skyboxes. These were all safely in the hands of the owners of the Arena, parking and skyboxes going toward defraying the costs of construction. The Blue Jackets could increase their revenues by renting out the Arena for special events but, as noted, there was stiff competition there from Ohio State's Schottenstein Arena, as well as the county fairgrounds and the convention center. But even without the competition, they would be struggling, since the Columbus market just was not big enough for a professional ice hockey franchise.[41]

But if the Arena could be publicly owned—that's right; here we go again—then all might be right again. The problem was: How to finance that takeover? The initial call in 2009 was for it to be funded by an increase in local sin taxes: cigarettes, beer, liquor, and wine. This was resisted, but the whining continued with the threat of the franchise being sold on to a group in another city. This got some local attention and a discourse complete with consultant reports that was quickly put together to show that if the franchise was a financial loser it was a loss leader, helping to sustain the Arena District and all the benefits it was supposed to bring to the city, not to mention, of course, Nationwide Insurance and the *Columbus Dispatch*.[42] And as serendipity would have it, this supposed public awakening happened to coincide with the arrival of the casino on the west side of the city—ironically, something that Nationwide and the *Dispatch* wanted to keep away from the Arena District—and the loot in tax revenues that it promised. No matter that the talk had been of how those revenues—a predicted $24 million a year for the city and about $16 million for the county—would go to

41. "Saving the Jackets," *Columbus Dispatch,* November 5, 2009. Professional ice hockey is weak nationally in comparison to the NFL and the MBA anyway: "In the grandiose world of American professional sports, the NHL All-Star Game might seem rather JV [as in 'junior varsity']. Although it is considered one of the 'big four' sports in North America, pro hockey is the straggler of the group. The NHL's most recent all-star showcase had only 1.3 million viewers. (The Major League Baseball and NBA all-star games had 11 million and 7.5 million viewers, respectively.)" (Sam Sturgis, "Can Columbus, Ohio Become a Sports Capital?," *CityLab,* January 7, 2015).

42. This was a profoundly dubious claim given the transfer of firms from offices from elsewhere downtown that had resulted in the supposed success of the Arena District in terms of jobs and taxes.

hire extra police and bolster local schools; more urgent issues were calling. By summer of 2011, things were beginning to shape up once more and a deal—for whom?—was being outlined.

The plan was for the city and the county to draw on a share of their casino tax revenues—up to a third of it—to finance the $42.5 million purchase of the Arena and its running expenses.[43] The Blue Jackets would get use of the Arena rent-free in exchange for a commitment to stay in Columbus until 2039. They would also get the revenues from naming rights. By investing more than $52 million in the Blue Jackets, Nationwide would assume 30 percent ownership of the team. On the other hand, it also stood to make money out of the deal since it was to be the contracted financer for it at a rate of almost 5 percent over twenty-seven years.[44] The new owner would be the Franklin County Convention Authority.

The immediate reaction from those outside the anointed few was not favorable. Columbus city schools saw it as a reduction in their property tax revenues since transfer to the county, a public body, meant that the Arena would no longer be liable for property taxes, though the franchise and Arena franchisees would be liable for some of their own.[45] More generally, there was popular dismay. Five times taxes to fund a public arena had been voted down, but it seemed that the so-called leaders of the city had triumphed once again, since there could be no popular vote on this particular tax stream.

This is not to say that there was no public attempt to overturn the agreement. A group calling themselves the Columbus Coalition for Responsive Government petitioned for a referendum issue that would have asked voters in the elections of May of 2013 to call a halt to city payments for the Arena. But it was too late: The contract had been

---

43. "Arena Deal Looks Good to Folks in High Places," *Columbus Dispatch*, September 16, 2011. "Folks in high places" indeed; nice touch.

44. It agreed to take its payments as the money came in from the casino taxes, sensing, wisely as it turned out, that they might not materialize to the degree expected—something that might have been avoided if the casino had set up camp next to the Arena District, as per their original plans. But delayed payments would mean increased interest.

45. Even, that is, the diminished stream that had resulted from Nationwide's successful challenge to the assessed valuation that had been assigned to the Arena. The Arena had cost $147.1 million to build, but they successfully argued that the valuation should be reduced from $129.7 million to $44 million. Nationwide did agree to turn over $1 million a year to city schools until 2015, but it was still a helluva deal.

agreed to two years previous and had survived the thirty-day period in which it could have been challenged.

The agreement, to use public money to bail out private entities, troubling and deeply ironic as it was, given the hysteria promoted by the *Dispatch* to keep the casino away from the Arena District, might have been the conclusion. But the saga opened up back in 1997 by the decision to build an arena and bring an ice hockey franchise to town shows no sign of ending. Because, guess what? As of 2015 the new owner, the county, is having trouble paying its bills, even with the money coming from the casino. Casino tax revenues had been well below predictions, and after paying the management company hired to run and market the arena, there was no money to pay for maintenance, let alone making any payments on the loan originally contracted to pay for it, so the interest payments due Nationwide continued to mount up.[46] The next step was to try to bilk the public further by asking the state for a property tax exemption, and this in a city where property tax exemptions already run riot (see chapter 5). Although owned by a public entity that did not automatically qualify the arena for the sort of tax exemption applying to other publicly owned properties like schools and state universities, if a tax exemption was indeed to be granted, the arena needed to be used for a public purpose and not for the benefit of a private entity like an ice hockey franchise. To make things even cloudier, the county, through its Facilities Authority, had given complete control of the arena to a private body, Columbus Arena Management, which, surprise, surprise, included as one of its four-member board, a representative of Nationwide. Meanwhile the school district that should have been a major beneficiary of these taxes had been missing out because of a 99 percent tax abatement on the arena, which had started with its completion in 2000 and was due to expire in 2016. And in fact, it decided in exchange for a payment of $586,000 a year to go along with the request for a tax exemption on the grounds—at least those that were publicly stated—that it was better to cut a deal than

46. "Casino Tax Money Falls Short for Nationwide Arena Debt and Maintenance," *Columbus Dispatch,* June 7, 2015. Moreover, by 2016 the *Dispatch* was singing a much more critical tune, a result of the fact that it was no longer owned by the Wolfe family but had been purchased in June 2015 by a national company, Gatehouse Media. For an indication of the more distanced and critical viewpoint subsequently adopted, see the editorial "Arena Profit Is Accounting Fiction," *Columbus Dispatch,* June 27, 2016.

Dumping on the Public *Ad Nauseam*

And the dumping on the public would increase. In May of 2018, the arena management was pleading poverty again. This time, it was a matter of capital improvements and repair projects that, given the shortfall in revenues from the casino—thank you, *Dispatch* and Nationwide for casting it into the wilderness of the far west side—could not be financed. The suggestion this time was a ticket tax of up to 8 percent on arts, cultural, entertainment, and professional sports events supplemented by some of the county's sales tax revenue.[1] A month later, there was a follow-up article,[2] presumably to soften up the public for what was to come. Eventually, after a great deal of contention, it would come to pass: a 5 percent tax on tickets to events at the Nationwide Arena.[3] As before, there was vigorous opposition to anything that smacked of a public bailout of the Arena, as indeed this does. There was a petition to put a charter amendment on the ballot in November of 2019 to eliminate the taxes and prevent future ones. It failed for lack of sufficient valid signatures: a common story at the Franklin County Board of Elections. But stay tuned. This is a story that keeps on giving. The latest is that the ticket tax is yielding revenue wildly below projections;[4] to put a figure on it, the tax on tickets for events at the Arena is yielding less than 12 percent of projections.

1. "Nationwide Arena Juggles Repair Projects while Awaiting Fate of Ticket Tax," *Columbus Dispatch*, May 28, 2018.

2. "Nationwide Arena Trails Competitors in Spending on Renovations," *Columbus Dispatch*, June 24, 2018.

3. "Columbus Ticket Taxes Set to Begin, Opponents Ready to Block," *Columbus Dispatch*, June 28, 2019.

4. "Ticket Taxes on Columbus Arts, Sports Events off to Slow Start," *Columbus Dispatch*, December 1, 2019.

risk nothing at all if, as seemed likely, the state granted the request.[47] Bottom line: You could not make this story up, even if you were drunk, and it continues (see "Dumping on the Public *Ad Nauseam*").

And Then the Crew

In the original plans for a downtown arena, put to a public vote in 1997, provision had been made for a stadium for the soccer franchise, the Columbus Crew. Since 1996, they had been playing at the Ohio

47. The value of the arena for tax purposes had also been disputed, and the prospect of legal wrangling also played into the school board decision.

Stadium. With the failure of the referendum in 1997 and the decision to go ahead with an arena for an ice hockey team, they were left on the outside looking in, and somewhat bitter about it too, judging from the lawsuits. Eventually a stadium would be built on the state fairgrounds some two to three miles north of the downtown. There was no public money and the team enjoyed more than a modicum of success, including winning the Major League Soccer (MLS) championship cup in 2008.

By 2017, though, change was in the offing. The news was not pleasant. The new owner of the franchise, Anthony Precourt, who had bought it in 2013, was threatening to move it to Austin. Apparently this had always been in the back of his mind when he made the purchase since a clause had been inserted in the contract that, in effect, allowed him to do that. His public explanation was that attendances at Crew games could be better. And despite the local uproar at his move, he had a point. In 2018, of all the Major League Soccer franchises, the Crew was bottom of the attendance table. While the average attendance at Atlanta United FC was a dazzling 53,000 a game, and at second best Seattle, over 40,000, the Crew could muster barely 12,500.[48] Precourt was not totally inflexible. Part of the price for staying was an arena closer to downtown. This would eventually happen, but by then Precourt was set on Austin. The "rescue" came from the Haslams, the owners of the Cleveland Browns, with an experience suggesting that they see the possibility of financial daylight at the Crew, and Pete Edwards, a local developer, and also physician to the team. The new stadium, on land donated by the city and some purchased from Nationwide Realty Investors, is expected to be completed by 2021.

By now, though, any professional franchise interested in the Columbus market has learned that the local politicos are a very easy touch. The initial announcement was that Columbus's contribution would be $50 million dollars, consisting of 6.6 acres of city-owned land and money for supporting infrastructure: notably roads and utilities. This would later increase by $25 million, generating considerable public angst and a concern of a replay of the Arena saga. There would, though, be more to come. For the project to come to fruition, there would have to be cooperation from Nationwide over the site of the stadium. This was because it was sitting on a large chunk of land and

48. "Major League Soccer Attendance," *Wikipedia* n.d. Available at https://en.wikipedia.org/wiki/Major_League_Soccer_attendance (last accessed 10/25/20).

would play hardball. Just how bad the news was would only emerge in early 2020.

Recall that, in the context of anxieties about retaining the Blue Jackets franchise in Columbus, Nationwide transferred the Arena to the Franklin County Convention Facilities Authority. Nationwide lent the Authority $42.5 million to make the purchase. The agreement was that if casino revenues did not suffice to pay off the loan, the loan would remain outstanding. Thus:

> At a contentious 2011 meeting in which the city approved making casino-tax revenue payments toward public ownership of Nationwide Arena, then-City Council President Andrew J. Ginther asked: "If the casino revenue goes away, what is the city's commitment to this going forward?"
>
> "None," replied then-City Auditor Hugh Dorrian—a stance that he repeated over the years in arguing that Nationwide was holding bad debt and the city had no liability.[49]

Evidently that was not how Nationwide saw it. In October of 2019, the city and the Authority had done a deal to repay the loan with interest. The city's share of about $65 million would come as tax abatements in the form of TIFs[50] for developing the Arena District. Not to be outdone in the realm of generosity, the county also got in on the action. The Authority's share of $51.5 million would come from annual surpluses—whatever that means—from operating the Hilton Columbus Downtown. This is owned by the county and leased to Hilton. In other words, Nationwide got the city over a barrel: The TIFs were the pound of flesh it demanded for negotiating purchase of the land that the city needed for the Crew stadium. But just why the County Convention Facilities Authority felt obliged to chip in is far from clear. After all, the original purchase agreement had been that if casino revenues did not suffice, the loan would remain outstanding.

We need to stand back at this point and consider the pros and cons of what has happened. To emphasize, back in 1997 city leaders

49. "Columbus, Facilities Authority, Quietly Reach Deal to Pay Nationwide for Arena Loan," *Columbus Dispatch*, December 24, 2019.

50. Tax Increment Financing or TIF: This refers to a concession to developers in which the taxes on the additional property value resulting from their development are dedicated to public improvements, like a freeway interchange, within an immediately surrounding area.

"stepped up" and announced that if the public did not want to finance the Arena, they would do it: Nationwide and the *Dispatch* would share ownership, with Nationwide chipping in 80 percent. But from the get-go, it was clear that this was more public-private than private. Not least, the city exempted the Arena from property taxes while, as we saw, the deal with the city for penitentiary land attracted opprobrium, as in the headline "The Great Land Giveaway."[51] This would set the scene for a much larger scale real estate development including various complementary land uses and rent extraction possibilities. When the ice hockey franchise threatened to leave for greener pastures, the city and county would intervene and purchase the Arena with a view to providing it rent-free to the franchise. The money for this was supposed to come from casino revenues. These have now been topped up with tax abatements and annual surpluses from the county-owned Hilton hotel. This is all money that could have been applied to public purposes much more attractive than keeping Nationwide happy. And one would have thought, given the past generosity of the city to the corporation, they could have been a little more generous in negotiating the twenty-one acres needed for the Crew. This is even more the case when one remembers that the nearest parking facilities to the new stadium will be ones owned by Nationwide. They cash in coming and going. Of course the city is complicit in this. It sucks up to the development community as a matter of course: Columbus Inc., as will become even clearer in the course of this book. Nationwide will turn around and say that they are investing in the district for the good of the city, including doing their bit for retention of the Crew. Perhaps. But they do it strictly on their own terms. And it continues. Office space downtown has a serious vacancy problem as tenants decamp for the fabled Arena District.

From one angle, the city's indulgence of Nationwide is puzzling. After all, it could scarcely consider moving someplace else. It is unable to pull up stakes like the ice hockey and soccer franchises threatened to, and quite plausibly. Nationwide is locked in and has been for a very long time. Its employment is quite massive. It might do a Boeing and transfer its headquarters someplace else, but abandoning its highly skilled workforce would be something quite other. Besides, it benefits in major ways from its knowledge of the Columbus real estate market; it has established pipelines of influence (evidently!) to the mayor's

51. *Columbus Alive,* June 1, 1997, p. 4.

office. Often overlooked is the way in which the various universities of the area, particularly Ohio State, are a proving ground for future employees. To establish the proportion of Nationwide employees who are Ohio State graduates would be a very interesting project!

To return to the Arena: Evidently it has proved to be a serious albatross for its new owners. Whether Crew Stadium will go the same route remains to be seen. The franchise owners clearly believe that a downtown location will turn attendances around, though the modest number of seats means that they can never approach the likes of Atlanta and Seattle. The question remains: Why have they been so mediocre? There *is* soccer interest in the city. According to a report in the *Washington Post* in March of 2016,[52] Columbus was the fifth most important market for watching English Premiership games on TV. The most obvious explanation is Buckeye mania. It is not just that Saturday evening games from late August on sometimes coincide with a game earlier in the day at Ohio Stadium; even when the Buckeyes are playing away, people will be congesting the highways making for a sports bar. Who wants to go and watch the Crew after all the excitement of *the* game? Time will tell and perhaps the new ownership has it right. But in any case, if history is anything to go by, the city will be a charitable backstop.

•

Columbus has a history of consolation prizes that have turned out to be damp squibs, most notably the America West mini-hub and then the Blue Jacket ice hockey franchise. Alas, it has been left with these because from the standpoint of achieving greater visibility, the geohistorical legacy has been unfavorable. In considering this, the problem of image is probably overrated. OK, so Indianapolis has the Indy 500 and is the amateur sports capital, while Austin has City Limits, if you like that sort of thing. But Charlotte? What is *its* image?

Rather, the way the city is wedged in between other major cities that were in a sense there first has been the major problem. Columbus could support a franchise in either football or baseball, but the NFL and Major League Baseball were spoken for a long time ago, and respective franchises in Cincinnati and Cleveland and even Pittsburgh

52. "Which U. S. Cities Are Watching the Premier League on TV the Most? We've Got Lists," *Washington Post,* March 21, 2016.

would oppose any move to encroach on what they see as their market. So Columbus has had to do with second best: the NHL and MLS. And for whatever reason—the Ohio State football presence, other limits to the local market—it has had to lay out money in order to retain these.

The same historical geography has condemned the airport to levels of service in terms of direct flights distinctly under par for an urban area of its size. This has been a big disadvantage as compared with peers like Kansas City and Charlotte and even Indianapolis. It has affected the ability of the city to attract major conventions. Despite the struggles to bring it about, the city now has a convention center that is competitive in terms of size to the point where it could host major national meetings. It even had the chutzpah to tender for the Democratic Party convention in 2016. One of the remaining strikes against it is that there is insufficient hotel space for that purpose.[53] But in that regard the city is in a catch-22 situation and the airport is again key.[54] Hotels will not invest until the big conventions show interest,[55] but that is unlikely to happen so long as airline service is so relatively weak.

There was a time, of course, when none of this mattered. Cities were based on industrial employment and railroads ruled the roost. Most of the population was sturdily blue-collar employed by some local champion, whether it be Ford, United Steel, Mack Truck, or Ingersoll Rand. All that has changed. White-collar populations have surged. Cities have shed their blue-collar employment, decanting it to branch plants in smaller towns, and more recently to China, while

53. Mike Mahoney, "Wanted: 1,000 Convention Hotel Rooms under One Roof," *Columbus CEO,* October 2015.

54. Also the old issue of image: "Columbus booked larger convention groups on average during the first half of the year versus the same period last year, but the challenges Columbus faces remain familiar: not enough suitable convention hotel rooms, and a lack of an image for the city among outsiders. . . . Experience Columbus sales director Angela Hammond said groups that consider Columbus as a finalist for their convention but end up choosing another city don't often say exactly why, but they know image is a factor. 'They come here and they love it, but then they say, 'How are we going to sell it to our attendees?,' Hammond said" ("Columbus Convention Visit Slowed in First Half of '18 by Familiar Problems," *Columbus Dispatch,* July 18, 2018).

55. An article in the *Dispatch* for September 23, 2016, "Effort Resumes to Add Big, Convention-Focused Hotel Downtown," underlines the continuing problems. The area close to the convention center now has two hotels with 631 and 532 beds, respectively, but this is still not enough to attract the big conventions. Conventions look for large hotels of 1,000 beds or more where they can negotiate discounts for large blocks of rooms ("Bigger Is Better," *Columbus Dispatch,* September 23, 2016).

retaining the corporate headquarters, banking, marketing services, and some of the research that sustain firm success. Firm headquarters need rapid airline connections. Meanwhile new functions have emerged as the convention traffic has soared. In short, cities have become postindustrial. What exactly that means and how Columbus assumed that status is examined in the next chapter.

CHAPTER 4

The "Postindustrial" City Comes to Columbus

IT IS A TRUISM that since the Second World War, cities have been utterly transformed. In 1945 they still relied heavily for employment on manufacturing; manufacturing, in fact, had been the key to the growth of cities anyway. In the nineteenth century, heavy industry demanding lots of muscle had dominated: iron and steel, heavy engineering, meat packing. Later, with the second industrial revolution of the early twentieth century and the rise of electricity, new waves of industrial investment would ignite growth in an equally new set of cities, including Columbus. Yet by the early postwar years, the lineaments of something quite different were emerging.

Industrial production had always involved more than factories, furnaces, workbenches, and assembly lines. Production had to be organized and administered. Increasingly, particularly with the advent of consumer goods industries, research and development of new products had to assume importance. Within the city itself, a division of labor with other sorts of enterprise was established. Firms needed finance, so there were banks. And everybody had to be kept healthy, which meant hospitals. There again, there was a need for public services, so people were employed in local government.

The emergence of new ways of organizing industry geographically started to transform cities. In the 1930s, Columbus, like many other cities, was a target of industrial firms as a site for their branch plants.

But electricity meant that the single-story plant could be substituted for old multistory ones where power was supplied by a system of belts connected to a steam engine. At the same time, the rise of assembly line production encouraged the single-story factory. In other words, factories would now consume a lot of space, which, in terms of site selection, put a premium on land prices. So it is no surprise that the new branch plants of the '30s and later preferred sites on the edge of the city, as indeed would be the case in Columbus. The idea of the central city as being the place of industrial employment was increasingly out of date. And so too would be the metropolitan area as, from the '60s on firms, partly on the back of the construction of the interstates, increasingly opted for sites in small towns, particularly for the lower-skill aspects of their production processes. This is what happened to Akron's rubber tire industry, but it was a common pattern.

What have remained in central cities are the headquarters of firms; the banks and businesses, like accounting, law, and marketing, that service them; hospitals and universities; and various branches of government, including state and federal offices. Old industrial buildings have been vacated, demolished, and the land redeveloped as offices, downtown sports stadia, hospitality districts, and increasingly expensive apartment and condo high-rises. In short, the city has become what is called "postindustrial," but there is an important sense in which its functions are ancillary to those of industry; they cannot exist without manufacturing somewhere.

Columbus is emphatically postindustrial. It was always less industrial than its state rivals, Cincinnati and Cleveland, and this is a difference that has endured over time, even while in all three, manufacturing employment has been decimated (table 4.1). In Columbus it declined by approximately two thirds in the half-century prior to 2000. What has taken its place is something quite different.

TABLE 4.1. Percentage of the labor force employed in manufacturing (urbanized areas)

YEAR	COLUMBUS	CINCINNATI	CLEVELAND
1950	23.8	31.5	38.8
1960	26.2	32.9	39.4
1970	22.9	31.2	35.1
1980	16.7	22.3	33.2
1990	11.6	15.4	23.1
2000	8.1	12.5	14.7

Among the largest forty-six standard metropolitan statistical areas (SMSAs) of the US, the Columbus area stands out in employment in two measures of its postindustrial status: "financial activities" and "professional and business services." One indication is the way in which it specializes in these relative to other SMSAs. Location quotients measure the degree to which a city's specialization in some activity is average, above, or below. "Average" is 1.0 and "above average" over 1.0. In financial activities, Columbus ranked eighth of all cities in 2012, and in professional and business services seventh, but it was clearly below average in manufacturing (table 4.2). Unsurprisingly, the two largest private sector employers are JPMorgan Chase Bank (20,475 employees) and Nationwide Insurance (13,000). What is a surprise, though, particularly given the presence of Ohio State and numerous other institutions of higher education with high enrolments, like Columbus State, it was no better than average in terms of employment in higher education, and sixteenth ranked in terms of the magnitude of its location quotient.[1]

TABLE 4.2. Select location quotients 2012

CITY	MANUFACTURING	FINANCIAL ACTIVITIES	PROFESSIONAL AND BUSINESS SERVICES
Columbus	0.81	1.30 (rank 8)*	1.24 (rank 7)**
Cincinnati	1.16	1.05	n.d.
Cleveland	1.35	1.02	1.0

Source: Chandan, Sam. "Performance and Timing of Secondary Market Investment Activity." Appendix D. NAIOP Research Foundation. November 2013.

*After New York, Charlotte, Phoenix, Tampa, Dallas, Minneapolis, and Salt Lake City.

**After Washington, DC, San Francisco, Raleigh, Detroit, San Diego, and Atlanta.

What was not included in the study from which these statistics were obtained was warehousing. The Columbus area is host to a plethora of distribution centers. According to a report in the *Dispatch,* the

1. Another study underlines Columbus's postindustrial credentials. In a study of the ratio of services to goods production across 364 metro areas in the US, it ranked fourteenth, wedged in between Denver and Chicago. See Richard Florida, "America's Most Postindustrial Metros," *Bloomberg CityLab* April 8, 2013. Available at https://www.citylab.com/life/2013/04/americas-most-post-industrial-metros/2815/ (last accessed October 25, 2020).

Central Ohio region has 35 percent more workers than average in the sector, bearing in mind the magnitude of the region's economy.[2]

More illumination of the city's postindustrial status comes from a list of the major private sector employers in the SMSA, but virtually all of this employment is in Franklin County (table 4.3).

TABLE 4.3. Major private sector employers in the Columbus metropolitan area, 2020

RANK	COMPANY	FULL-TIME EMPLOYEES
1	JPMorgan Chase & Co	20,316
2	Nationwide Mutual Insurance Company	12,862
3	Honda of America Mfg., Inc.	11,077
4	Limited Brands Inc	7,662
5	Cardinal Health	5,075
6	Huntington Bancshares Incorporated	4,921
7	Amazon	4,828
8	American Electric Power Company, Inc.	3,627
9	Alliance Data	3,000
10	Abercrombie & Fitch Co.	2,598

Source: https://columbusregion.com/market-research/largest-employers/ (last accessed April 30, 2020).

Financial services companies figure prominently: four of the top ten spots. Limited Brands and Abercrombie and Fitch are both headquartered in Columbus and are apparel companies. Limited Brands is the brain child of Leslie Wexner and has a variety of operations in the Columbus area, ranging from distribution through clothing design to administration. Significantly, in a study of location quotients for fashion and design in 2012, Columbus came in third, after New York and Los Angeles.[3] The major exception in a list dominated by finance, headquarters, and service industries, the only manufacturing company listed is Honda located in Marysville in Union County, adjoining

2. "Distribution Centers Put Central Ohio at Forefront of Retail," *Columbus Dispatch,* February 23, 2014.

3. Columbus's location quotient was 3.37, which means that given its total share of all employment across all SMSAs, its share of fashion and design was 3.37 times more than expected—compare with New York at 4.84 and Los Angeles at 3.82. See Richard Florida and Sara Johnson, "The World's Leading Cities for Fashion," *Bloomberg CityLab,* September 7, 2012. Available at http://www.citylab.com/work/2012/09/worlds-leading-cities-fashion/3182/; last accessed October 25, 2020.

Franklin County on the northwest. These companies are *not* the largest employers, though. Pride of place goes to the public sector, with Ohio State University clocking in first with almost 33,335, the state of Ohio with almost 21,342, and OhioHealth with 23,836.[4] On the other hand, one wonders just where Columbus would be without the flows of money from the rest of the state into state government and a very large state university. But bottom line, and without mentioning a research and development presence in the form of the Battelle Institute and Chemical Abstracts, Columbus's postindustrial status is evident.

On the other hand, industry, even in a somewhat depleted state, is not far away in counties contiguous to Franklin County. Table 4.4 shows a general decline over time, but the proportion employed in manufacturing remains above that in Franklin County, and in one instance, to a quite spectacular degree.

TABLE 4.4. Percentage labor force in manufacturing

COUNTY	1960	1970	1980	1990	2005
Franklin	26.2	22.9	17.0	12.2	5.4
Delaware	26.0	28.1	25.0	19.0	6.2
Fairfield	41.3	40.5	33.3	21.0	9.2
Licking	35.7	32.8	28.4	19.6	11.3
Madison	27.2	26.6	23.6	19.7	15.1
Pickaway	24.5	30.0	29.4	24.3	12.9
Union	42.0	34.7	35.3	31.0	31.8

Honda, based in Union County, is a major presence in the area as a result not only of its assembly operations in Union County but also because of its numerous components and parts suppliers, attracted by Honda's just-in-time delivery system, which puts an emphasis on proximity.[5] Figure 4.1 indicates the locations of firms differently positioned in the Honda supply chain. Original equipment manufacturers, or OEMs, supply directly to Honda in Marysville; Tier 1 firms supply the OEMs with materials for further fabrication, while Tier 2 firms supply Tier 1. The relatively dense interstate network in the region is

4. "Here are Central Ohio's largest employers: Our ranking found 120+ organizations with 100+ workers." *Columbus Business First,* July 12, 2019. Available at https://www.bizjournals.com/columbus/news/2019/07/12/here-are-central-ohios-largest-employers-our.html (last accessed October 25, 2020).

5. Mair, Florida, and Kenney 1988, 364.

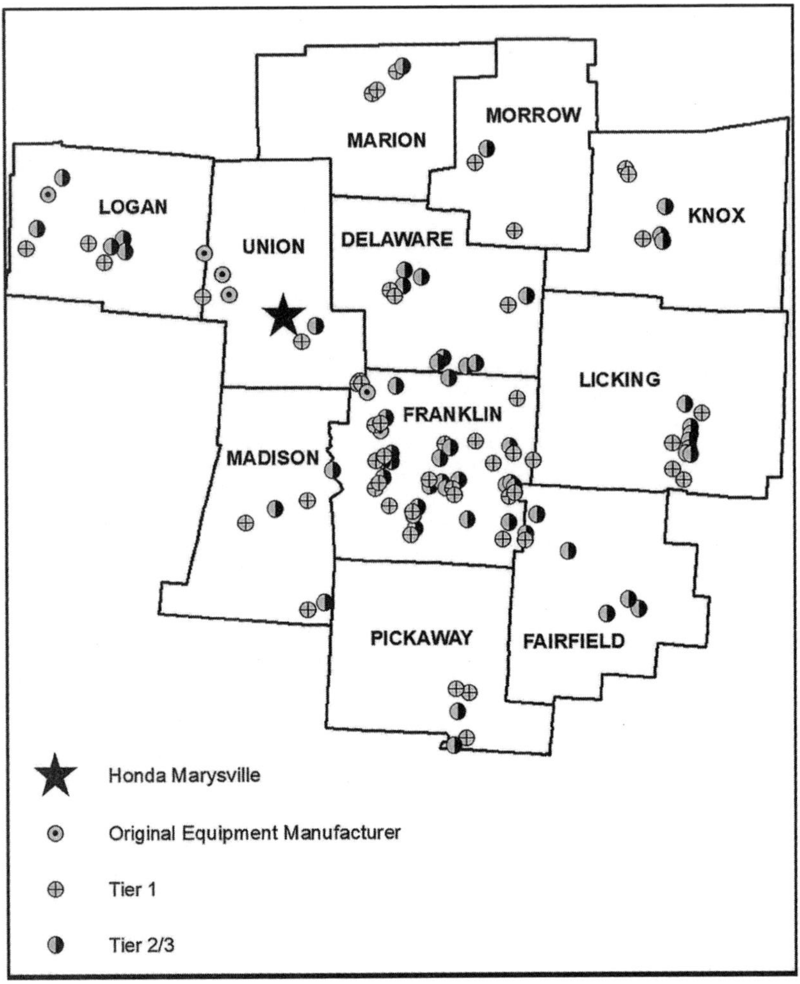

FIGURE 4.1. Honda's Central Ohio supply chain. Map by Jamie Valdinger, based on Mair, Kenney, and Florida (1988), p. 364, figure 4.

obviously a plus, but so too is Columbus since it has at least some of the airline connections important to a global firm[6] as well as the sorts of exclusive suburbs, with their prized school systems, attractive to the managerial and technical class. Just what the synergy is between the financial and business services of Columbus and surrounding industrial firms would warrant further investigation. The connections surely

6. Though obviously not as good as might be desired. Significantly, when The Ohio State University was contemplating the future of its airport, Honda officials expressed concern as they use it for their own private planes.

exist, cementing a regional division of labor between Columbus and an industrial periphery beyond the suburbs and in small towns that offer not just cheaper sites for big space-consuming plants but also cheaper labor: an artifact of lower costs of living, particularly housing, and workers often recently engaged in small-scale farming, perhaps still owning land but renting it to someone else, and with all the prejudices about unions that that often entails.

Such is the current state of geographic play in Central Ohio: a clearly postindustrial city at its center and where industry is a bigger presence in surrounding small towns, but in a synergistic relationship with one another. The question is, how did it happen? Obviously Columbus represents a wider American urban experience. But there had to be people involved, and there were struggles over the city's future, both winners and losers. There are continuing struggles to cement that postindustrial status and the rents that developers have been able to reap from the change and from recycling the old industrial sites. It is to those struggles that I now turn.

Future Contested

There is never anything "natural" about urban change. The supposedly irresistible pressures of the market get channeled in particular directions. Politics plays a massive part. So too is that the case in the transition from the industrial form assumed by large American cities a century ago to a more postindustrial character after the Second World War, with delays in some instances and, in any case, quite unevenly. Columbus is no exception; in terms of its economic base, its destiny was never written in stone but was fought over.

At the beginning of the twentieth century, Columbus had a considerable industrial base. This is underestimated by census statistics since many large factories were located beyond the city boundaries, partly for purposes of tax avoidance, partly because they required large acreages. There were some major employers. In 1920, Jeffrey Mining and Manufacturing, which *was* within the city boundaries, oriented to producing machinery for the coal mines of Appalachia, employed over 3,000. Buckeye Steel Castings *had* been closer to downtown Columbus but relocated to a site much farther south, to what was until very recently its current location. It employed over 2,000. These were homegrown industries. But from the late nineteenth century on, major corporations based elsewhere started to locate branch plants in other parts of the country. This provided the necessary condition for cities to boost their economic base by attracting them in. So it was in Columbus from the very start of the twentieth century, with the Board of Trade initially taking the initiative and then from 1910 on, the newly formed Chamber of Commerce. From the 1920s to the late '30s, though, this branch plant policy became controversial with some of the larger local firms. Delmar Starkey, who worked for the Chamber and who would eventually take over the inward investment policy, has remarked about that period: "I saw case after case of a prospective industry or big business come in and talk with my boss, the chief executive at that time, and several times they'd stop at my office when they were leaving and say they couldn't understand why they got no encouragement. They were all discouraged."[7]

At that time, it seems, policy making at the Chamber of Commerce was dominated by the Wolfe family, who were owners of the *Dispatch,* the Ohio National Bank, and a shoe factory, along with the owners of the dominant department store Lazarus and the large Jeffrey Mining and Manufacturing, and Buckeye Steel Castings firms. Their major concern was how new investments from outside would affect local labor markets: not just the pressure on labor markets that could result from sudden jumps in demand subsequent to the arrival of a large employer, but also the possibility that the branch plants of major national corporations would be the Trojan horse through which labor unions would enter the area. But for many other, smaller Columbus firms, dependent on local linkages, new businesses were welcome, and from 1937 on, Starkey managed to turn things around, partly through stacking the Chamber of Commerce board in his favor.

This shift in policy was symbolized by the arrival in 1941 of Curtiss-Wright, an airplane manufacturer, employing in excess of 25,000 (!) in a labor market employing only 140,000 at that time. This created waves among the bigger businesses of the area. According to an interview that Mair conducted with Starkey, one of the Lazarus brothers called a meeting of the city's major industrial and retail establishments to protest the Curtiss-Wright plans[8] and some chamber members stopped paying their dues.[9] Curtiss-Wright was unionized and the feared conta-

7. "City's Chamber Had Many Roles in Past 100 Years," *Columbus Citizen Journal,* January 24, 1984, p. 19.

8. Mair 1988, 189.

9. Ibid., 190. Even while, of course, Curtiss-Wright was producing planes for the war effort. Seemingly, concerns about labor unions trumped patriotism.

gion did indeed occur. At the then-1,300-employee Buckeye Steel plant an organizing drive got underway in 1941 to be successful the following year, while the demand for workers from Curtiss-Wright weakened the leverage of employers on the union question.

After the war and the rundown of production at Curtiss-Wright, the policy of attracting in new industry continued. Milestones included:

- A General Motors Fisher body plant opened in 1946,[10] employing 4,000 by 1950.
- North American Aviation purchased the Curtiss-Wright plant in 1950 and by 1953 was employing 17,000.
- Westinghouse arrived to manufacture electrical appliances in 1953, employing 5,000 by 1955.
- Western Electric, producing telephone equipment, opened a 4,000-employee plant in 1959.

The locational emphasis was east-west: Fisher Body and Westinghouse close to Broad Street on the west side, and North American Aviation and Western Electric on the east. The Western Electric plant, though, would turn out to be the high point of the industrial drive. Only one major plant opened after that and that was the Busch Brewery on the (then) far north side in 1967, employing 1,000. A signal event had come in 1955–56 with the failure to secure the location of a Ford plant that would have employed 3,000 to produce steering gear and small components. The site in question was at the intersection of Sinclair and Morse Roads, about six miles north of the city center. It needed a rezoning and it failed city council 4–3, supposedly as a result of opposition in the neighboring Beechwold area. But turning down a major employer on rezoning grounds just does not happen; a way will be found. So what was the issue? It was later claimed with some authority that "Ford was discouraged from coming in," and "according to some recollections," there was the suggestion that the discouragement originated in "the city's downtown leadership,"[11] while Starkey in Andrew Mair's interview with him in 1987 emphasized the opposition of the Wolfe family.[12] And then, if there had been any doubt about the direction of economic policy in Columbus, a vision for the future of its economic base, it would be resolved some twenty years later, when

10. See Hunker 2000, 55.

11. "Selective Growth Shaping Future for Columbus," *Columbus Dispatch,* October 10, 1977, p. A1.

12. Mair 1988, 197.

Volkswagen was considering buying the then-vacated Westinghouse site for an auto assembly plant. One Chamber spokesperson claimed that Columbus was the priority site. However: "I'm not a great backer of developing heavy industry here," explained one prominent business leader in off-the-record remarks. "I didn't hear any basket of tears being shed in Columbus over the Volkswagen decision (to locate in Pennsylvania). And I must say, there wouldn't have been unrestrained jubilation if we had gotten the plant in Columbus."[13]

The fact was that after the Second World War, it became increasingly clear that expansion of the local economy was more likely to occur through "postindustrial" activities. In this, Columbus was advantaged in a number of distinct respects. The first is that state employment has always loomed large in the city (table 4.5). Shifting census definitions make it difficult to put together a more complete set of data, but the contrast in government employment, a contrast that presumably is owing to the strong state presence in Columbus, is clear across the three major urban counties of the state, and therefore among Cincinnati, Cleveland, and Columbus. As of 2017, employment by the state in Columbus amounted to over 6 percent of its employment. And then, in addition, there has been the weight of Ohio State University, which is a massive local employer: over 30,000, or over 8 percent, of employed workers (see "Coveting the Advantages of the State Capital").

TABLE 4.5. Percentage of employed workers in government employment: Cuyahoga, Franklin, and Hamilton Counties

COUNTY	1970 % GOV'T	1980 % GOV'T	2005 % LOCAL, STATE, FED GOV'T
Cuyahoga	13.0	10.2	11.5
Franklin	19.9	20.8	15.2
Hamilton	12.9	14.9	10.1

Both state and university employment boomed after the war. So too did that of other major white-collar employers. These included the city's numerous insurance firms, buoyed by increased home ownership and the victory of the automobile, with their particular property insurance requirements, and its banks, one of which would emerge as a quasi-national bank subsequent to the deregulation of banking in the

13. Ibid.

Coveting the Advantages of the State Capital

The concentration of state employment in Columbus has not gone uncontested. In 1994, there was an attempt to give some steam to a movement aimed at what was believed to be a more equitable distribution of state capital expenditures and the decentralization of state functions from Columbus. The proposal was to move departments like the Department of Natural Resources and the Department of Liquor Control to other locations in the state. This was "The Other Ohio," organized for the most part from Toledo by the publisher of the *Toledo Blade*. In the event, it did not gain much traction. It did, however, suggest the existence of tensions around the way in which Columbus has benefited from the location of state office employment.[1] This issue had been brewing for a couple of years.[2]

1. "The Have-Nots Want a Little More from the Haves," *Columbus Dispatch*, October 23, 1994, p. 1B.

2. See "Being State Capital Has Its Benefits," *Columbus Dispatch*, December 20, 1992, p. 1A.

1970s. Little wonder, therefore, that the Ford decision could be taken with such seeming insouciance. But one can also see why there was more than insouciance; there was downright opposition. Postindustrial cities, if they are to expand, and continue to attract other postindustrial activities, have to produce and reproduce an appropriate labor force. White-collar families will do that particular trick, while blue-collar families lack the sort of cultural capital necessary to creating underwriters, bank lending officers, claims officials, people to work in the state pension offices, and the like. Postindustrial cities have particular structures of feeling, which results in different public images. San Francisco is not Oakland and nor is Columbus, Cleveland.

The Postindustrial City as a Real Estate Opportunity

"MAJOR LEAGUE"

One of the more concrete slogans that has gone along with the emergence of the postindustrial city and given developers a more concrete goal through which they can exploit that emergence has been that of the "major league city." I have put it in scare quotes since it needs some critical examination. If you Google it, what you get are references to which cities have major league franchises, which lack them, and why that is or should or should not be. There is, though, a wider penumbra of meanings. Cities are "major league" if they have a national and positive visibility: a city with a vibe that can attract the corporate headquarters of firms or visitors to conventions. Major league franchises can help, particularly in attracting corporate headquarters and their entertainment needs, but obviously there is more to it than that. Los Angeles has done very well for a while without an NFL team, and now that they have two of them, the locals seem pretty indifferent to their arrival. Take away its baseball and football franchises and New York would still be "major league." So while a franchise may help cities that aren't "major league" become so, they are not always necessary to maintaining that status. To become a major league city in this wider sense, you need not only the franchises but also the convention center and associated hotels and the airline connections that can persuade those locating corporate headquarters and choosing convention locations—which brings us back to Columbus and *its* major league ambitions.

As outlined in chapter 3, the major league city agenda there included three priority items: a convention center, a major league franchise, and improved airline service. All have been achieved to some limited degree, if not without a struggle in the case of the convention center and major league franchises, and not in the spectacular fashion that growth interests in the city would like to have seen. The convention center still lacks the big hotels that would allow it to host major conventions, the major league franchises are not in either of the three major spectator sports in the US, and the airport still lags rivals like Indianapolis (a bit) and Charlotte (hugely).

On the other hand, the location of the convention center and the arena complex in the Arena District have had useful synergistic effects, not least in the Short North, enhanced gentrification in the area, and the prospect of stretching out those effects farther north. This synergy has come at something of a cost, though, in terms of the coherence of the downtown. Even before the Arena District had started to take shape, notably before the arrival of the arena that would give it its name, Leslie Wexner was critical of the dispersed nature of redevelopment.[14] As he said then:

14. "A Different View of Downtown," *Columbus Dispatch,* May 15, 1983, p. G-1. This view has been echoed more recently by the current (2017) mayor, Andrew Ginther: "We still struggle with the fact that it is one of the largest, most spread-out downtowns of any city our size in the country," Ginther said. "Many other big cities

> There is no nucleus; there is no heart; there is no center; there is no crossroads. You just have a bunch of people just spread out.

And:

> A lot of special interest groups have gone out in fragmented ways. How does any community control the real estate developers in an orderly way? There is a collective wisdom in the community that decides how the city is going to grow, whether it's tax abatements, tax incentives, strong zoning, strong leadership in the private sector. But that's what you didn't have here. You didn't have the city and the private sector working towards a common objective. You had the city cooperating with individual segments, each going his separate way.

If anything, the lack of cohesion has worsened. There is now a northern pole anchored by the Arena District, and the Short North just to the north of it; a considerably less vibrant southern nucleus focusing on the county office buildings and the Brewery District, a revivified area of former breweries offering loft living and numerous bars and restaurants; in between is the historic downtown around Capitol Square and consisting largely of office and hotel developments, along with an emergent set of residential towers for the wealthy to its south (see figure 4.2). If the hotels were closer to the convention center, that would be a help, and residential growth might be all the more rapid if there was more nightlife in the immediate vicinity, which was the inspiration for a free shuttle bus service now in operation: the CBus.[15]

The crowning glory of major league status would be to attract the corporate headquarters of a Fortune 500 firm. As of 2019, Columbus had four of these: Cardinal Health (16), Nationwide Insurance (73), American Electric Power (192), and L Brands (241), which at least testifies to its ability to retain them. But it lost a big one in Banc One. This was a bank, at one time known as City National, that had grown mightily on the back of bank deregulation. In the mid-'60s, it did not even have a branch outside Franklin County, and the reason was, by law it was not allowed to. Once the barriers to branching across county and state lines were progressively dismantled, it bought up banks not just elsewhere in Ohio but in twelve other states, including Arizona,

---

have much more dense, highly concentrated downtown areas" ("1 Million More People? Columbus on Verge of Growth Spurt," *Columbus Dispatch,* June 23, 2017.

15. https://www.cota.com/how-to-ride/cbus/.

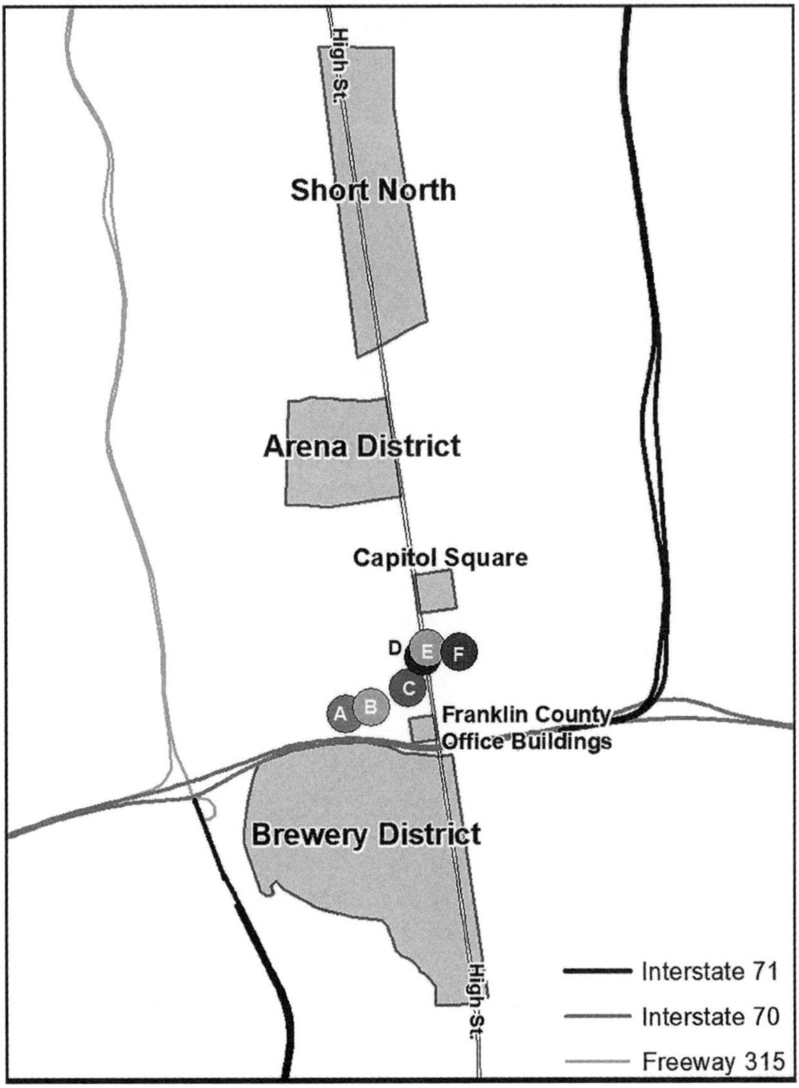

FIGURE 4.2. Stretching out the downtown. Key to residential towers—A: Miranova; B: Waterford Tower; C: Julian Apartments; D: LC River South; E: Highpoint on Columbus Commons; F: 80 on the Commons. The distance between Capitol Square and the Franklin County Office Buildings is about half a mile. The distance from Capitol Square to the Arena District somewhat over that. Map by Jamie Valdinger.

California, Illinois, Michigan, Texas, and Wisconsin. It then merged with First Chicago NBD in 1998, and part of the deal was that the headquarters move to Chicago, which in banking makes a sort of sense given the strongly agglomerative nature of its headquarters' business, like access to major business clients, though Charlotte seems to have thrived regardless.[16] The agglomerative logic then led to the new Bank One as it was, being bought out in 2000 by Chase Manhattan. This does not mean that Columbus has, in consequence, lost employment. In fact, Chase Manhattan has expanded considerably, to the point at which it now employs 20,000 people, which is a big chunk, whatever the size of the overall labor market: two and a half times what the old Bank One had employed almost twenty years ago. Furthermore, it is by no means all back-office employment, as the consumer banking administration is located there.[17] Nevertheless, the top brass are elsewhere.[18]

THE UNWANTED—AND THE WANTED

The creation of the postindustrial city entails massive changes in land use in the downtown and its immediate vicinity. To some degree, this occurs through the recycling of old industrial and railroad sites and, at least in a state capital like Columbus, the conversion of former state-owned land: With respect to the former, think of the replacement of the old Union Station by the first incarnation of the convention center, and with respect to state uses, the Arena District and the old state Pen. But there are other uses that have to be fended off, like homeless shelters and bus stops that attract the poor as they wait to change from one bus to another. By the same token, there are other uses that the promoters of the postindustrial city want to attract in from elsewhere in the metro area, and regardless of the consequences for the neighbor-

---

16. Exactly what led to the takeover of First Chicago and the move of the headquarters (HQ) to Chicago is still unclear. Acquisition in 1997 of First USA, a Dallas-based issuer of credit cards, was perhaps a step too far since it resulted in considerable business losses. Acquisition of First Chicago the following year may have been an attempt to right the ship, the cost of which was to move the HQ. This is speculation. What isn't, though, is that First Chicago insisted, as part of its price, that the HQ should indeed so move.

17. See Polya Lesova, "Why J. P. Morgan Is Adding Jobs in Columbus," *Market Watch,* September 20, 2012.

18. Hopes were raised again in 2011, when Sears was apparently contemplating moving its headquarters, along with 6,200 employees, from a Chicago suburb. Its rival was Austin, Texas. Quite colossal financial incentives were offered: "A $400 Million Carrot for Sears? Ohio Bids for HQ," *Columbus Dispatch,* December 1, 2011. But almost certainly, rumors of moving on the part of Sears were simply a bargaining tactic designed to put pressure on the state of Illinois, which had earlier demurred. In the light of the ongoing downturn in traditional retail and Sears's business struggles, this may have been a corporate HQ to be avoided.

hoods affected. Columbus, like many other American cities experiencing the developer-mediated transition to the postindustrial form, has known all of these.

The emergence of the postindustrial city has, for a variety of reasons, been accompanied by a rise in the homeless population. Exactly why is beyond the scope of this book, but the closure of state mental asylums on the dubious assumption that people could be medicated into sanity has certainly been one of them. The problem for the developers who slaver over the rents to be gained from high-rise office buildings and new residential towers is that the homeless tend to congregate downtown, and they do it for good reason: There are sidewalks and lots of foot traffic, which enhance the returns to panhandling. Further, social service agencies that provide help are attracted by the old warehouses and former retail outlets that have yet to be converted, so unsurprisingly, those catering to the homeless in the form of shelters likewise tend to cluster there—if they can. And in Columbus, they have collided with sites cherished by the developers, notably in the Short North and in the vicinity of the North Market in the early '80s, both of which as attempts to find somewhere for the homeless were vigorously rebuffed.[19] Since then, our city builders have been able to sleep easily in *their* beds.

But the great unwashed simply won't go away. They tiresomely congregate in the vicinity of the major crossroads of the downtown at High and Broad, with overflows both north and south, as they wait for buses to take them home from jobs, which incidentally are not ones that might provide them with the money to buy a car. In 2010, this issue found its way onto the city's agenda:

> Downtown developers have complained that COTA passengers waiting for transfers near Broad and High streets, and buses lining the curbs make the area less attractive for retail stores and their customers.
>
> It's an issue raised at least twice in a 10-year Downtown strategic plan endorsed by the Downtown Commission and the Columbus City Council this year. That plan calls for a Downtown transit center where people can wait for buses protected from the weather and away from High Street.
>
> In another recommendation that outlines ways to improve High Street, the plan singles out buses as a problem there: "The bus transit

19. Mair 1986.

> mall that occupies High Street increases bus congestion, blocks storefronts and prevents on-street parking."[20]

Frank Kass, prominent local developer, claimed that the downtown section of High Street—where he not uncoincidentally happened to own property—was the only "dead place" in a glowing highway of prosperity stretching from the Brewery District in the south to Worthington in the north.[21] What he failed to add, of course, was that one of the reasons it is dead is that the big pole of attraction for the office tenants is now the Arena District and, to a lesser degree, the Brewery District in the south—part of the dispersion effect that Wexner complained about. So instead of blaming the buses, he might blame Nationwide, the principal developers of the Arena District, who, again and not by coincidence, once occupied a major chunk of office space much, much closer to the intersection of Broad and High than where they are now. In the event, the Central Ohio Transit Authority, or COTA, resisted the idea of a downtown transit center away from High Street on the grounds that it would affect accessibility to the buses, and the transit center idea would eventually bite the dust in a compromise that took some of the buses off the main artery into parallel streets a block away.[22] So a minor win for the developers, though not before some of the usual extravagance from the *Dispatch* editorial writers: "End the Bus Blockade," they boomed.[23]

But there are also activities that the developers want to pull in from elsewhere to complement what they already have and to burnish the postindustrial city-in-the-making. The outstanding case of this has been the baseball stadium. Cooper Stadium, west of downtown

20. "All Those Buses and Riders: Bad for Business," *Columbus Dispatch,* November 2, 2010.

21. Ibid. This was a claim echoed in the same article by another local development advocate: "There are forty-five empty storefronts between Nationwide Insurance and the Franklin County Courthouse, according to Guy Worley, president and CEO of the Columbus Downtown Development Corp. They're less attractive spots for businesses, he said, because the wall of buses makes them invisible."

22. This would not be good enough for one of the members of the COTA Board of Directors—an appointee of the mayor who had come out publicly for a "solution"—who wanted a more radical dispersion of bus stops. In this way, he claimed, the crowds that gave cover to drug deals and attention seekers would be broken up. So full marks for an ingenious justification, as well as one that reinforces the stereotypes ("End the Bus Blockade," *Columbus Dispatch,* February 5, 2010).

23. Ibid.

in the somewhat rundown Franklinton, had long been the home of Columbus's minor baseball team, the Clippers, and was owned and operated by the county. By the early 2000s, there was debate about the future of the stadium.[24] Opinion seemed to be veering toward an entirely new stadium rather than renovating the existing one. Two possibilities emerged: first, one to the south of the downtown between the City Center shopping center and a nucleus of development focusing on the county courthouse and spilling over to the Brewery District to the south, the Mound-High Street site. This was supported by those anxious to promote the redevelopment of the center city, as well as the owner of the land, one of the Schottenstein family involved in development. And second, one next to the Arena District: pushed by Nationwide Realty Investors, for whom the summer, by virtue of the lack of ice hockey activity, was a downtime for the various bars and restaurants in the area. It was also recognized by the county commissioners that if the stadium moved, a use would have to be found for the existing thirty-eight-acre site: "There's no way we can leave Franklinton without a plan for what to do there," O'Shaughnessy said. "That's not fair to the people there."[25] Famous last words.

The decision, arrived at five years later, in 2007, would be to build a new stadium in the Arena District. This would be financed by county-backed bonds, with the debt to be paid off with a mix of revenue from corporate sponsorships ($30 million pledged) and stadium operations, a $9 million grant from the state, and proceeds from the sale of Cooper Stadium. The move was completed by 2009. The question then became, what to do with the old site? By the time the move was completed, there was a potential buyer. This would be Arshot Investment Corporation, owned by a local developer, William Schottenstein, which planned for the forty-six-acre site, an auto racetrack, though later modified to include a hotel, conference center, and restaurant and exhibition spaces. The news was met with general resistance[26] as the noise such an amenity was likely to make became an issue. Seven years later, with all the approvals needed and requests for incentives granted, the site was still undeveloped. But bottom line, who among those so

24. "New Downtown Baseball Park Back in Play," *Columbus Dispatch,* September 19, 2002, p. A1.

25. Ibid.

26. This included opposition from residents, businesses, and realty interests in adjacent German Village, a gentrified neighborhood of elevated incomes, and the Metropolitan Parks Board, concerned about disturbance to its bird-watching facilities.

Pulling in and Pushing Out

It is all a matter of making room for the desirable, and that might mean getting some uses pushed out elsewhere. In November 2012, there was an odd news story. The city of Columbus was threatening the use of the right of eminent domain to secure the sale of a property of just less than seven acres on McKinley Avenue, a light industrial area to the west of the downtown. It seemed that the owner had earlier agreed to a sale and then decided to sell it to someone else and, to add insult to injury, for less than the city was offering. The city wanted the land as a site for code enforcement and public utility crews currently located in the Arena District. In the end, the land would be transferred without the city drawing on that power. No reason was given for why the city wanted to so relocate, though toward the end of the saga, it was stated that it wanted to move "out of the congested Arena District."[1] That may well have been. The questions are: Was it pushed so as to release valuable land to developers? And if so, did it obtain a fair market price? Or was it another case of socialism for developers?

1. "Columbus to Start $11 Million in Work on Land Where It Forced Sale," *Columbus Dispatch*, September 29, 2014.

keen to build the postindustrial city gives a damn? To paraphrase from the Vietnam War era, just a bit of "collateral damage" (see "Pulling in and Pushing Out").

THE RETURN OF THE MIDDLE CLASS

Gentrification, the slow conversion of older housing, typically regarded as of some architectural merit, from occupation by a working-class population to use by a more affluent stratum, has become a distinguishing trait of the postindustrial city. The obvious reason for this is a demand for convenient housing subsequent to the growth of white-collar employment in the central city, particularly in financial services, law, and, in some instances, higher education. It is, though, a little more complex. The changing contours of the life cycle, particularly for the better heeled, has clearly made a difference. The growth of the single-adult population and delayed child rearing have certainly played a part, if only because for these groups, the issue of city schools that invariably attaches to central city living either does not apply or can be put off to a distant, yet-to-be-defined, future.

As a paragon of the postindustrial city, Columbus is home to numerous cases of neighborhoods undergoing this sort of conversion, but at different stages. These range from German Village to the south of the downtown, which is virtually complete, through Harrison West and Victorian Village and then more intermediate cases like Italian Village, to ones like Olde Towne East and more recently East Franklinton,[27] where the process is still in the initial stages. Originally it was more serendipitous, bottom-up, promoted by fixing-up home buyers, attracted by the domestic architecture of a neighborhood and perhaps some shared features of it, like shaded streets, who happened to find themselves in close proximity to others just like them. German Village, dating from the early '60s, and Victorian Village, starting in the 1970s, fall broadly under this heading. German Village was an area of small, tightly packed houses bordering cobbled streets, dating back to the mid-1800s, and once home, it is commonly claimed, to German artisans. It is now something of a tourist attraction, with its distinct architecture and "olde worlde" feel. What is now Victorian Village, on the other hand, dates back to the first two decades of the twentieth century, when it was *the* place to live in Columbus.[28] In both cases, chance played an important role: not just the fact of doer-uppers doing-up at the same time in the same general area, which would form the basis for the creation of neighborhood groups to lobby the city for tree plantings, code enforcement, and restoration of cobbled streets, where they had been torn up, as well as pressuring banks to lift their lending restraints on the areas concerned. Both areas also benefited from the proximity of very attractive city parks. In the Victorian Village case, the way had also been cleared by one of the very few instances of urban renewal in Columbus back in the 1950s. This had been the clearance of Flytown, a supposed slum, on the southern edge of what would become Victorian Village in order to make way for freeway construction, a high-rise retirement community, and a small shopping center; this would then go on to anchor the rehabbing to the north—a nice "safe" area, in other words.[29]

---

27. The term "East Franklinton" is interesting, suggesting an attempt to differentiate from "Franklinton," which has a less than salubrious reputation.

28. "The homes are noted for their stained and leaded glass, soaring turrets, elaborate porches and carriage houses" ("Victorian Era Lives Again," *Columbus Dispatch*, September 6, 1981, p. K-6).

29. For a useful discussion of the Victorian Village case, see Lenore Egan Brown, "Victorian Village: A Once-Grand Neighborhood Fights Back," *Columbus Monthly*, June 1975.

Starting in the '80s, though, what attracts attention is the way in which gentrification becomes more engineered, more intentional, more corporate, and responding to a more coherent vision, if one can apply such a positive sounding term to such a dodgy process, and harnessed to other agendas. While in the German Village and Victorian Village conflict had been muted because displacement had been more gradual, this would change. Gentrification, as elsewhere, would become almost a dirty word, giving way to more anodyne expressions like "redevelopment" and "revitalization": in other words, the "something for everybody" that is exactly that—pure pie in the sky.

A taste of things to come would be the so-called Renaissance District—in its label, not exactly "revitalization," but pretty close.[30] This would be to the northwest of Victorian Village and even overlap with it, providing further impetus to the latter through its synergistic effects. The "coherent vision" in this instance would be that of the Battelle Institute, a private research organization that at that time had over 1,000 employees and was, and is, located on the northern edge of the area that would be gentrified. Starting in 1960, Battelle had acquired a quite massive number of houses to its immediate south: In fact, it would eventually own just short of two-thirds of all the houses and a few vacant lots in an area of at least seventeen blocks.[31] The intent was to hold the housing as part of Battelle's plans for future expansion. The area consisted of numerous visually attractive houses that had been subdivided into apartments for students and the working poor. It was a center of gravity for Appalachian immigrants, and a relatively transient neighborhood. But by 1975, Battelle's calculations regarding the area had changed.

On the one hand, it had revised downward its expansion needs. On the other, it had been the object of a financially punishing court decision. The institute had been created by one Gordon Battelle in 1923. It was his will that led to the establishment of a nonprofit institute, but the will had also specified that part of its revenues had to go to charitable enterprises. The latter would come under the spotlight in the 1970s. Battelle, it was argued, had neglected its responsibilities. The settle-

30. Adrienne Bosworth, "Renaissance: The Controversial Rebirth of a Neighborhood," *Columbus Monthly,* January 1983.

31. Depending on how one defines "block"; those who want to check it out on Google Maps should look at the area in question, which was bounded by King Avenue on the north, Neil Avenue to the east, Third Avenue on the south, and the Olentangy River on the west. Pretty impressive, in other words.

ment was worth over $80 million.[32] The federal government would then step in and confiscate the institute's tax-exempt status, which required the payment of some $46 million in back taxes. This was the somewhat complex background to trying to withdraw from ownership of this housing stock, but at a financial advantage.

Smoothing the way, and helping to quell the uproar over displacement, there was money from the federal Department of Housing and Urban Development, which was looking for a rehab project to finance in order to show how a neighborhood could be revitalized without displacing low- to moderate-income households: $2 million used for mortgage assistance to those who could afford it, relocation expenses for those who could not, along with some physical improvements to the neighborhood. In the event, some 110 moderate-income families were indeed assisted in becoming homeowners, but two hundred others were displaced. There would still be contention, largely around plans for demolishing housing to make way for a five-acre shopping center in the area that would, in fact, be rejected by the city council on a rezoning issue.[33]

To repeat: This was a foretaste. It would be a foretaste, not just of engineered gentrification but of the role that major institutions can play in using gentrification for their own purposes. For others, it would be a matter of securing their boundaries. This would be the goal of the Ohio State University. Its project would be on the southeast border of the university, including something to be called Campus Gateway and also the "revitalization" of neighboring Weinland Park. What had sparked this off was the murder in 1994 in the area of a student, Stephanie Hummer. After the usual encomia of sympathy and regret, the university realized that the problem was quite a bit broader. The threat of death by violence might not put off students from going to Ohio State,but their parents were a different consideration altogether.[34] The immediate goal, working through a development agency created

32. As discussed in chapter 3, this would be significant in financing the first Columbus convention center; so much for "charitable enterprises"!

33. "Near Northsiders Fight Shopping Plaza," *The Lantern,* June 9, 1980.

34. "Hummer's death was obviously a tragedy, but for Ohio State it was also a full-fledged public-relations crisis. Parents want to believe that when they send their kids off to ol' State U., they'll be safe. But South Campus—awash in rundown student housing, seedy bars and drug dealing—wasn't safe. And because the neighborhood wasn't university property, OSU officials didn't deal with the gathering danger" ("The Gateway Gamble," *The Other Paper,* March 3–9, 2005, p. 1).

by the university, Campus Partners (as in "partners with whom and for whom?"), was to replace an area of bars with office space, grad student housing, and what was initially described as "a better mix of retail."[35] This would be part of a larger plan to "revitalize"[36] the entire adjacent area surrounding the campus and to encourage homeownership.

Drawing on the right of eminent domain granted by the city, or at least its threat, to assemble the land, the immediate result would be a largely retail development spread over 7.4 acres. Attention then shifted to "upgrading" Weinland Park, an effort stimulated by a desire to rid the area of a population of low-income renters, largely African American, seen as posing a threat to the security of students. The specific form of the initiative was the Weinland Park Collaborative (WPC), formed in 2010 with the goal of "revitalizing"[37] the neighborhood and bringing together the university, the city, the Columbus Foundation, JPMorgan Chase—a firm with a presence in the city as a result of its takeover of BancOne, and with numerous employees—and others. The publicly announced goal was a mixed-income neighborhood without displacement. The emphasis would be on the development of abandoned property, an industrial site requiring brownfield remediation, and foreclosed homes. This has actually occurred, though how durable the fix will be remains to be seen.

Weinland Park had a lot of Section 8 properties: apartments rented to holders of Section 8 vouchers. Section 8 has been an attempt to privatize subsidized housing for the poor. Instead of living in housing owned by a state agency and built explicitly for those of low income, the effort has been to distribute vouchers that cap the rent the holder has to pay the landlord, the remainder being paid by the federal government. The presence of so many poor people and the pathologies that they often attract was clearly a problem for the Weinland Park Collaborative. Certainly there was support within Weinland Park for getting rid of them so that gentrification and their property values could flourish, and indeed some of the (now former) Section 8 properties have been converted to homeownership. A very large number

35. "Big Plan on Campus," *The Columbus Guardian,* August 3, 1995.

36. Ibid.

37. In scare quotes because it is such a deceptive word that hides as much as it reveals, and that can mean different things to different people. For an existing homeowner, it can mean getting rid of "them"; for the poor, it can mean improved public infrastructure; and for real estate investors, gentrification.

were owned by a private entity, Broad Street Management Inc., which was seen as part of the problem: supposedly lax in property upkeep and tenant surveillance. This portfolio of properties was purchased by the Weinland Park Collaborative. The properties were rehabbed and Section 8 tenants relocated elsewhere. What is interesting, though, is that, for whatever reason, they have been allowed back in to the rehabbed housing but on quite strict conditions: that is, a very strict vetting process for criminal records, the criminal records of relatives (!), and substance abuse. On return, they had to agree to a code of conduct, allowing the organization to whom this aspect of the initiative had been delegated to enter at any time and inspect for criminal activities or undocumented residents. Just what is going on here is unclear. Has the university bent to criticism of displacement subsequent to the process? Or has it a longer-term strategy in view? Certainly, if you can have tenants without the dysfunctionalities, then the area will be more attractive to those with money who are looking for housing. In other words, a more liberal approach might ultimately achieve a more complete gentrification, with the present tenantry a mere holding pattern. Meanwhile, there is money for existing homeowners to rehab property exteriors—up to $20,000, depending on income, and down-payment assistance for university employees who would like to buy property there.

Some summary observations can now be entered. First, in what might be called "Stage 2" gentrification, institutions like the university and Battelle have played an important role. The city has supported these initiatives for its own fiscal reasons; it likes the idea of the higher home values that come in the wake of the process. There was, in consequence, disappointment when a major hospital, Mount Carmel, announced its decision to pull up most of its stakes from a neighborhood on the near west side, long targeted by the city for "revitalization," Franklinton, in favor of a location in suburban Grove City.[38]

Second, there is the question of displacement, for which gentrification is notorious. German Village proceeded without much opposition.[39] Over time, this has changed. One instance, the gentrification

38. "Mount Carmel Moving Inpatient Hospital to Grove City as Part of $711 Million Investment," *Columbus Dispatch,* March 12, 2015.

39. In 1978, though, there was an anxiety that an extension of German Village boundaries, with all the property value implications it would entail, would result in displacement. See "Expansion of German Village Dies in Vote by Columbus City

of Olde Towne East, which included a large number of poorer African American households, received wide publicity in a much acclaimed film, *Flag Wars.* The movie documented not just the fact of displacement but also cultural tensions. There was, for instance, gentrifier opposition to a sign for a community gallery carved in African relief—supposedly in violation of housing restrictions implemented when the area was declared, with the prompting of the middle-class rehabbers, a historic district.[40]

Just where those displaced move to raises interesting questions that have yet to be researched. Presumably the areas are ones where the housing is more affordable than it becomes with gentrification, which means areas with relatively low or declining home values: Think, for example, of those devastated by the fallout from deindustrialization, like Hilltop, the South Side, and increasingly some areas in southeast Columbus. This in turn suggests that gentrification, much as its glories are trumpeted by the developers and the city with talk of "revitalization" and "redevelopment" is no solution to the question of dilapidated housing; it simply gets moved around. Not, though, that they would seem to care:

> Developer David Pierson, an Italian Village commissioner, said it is inevitable that some low- to moderate-income families are forced out of the village. "In any situation like German or Italian Village, any time you come into any area and improve it—those [low-income] people are going to have to go somewhere. I don't know where that is going to be, out east or out W Broad Street or something," Pierson said.[41]

Council," *Columbus Dispatch,* March 28, 1978, p. B-5; "Council Denies Annexation," *The Lantern,* May 26, 1978, p. 5.

40. There is a good description of the movie in the Wiki entry: "Flag Wars," *Wikipedia,* n.d. It used to be available on YouTube, but apparently no longer.

41. Bill Eichenberger, "Italian Village, Tradition, Transition," *Capitol Magazine,* February 22, 1987, p. 10. In the same article: "Aristotle Matsa, also a village commissioner, said the neighborhood has done well housing the poor and elderly. 'We have more and better housing for those with low and moderate incomes than ever before.' Matsa cited the Bollinger Tower and Taylor Terrace senior citizen complexes, as well as 100 or more Section 8 [low-income] housing units as examples of the neighborhood's success" (p. 10). The reference to Bollinger Tower is interesting. As we will see in chapter 7, it too would bite the dust as "better housing for those with low and moderate incomes" as gentrification of a commercial sort has surged in its vicinity.

This is to view the process as a process in itself, and not so much an aspect of the creation of the postindustrial city. In that regard, and bracketing the displacement of the poor, it is a highly contradictory one. This is because it brings back into an area of the city, undergoing all manner of redevelopment, a stratum of people who, when it comes to where they live, are not about to be pushed around. These include more than the usual proportion of professionals able to articulate an argument in a way that attracts the attention of city officials, along with lawyers and civil engineers who can bring expert knowledge to bear. There is a history of concern on the part of the Victorian and Italian Village gentrifiers at the parking implications of projects like the convention center and later plans for a city-sponsored arena. The rise of the commercial district known as the Short North has been a more recent provocation, again on parking grounds. Even gentrifying areas not so close to the major action have revolted. Such was the case of German Village when it opposed the plans for redeveloping the old Clippers stadium site on account of the noise that would be generated by a proposed high-speed auto-racing track.

There is an old view of the American city, according to which the poor live closer to the city center and the wealthier live out in the suburbs. As employment shifted out to the suburban fringes in the 1960s, this led to the idea of a spatial mismatch: The poor who needed the jobs had a long way to get to them. This was always an oversimplified view, not least because there were blue-collar suburbs, and with the elapse of time it has become more and more an exception rather than the rule. Then again, there were always directional biases in the way urban expansion proceeded; suburbanization proved easier in some directions than in others. So in Columbus, there has always been a northward bias in the suburbanization of the population, slightly less to the west-northwest and east-northeast, and very little to the south, which has to do with the physics of sewage flow: The treatment plants are in the south, the river basins that the city straddles slope in that direction, and pumping sewage against the topographic grain is very expensive.[42] The postindustrial city has accentuated some of these features and introduced new ones into the city's social geography.

In Columbus, one of the most obvious changes has been gentrification and latterly the development downtown of residential towers for the wealthy. As the city has become more postindustrial, so indus-

42. Hunker 2000, 28.

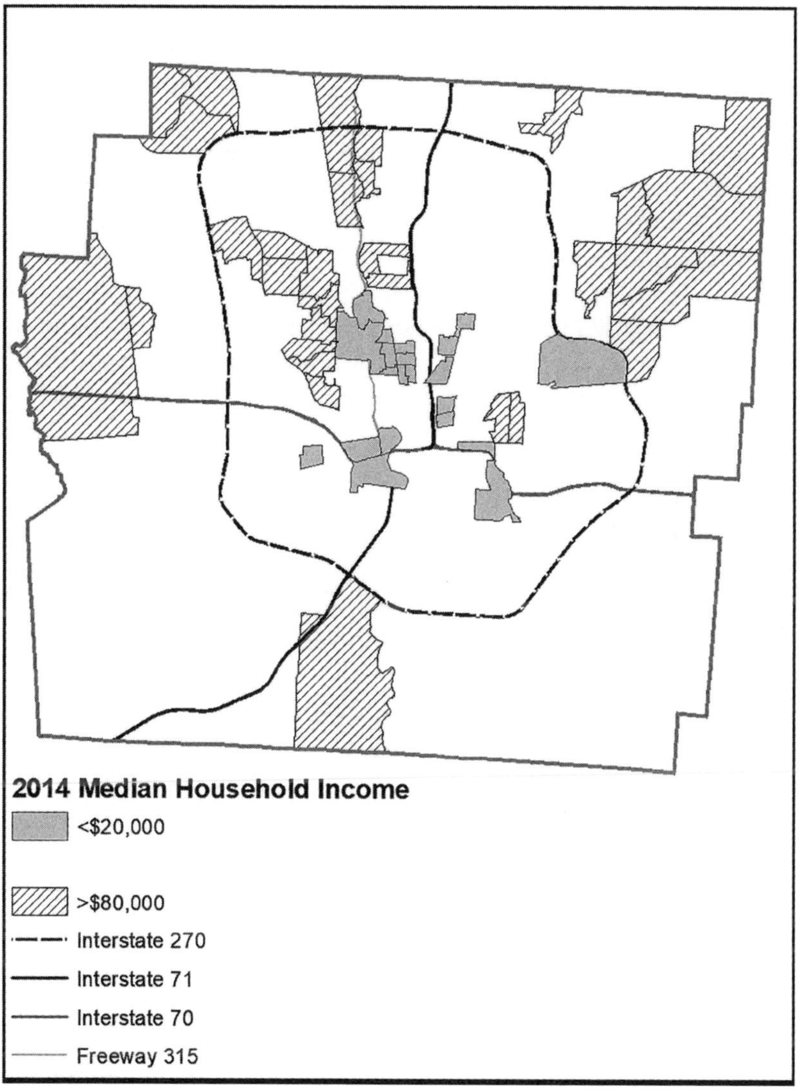

FIGURE 4.3. Median income, 2014. Wealthier along a northern arc from west to east, poorer in the center, and middling everywhere else. Map by Jamie Valdinger.

trial employment has greatly diminished, leaving in its wake rust belts. Meanwhile, the growth of a more affluent stratum has been manifest in what can be described as "the golden arc": a belt that follows approximately the Outerbelt from the west side around the north to the east (see figure 4.3). This is where the more affluent of the suburbs are located: Hilliard, Upper Arlington, Dublin, Worthington, Westerville, and Gahanna, and, at some remove, New Albany and now pushing still farther east into Licking County. There are also the large swathes of the city of Columbus located in those suburban school districts that grew rapidly in the wake of busing for racial balance, as we saw in chapter 2. It includes major nodes of office employment at intersections of the Outerbelt at Dublin, Worthington, Polaris (just to the north and off I-71), and Easton. The counterpart to this in the southern part of the city is the efflorescence of warehouse, distribution center, and associated trucking depot and truck-servicing employment, notably around but not necessarily in the Rickenbacker development, to the east of the airport, taking in Reynoldsburg, which is home to a very large distribution center for The Limited,[43] recently slopping over into Licking County,[44] and on the west where the Outerbelt intersects with I-70 (see figure 4.4), and generating a very different built environment.[45]

The label "postindustrial city," of course, signifies that manufacturing industry is a thing of the past and Columbus, like its peers, has been affected by a rash of plant closures. It is no accident that these have occurred in areas that are now some of the poorest in Columbus: the city's rustbelts, in other words. Areas particularly badly affected by this have included the following:

- The West Side, which had been the site of a number of large assembly plants: White Westinghouse closed in the late 1980s, and Delphi, at one time a GM body plant, Fisher-Body Ternstedt, in 2007. As remarked above, these had initially been large employers.
- The South Side: Closure of Federal Glass in 1979 left 1,500 without work, and the slow rundown of employment at Buckeye Steel Castings, which eventually closed for good in 2016, had employed 2,000 in the '50s but was eventually down to 650.
- The Near Northeast Side:
    - Timken: 2001, just over 200 employees at time of closure, effectively closed 1986.

43. Employing 3,700 in 2020: https://en.wikipedia.org/wiki/Reynoldsburg,_Ohio.

44. A newly announced Amazon distribution center in the western part of Licking County will reportedly employ 4,000 workers" ("Online Shopping Growth Spurs Big Job Gains Here," *Columbus Dispatch,* November 20, 2016). It is now up and running.

45. One should be careful not to exaggerate this. There are numerous pockets of the less well-off along the northern arc but also areas of more affluent housing in the southern and western suburbs, notably in Grove City and Pickerington.

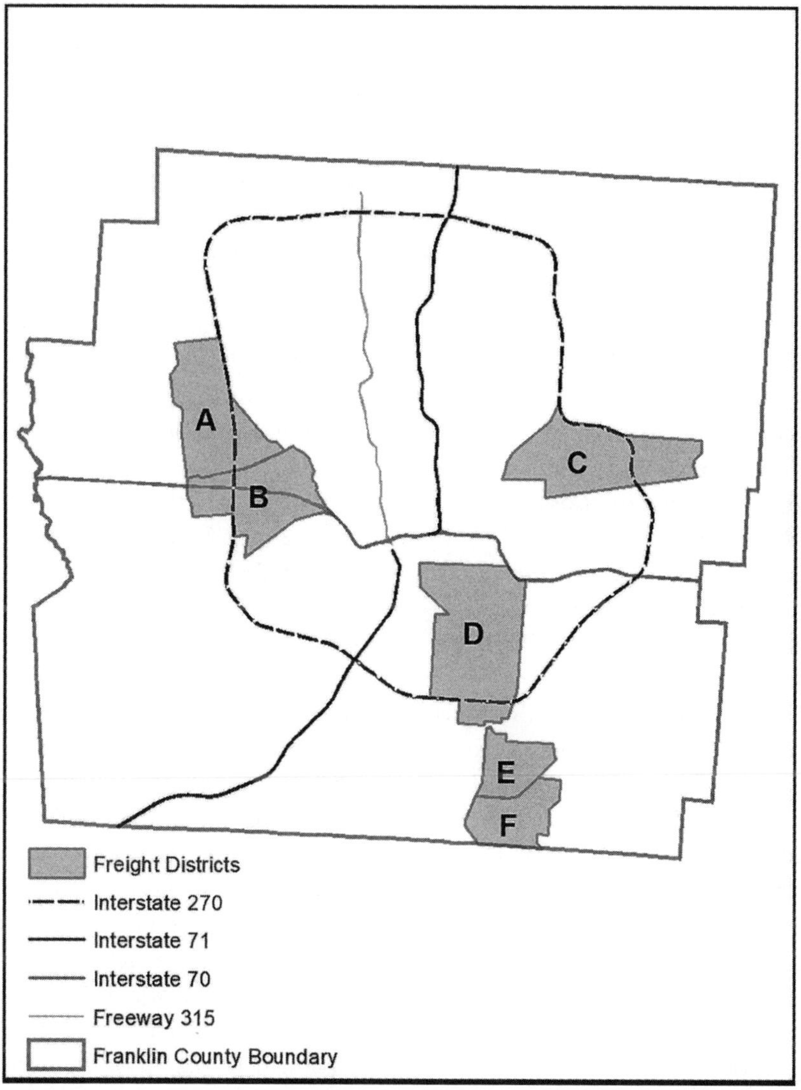

FIGURE 4.4. Freight districts in Franklin County. Key to districts—A: West Belt North; B: West Belt South; C: Port Columbus; D: Discovery Park; E: Rickenbacker North; F: Rickenbacker South. Map by Jamie Valdinger.

- Jeffrey Mining and Manufacturing: 1974 sale by Jeffrey family to Dresser Industries; closure in 1995 with employment of 100.
- Columbus Coated Fabrics: closed 2001; 250 employees at the time.

On the other hand, the fact of the rust belt appearance of many of the areas surrounding what were once thriving industrial plants is more complex than might initially appear. Commuting geography is always too complex to assign the employees in a particular neighborhood to a particular employer. The effects of closure for immediately surrounding areas cannot have been good, but the age of the housing also needs to be taken into account. Manufacturing, in testimony to its relative age in Columbus, was in what are now regarded as older parts of the city. Much of that housing has long since lost favor with the growth of newer models with more modern amenities, including garages, farther out. In consequence, areas like Hilltop and Lincoln West, the South Side or the area on the northeast around what had been Jeffrey Mining and Manufacturing and Columbus Coated Fabrics, are, apart from the aged who are in a sense marooned there, the last resort of those who are unable to afford anything better (see "Where Do the Displaced Move To?"). Some of it is favorably located so that it can take advantage of the gentrification boom; Victorian Village, close to what had been the Jeffrey plant, is a case in point. Again, the Jeffrey site has been leveled and is being redeveloped for a more affluent clientele: Jeffrey Park.

The way in which the division of labor in manufacturing developed also bears emphasis. Some were always at the end of the queue, most notably African Americans, whether through racial discrimination in employment practices—common before the '70s—or simply, by virtue of a recent rural Southern background, lacking in basic education. Accordingly, African Americans always made up a disproportionate number of the unemployed. The way in which social life outside employment was racially structured also did not help. A good deal of blue-collar labor, particularly assembly-line work, has always been recruited through word of mouth; given the fact that African Americans are a minority—less than 14 percent in the city of Columbus[46]—and that social networks tend to be racially homogeneous, the likelihood of an African American hearing of a job is much lower than for whites.

The obverse to this set of rust belts is what might be called the "golden arc" described above. The employment base is very different, though obviously that does not mean that people living in these places work there; there is in fact a huge commute along the Northern Outer-

46. Census estimate for 2016.

Where Do the Displaced Move To?

Just where those displaced by gentrification end up would be worthy of study. The epicenter of Appalachian Columbus used to be what is now Harrison West and Victorian Village: gentrified areas, in other words. There were, in the 1960s, numerous Appalachian bars on North High Street where one could observe traditional dancing of the clogging variety. The Appalachians have gone, so where did they go to? Hilltop is a possibility. According to a very brief report of 2013 by Christina Drain, the population currently is predominantly "Appalachian white."[1]

1. "Hope for the Hilltop," https://engage.osu.edu/newslist-items/hope-for-the-hilltop.html.

belt connecting them to various concentrated areas of white-collar employment. Each of the freeway interchanges has major office developments around the Tuttle, Sawmill, Worthington, Westerville, and Easton exits and then north along I-70 to take in the massive office developments at Polaris. Aside from the nucleus of office employment downtown, which remains very considerable, with Nationwide Insurance employing at last 13,000 there, this is where the job growth is. The top five office parks are listed in table 4.6.

TABLE 4.6. Top five office parks, Columbus area, 2015

OFFICE PARK	OFFICE SPACE (SQUARE FEET)
Polaris Centers of Commerce	4.50m
Easton	3.76m
New Albany Business Park	3.07m
Tuttle Crossing Business Park	2.70m
Arena District	1.78m

Source: "Office Parks," *Columbus Business First,* January 2, 2015. Available at https://www.bizjournals.com/columbus/subscriber-only/2015/01/02/office-parks.html (last accessed October 25, 2018).

Median income, of course, is a key variable in tracking the unevenness of development in the Columbus area, and the golden or northern arc is where the more affluent tend to concentrate. It is the obverse of the city's rust belts. Accordingly, it has become the fount of developer fortunes and, with its growing, affluent populations, a crucible of local politics. The die was cast quite early with Columbus's annexation policy, starting in the 1950s. The major push has always been to the north, capitalizing on the demands of developers for access to services for their projects. It would be along the northern arc that the conditions would be laid for the explosive schools annexation issue, for it was here that the city had advanced into the suburban school districts on a quite massive scale, as discussed in chapter 2. The rapid shift of population to the north, and the growth of Delaware County, has set the stage for the mall wars to be discussed in the next chapter. Westland and Southland went quietly, but the Northland case would be dramatic. And in addition, as one might expect, it is along the northern arc that issues of congestion have been most pressing and, despite massive state investments in alleviating road works, continue to press. There is no end to it because capacity-increasing infrastructure merely encourages more development and more car use. Accordingly, developers have been central to what has transpired in this part of the city. It is to their role in the politics of development that we turn next.

CHAPTER 5

Property Development and the Pursuit of Rent

The Developers

There is clearly a genre of business called "development," and the people who commit resources to it are known as "developers." They have been a major focus of the discussion so far. Now we need to take a closer look at how they make their money. First off, we should notice how complex the development industry is. In the jargon of the economist, it exhibits all manner of degrees of vertical integration and disintegration. There are firms, often titled "land companies," that do little more than buy up land, holding it until it is "ripe" and can be sold to someone who is going to build on it. There are the so-called housing developers who buy the land, subdivide it, insert the roads and utilities, and then sell lots to individual builders. Some, on the other hand, embrace all parts of the process: buying the land, inserting the utilities, and carrying out the building, though perhaps subcontracting to someone for that purpose. In other words: a huge diversity of combinations, and some developers even have their own realty companies in charge of finding tenants. Then again, there are firms that specialize in different sorts of development. Don Casto is the major developer of shopping centers not just in Columbus but in the rest of Ohio and beyond, though not, it would seem, of mega-malls like Fashion Place at Polaris. Don Kenny specializes in rental housing. The primary concern of Nationwide Realty Investors has been offices, though in the Grandview Yard case, it has also been involved in housing. And so on.

Ultimately what is at stake is the provision of premises, either for rent or sale. Some properties may be retained by the developer as a source of rent, while others are sold on to release capital for further projects. Housing is sold to households, but apartment complexes may be sold to firms that are specialist landlords, who may then subcontract to a property management company. Insurance companies like office and shopping center developments because of the relatively stable stream of revenue that they provide: something that helps see them through sudden bumps in claims. They then rent space to individual retailers or firms needing offices.

This is how we know development today. It bears emphasis, though, that prior to the Second World War, it would have been much harder to discern. It was only afterward that the development industry blossomed into something that we would now recognize as such. Business always had specialized industrial, financial, and commercial sectors; only later would it acquire what is known as a property sector.

Accordingly, and prior to an examination of how they make their money, this chapter opens with a discussion of this historical background and the logics of property capitals—the sorts of practices they engage in, how they engage in them, and why. These practices are aimed ultimately at making money, but how they do that varies, and this variation needs to be acknowledged. On the one hand, they work on their own, getting the cooperation of local government, designing their developments so that they can maximize the take from particular sites, like sites on golf courses or lakes, in the case of housing. They also work together to maximize their profits. Some of this is utterly intentional. They may combine forces, spreading the risks involved in large, long-stay projects. They also know what they are doing when they support each other in combating the threat of impact fees. In other instances, the effect is unintended. What they build has advantages over earlier vintages of housing, shopping center, office development, and the like. This places the latter at a disadvantage, to the point at which they may have to lower their rents. Ultimately, older developments get abandoned: what I refer to as the "scorched earth" effect. This is not something that developers intended, but by thinning out the competition, it certainly works to their advantage.

This is the substance of this chapter and the one to follow. In this one, I provide some historical background that helps shed light on developer strategies. This is followed by some examples of these strategies in action. In the following chapter, I explore the various ways in which developers combine, both intentionally and otherwise, to bolster their profits.

Property Capital and Development Politics

As might have been surmised from various references earlier in the book, property developers are hugely important to the politics of development, not just in Columbus but throughout the US. This is something that is very American. It is much less the case in the cities of Western Europe, where the balance with local and central government has tended to be different. But even in the US, it was a power that only became apparent subsequent to the Second World War. In the nineteenth century, things had been quite different. What might be called a property sector did not exist, at least in the contemporary sense. Provision had to be made for housing and premises of various sorts, but it was handled differently. If a factory was to be built, it would be the industrialist him- or herself who would locate the land, find an architect and builder, and pay for everything, either out of pocket or on the basis of bank loans. Manufacturing companies did not rent their premises any more than retailers. Renting, rather, was something people did to get a roof over their heads, but even then, the landlord was a very small operator, perhaps living on the same block or even under the same roof, and not at all "professional" in the modern sense, since he or she would often have some other job or business, like owning a small neighborhood grocery. If you were planning on owning a house, you would likely buy a piece of land and have it custom built. The professional developer, building ahead of demand, holding for rent that could then be ploughed back into more development, was, for the most part, sometime in the future.

But "sometime," and not a long time. In the first two decades of the new century, there were more than straws in the wind. For a start, the precursors of the modern shopping center were beginning to put in an appearance. One of the best known is Kansas City's Country Club Plaza, which was in operation by 1923 and geared to the shopper arriving by car. Something similar, if not quite so ambitious, was located in Main Line, a wealthy suburb of Philadelphia.[1] This was Suburban Square, developed close to a railroad station during the 1920s by

1. Dyer 1998.

a syndicate of local businesspeople, including ones with interests in real estate and banking. As in the case of Country Club Plaza, a notable feature was the way in which it managed to attract branches of department stores already well established in the downtown: another portent for the future. In a discussion of "organized factory districts," Harris and Lewis point out how

> these were planned privately by railway and real estate companies and supported by local government. Of small account before World War I, there were 122 such districts in 84 cities by mid-century [in North America]. Places such as New York's Bush Terminal offered manufacturers cheap land, low taxes, direct freight car service, building design, financial assistance, and other external economies.[2]

And then there was housing. There were large planned developments sometimes covering hundreds of acres, like the Columbus suburb of Upper Arlington. These were the product of what Marc Weiss (1987) has called "the community builders," subdividing, inserting utilities, making provision for parks, sometimes doing the actual building and speculating on customers. They would then be immensely important in a national organization, NAREB, or the National Association of Real Estate Boards. It would be NAREB that would put pressure on the Federal Housing Administration (FHA) in the 1930s for a tightening up of zoning standards so as to protect the investments of their members. They would be important in the decision to set up the FHA in the first place and in its decision to insure mortgages and so turn on the spigots of mortgage finance and lay the basis for the postwar wave of suburbanization—something from which they would benefit immensely.

By then, property development had emerged as a clearly defined sector of capitalist enterprise. While industry produced the goods, the retail sector distributed them, and the banks financed investment and, increasingly, customer purchase, the property sector provided the premises and collected rents: rents from corporations located in office parks, rents from retailers occupying shopping centers, and rents from industrial corporations seeking a modular unit. A similar pattern repeated itself in housing. Firms needed workers and workers needed housing. So there were increasingly large apartment developments as

2. Harris and Lewis 2001, 281.

well as a lot of housing for purchase, in which case it would be the bank that would collect the rent, albeit in the form of mortgage interest.[3] Rent was increasingly the name of the game, though to finance additional investment a lot of apartment developments, shopping centers, and office parks would find their way into the portfolios of companies in need of a fairly constant source of revenues, most notably insurance companies and pension funds. Property development would become a highly specialized business, though that did not mean that others might not get in on the renting game, like hotels, universities, and hospitals. And they would in Columbus, of course, where health and higher education have been growth industries: Think of the recent rash of high-rise apartment developments for students opposite the university, not to mention the expansion of dormitory facilities engaged in by the university itself.

Development has become a highly competitive business. Office buildings, housing, and shopping centers are built without any assured tenants or customers, though if banks see a glut of property, they may withhold loans until there are guarantees of a major tenant like, in the case of a shopping center, an anchor store. Cost competition is important in snagging the buyer, but pushing the rivals out of the game is not necessarily the result, which is where product competition comes into play. Developers try to ensure their future by innovation. Property development has become a matter of introducing something "better" than what had gone before. The history is easy to observe: two-car garages instead of one-car, and later three-car garages; apartment developments with community centers, health centers, and swimming pools; malls replacing shopping strips and covered malls replacing those that were open to the air; housing developments around golf courses, then around lakes, then with bike paths and jogging trails. Then there are the more specialized developments: residential complexes for the retired, like Friendship Village in Dublin, where you can change your arrangements as your condition deteriorates, but stopping short of an on-site crematorium.

There have been tendencies to more integrated forms of development, too: If you are building housing, make provision for a small shopping center and snag the rents that someone else would if you

3. Rent is equivalent to the rate of interest; why otherwise build to rent out, when the money itself could be loaned out at a higher rate of interest? In other words, there has to be a close relation between the rate of interest and rents as a proportion of what it cost to put some building up.

left it out;[4] hotels go with restaurants and cinemas; and so on. What innovation and integration of land uses has meant is a tendency to developments covering ever larger acreages, and this affects the geography of development. It pushes it out to the periphery of the urban area, where land is easier to assemble simply because there are fewer owners, and ones owning larger areas of land in the first place, to deal with. Closer in to the center of the urban area, it is not just that land is already developed and would need clearance, possibly involving negotiation with existing tenants and issues of unclear titles, because not all the land is. But the still-to-be-developed land comes in relatively small pockets and fitting in a big development is much more difficult, which is one of the reasons that as you get closer to the center of the city, building elevation increases.[5] There are other advantages to the periphery, particularly for residential development. Over large acreages, the housing developer can control a great deal—the layout of the development, its density, the inclusion of features like some parkland—though there is also stuff that one cannot control, like, even notably, the schools. On the other hand, on the edge of the built-up area, the chances are higher that you as a developer can, in effect, colonize a school district that so far has few children, and your development is going to change everything, even while you may have to help out with the construction of new schools. In other words, as a developer you put yourself in a position where the name and hopefully reputation of the school district can be one more source of rent, rather than, as in big city districts, threatening to lower it.

In the search for rent, innovation is a crucial part of the game, but only one part of it. Development can be a lengthy process. Land is bought, hopefully cheaply, and in anticipation of the advancing wave of development. It then has to be held for an indeterminate period of time. The problem is, holding land can be expensive. Above all, taxes have to be paid. And it may be the increasing property taxes on land that is subject to an anticipatory rise in its value that persuades farmers to sell. How convenient, therefore, if there is a state law that says agricultural land should be assessed for tax purposes as agricultural land

4. An example from the Columbus area is Worthington Square, developed by Planned Communities alongside their residential developments in what is now Worthington Estates.

5. In other words, not just a matter of spreading high land costs over more units. A small supply of lots, though, does force up prices, which lends further impetus to building upward.

and not, as has been the previous practice, as urban. Numerous states, including Ohio, have this legislation since farmers, through organizations like the Farm Bureau, can be powerful lobbyists. In Ohio, it has been in effect since 1974. Land under farming has to be taxed at what is called its current agricultural use value. The county auditor grants the break on receipt of a request, and as long as the land stays under agriculture for four years, the subsidy applies. But developers have taken advantage of it, buying the land, renting it out to someone who will put a few cows on it, and then claiming it as agricultural. A nice windfall for the developer, therefore. There was something of a flurry of critical interest in this in the late '70s, but the original legislation emerged unscathed.[6]

Pushing costs on to others is taken for granted. Private development depends on various forms of public provision, like new schools to accommodate the children and widened highways to take the increased traffic. The problem is: Who is going to foot the bill? Externalizing the costs of a development while internalizing all the profits is an old game, but played with grim earnest. Local government may try to recoup these costs by requesting a fee for each house constructed, something known as an impact fee. In some instances, where the housing market is so tight that the fee can be passed onto the purchaser, there may be minimum resistance. But if the developer has to swallow it, the opposition will be stiff as the developer comes to the supposed defense of the buyer: how it will push up the price of the house and exclude the less affluent, when on the contrary, the developer is in a situation where he or she simply lacks that sort of market power. As we will see, this has been the case in Columbus, but that has not stopped the developers and their lobby from proclaiming the opposite and shedding crocodile tears for the buyer, even while the buyer can relax because in actuality it is the developer who is going to have to find the money for the fee or fees. And the claim that developers will simply decamp and move elsewhere is just not on; they are too embedded in a particular housing market, too dependent on banks that know them, builders who have learned to trust them, or if they do the build-

6. "Franklin County developers and land speculators have chopped their property tax bills by an average of 83.5% by taking advantage of a 1974 law designed to help farmers, a spot check by *The Dispatch* of county auditor's office records reveals" ("Land Developers Are Using Farmers' Tax Break Law," *Columbus Dispatch,* December 18, 1977, p. A-8).

ing themselves, on subcontractors they can trust to give this serious consideration unless they are desperate.

So impact fees get resisted. In other cases, it is a matter of the begging hand. Instead of meeting the public costs of their developments, developers will turn around and request tax abatements as the price of allowing them to come in and congest the local highways, overload the utilities, bolstering their case with all manner of inflated claims about the public benefits of their developments: the jobs that a shopping center will generate, without mention, of course, of those that will be destroyed elsewhere in the city, and the tax revenues that will be generated if lots of dubious assumptions about the ability to land tenants and the like, and the absence of competing malls, hold true. Developers and their spokespeople are seemingly nothing if not optimists. Of course, anxieties about resulting congestion can be turned on their head by asking for local government to provide a TIF, or tax incremental financing district: an area surrounding the development into which the tax revenues resulting from the increased value of the property can be returned in the form of improved public infrastructure, notably highway improvements. So much for the claims about tax revenues working to the benefit of a wider public.

Then there are the re-zonings. Again, they are part of the game. Zoning maps are supposed to provide assurance to property owners as to the future of the immediate environs, but it is of course a false assurance and bound to create disappointment and anger on the part of those who saw it as more secure than it really was. Zonings get changed, and only in part because of developer greed. Zoning maps are political documents representing the wish lists of people who own land there, including the land on which their various improvements stand. They might—just might—also represent the balance of demand for different sorts of uses. So the allocation of such and such a percentage of the land to residential uses and such and such to commercial might in fact closely reflect the demands of developers for developable land. But those demands tend to shift, so creating shortages of land zoned for certain uses, and excesses of that zoned for others; some uses are overzoned and some underzoned. So if you are a developer of tract housing at a density of, say, eight houses per acre, and land zoned for that density is in short supply, it makes perfect sense to buy land zoned for housing at two houses per acre for which the demand is very limited and seek a rezoning. Instead of paying over the top for your land, you will get it cheap, and since land zoned for dense housing is still in short supply, you can not only cut your costs, you can make the customer pay a little extra. Meanwhile the neighbors are up in arms, claiming that the high-density housing is going to lower their property values. They may be right, but compensation for their losses is not something that they can expect from the developer, aside, that is, from a few earthen mounds and tree plantings to obscure the now not-so-desirable view.

So developers work with local government; in fact, they *have* to work with local government since it is local government that has responsibility for land-use planning, water and sewer, and local highways. There can be tensions, but nothing that cannot be worked out, because local government too is part of the grander scheme of things: a willing accomplice, and for its own reasons. For a start, they are anxious about their own revenues. Property tax revenues are part of it, and the juicier the yield of a development relative to the municipal expenditures it will require when up and running, the better: So, the low-density housing referred to earlier has its advantages, but so too does a high-density apartment development of one-bedroom apartments, since it is likely to generate very few children who then have to be educated at local expense. A shopping center can be even more attractive: not just property tax revenues but sales taxes as well, no children to educate, and aside from the occasional police run to keep the shoplifters in line, not much else in terms of ongoing public outlays.

Local governments also invest money in long-term capital projects. Paying for them requires a stream of revenue, but this can be in the form of user charges, as with water and sewer. Without the users, who is going to help pay off the bonds sold to expand the waterworks or sewage treatment plant? And many of these are constructed speculatively, as in "build and they will come"—but they might not. So local government has to make sure that they do, by promoting the area as developer-friendly—as in the ready offering of TIFs and tax abatements.

Finally, city councilors and township trustees can have personal stakes in development. Township trustees on suburban peripheries are typically well-known local people. They are well known because family members go back a long way. That often translates into land ownership. Charges of conflict of interest are unlikely, since their own land may not be immediately affected. But promoting development elsewhere in the township can make it easier to sell their land in the future. Not all of them own land so that their positions are compromised in this way, but many of them do, and stories of actual conflict of interest are just too common to be ignored.[7] Likewise, all the insurance agents and realtors who put their names forward for city council, particularly in the suburbs, may have no ulterior motive, but being on council will certainly present them with opportunities of serious interest. Developers seeking rezonings will, if they are granted, need property insurance. Realtors have their own interests in promoting the development of a suburb, and supporting a bond issue for capital improvements is a no-brainer.

But as far as the socialization of the costs of development goes, and the privatization of the benefits, this only scratches the surface. In its geography, development has a strong movement outward. It is not too far-fetched to think of it as a frontier movement—waves of residential areas, their shopping malls, succeeded by ever-newer models farther out. As it expands at its edge, development leaves behind housing that is older, less contemporary in style, and *démodé* shopping centers, all of which have to compete with the newer versions. This is aggravated by the speculative character of the property sector, which means that there is a continual tendency to overshooting: a supply in excess of demand. Meanwhile, and to add to the effect, older industrial properties, which find it hard to expand, get vacated in favor of new factories on the edge of the city or in a small town. This can and does leave in its wake abandonment of properties: abandoned housing, which is a story going back to the '60s, and abandoned shopping centers.[8] In effect, housing is sold on by the developers to people who think they have a rock-solid asset, and its increasing value is then compromised by ever more production.

---

7. Compare Mason Gaffney: "The LG [local government] . . . is a group of landowners in league to preside over the collective capital that they use jointly. The LG is a halfway house between the individual landowners and the state. Landowner control is modified by democracy, which gives the whole system some of its characteristic tensions and compromises. But landowners, as the permanent party of every LG, take a strong and steady interest in local government out of all proportion to their numbers. It is reasonably accurate for many purposes to think of the LG as a collective landowner, maximizing land income" (Gaffney 1973, 117).

8. For a short video on the problem in Columbus, see "Columbus Vacant House Epidemic" (https://www.youtube.com/watch?v=UQQSufF58-I; last accessed April 30, 2020). What is not mentioned there, is how fundamental abandonment is to sustaining the prices of newer housing further out: It is not a conspiracy, but just the way the housing market works.

As in the last chapter, what has recently worked to mitigate this tendency has been the redevelopment of city centers. Once property values have dropped below a certain level, they become attractive to the gentrifiers, the redevelopers of all sorts, and old industrial properties close to one another can be converted into chichi residences, as indeed in the case of Columbus's Brewery District. This has been stimulated by the postindustrial city effect, though this can vary significantly from one city to another: Detroit is not Chicago! And not all of the neighborhoods can or will be gentrified. In other words, the particular form of development in the American city has very deleterious effects on what it leaves behind in its wake. It is like, to paraphrase the urban economist Edward Mishan (1967), rolling out a carpet of opportunity in front, as it gets rolled up behind, and Columbus has been far from exempt.

Case Studies

All the major regional shopping centers in Franklin County are in the city of Columbus: testimony to the vigor of its annexation policy as discussed in chapter 2. Significantly enough, compared with some earlier genres, like Northland, Westland, and Eastland, they are all multiuse projects. The developer spreads risks across a diversity of land uses: a strategy that is clearly going to pay off at a time when conventional retailing is struggling. On the other hand, the residents, the hotel visitors, the lunchtime crowd, can patronize the restaurants that are part of the development. In order to accommodate the complementarities, these sorts of development require lots of land: hence their peripheral location, though as further development has enveloped them, they look less so. Their size also imposes accessibility challenges. They need to attract shoppers and the workers in their offices from a wide surrounding area. A freeway location is an absolute necessity. But then you may have to get a new set of off- and on-ramps, which is where the politics can get interesting, as we see in the first two case studies.

The third case study, of the Villages at New Albany, is different because the emphasis there has been residential. Again, it helps if you have the accessibility, but schools are now much more important. Size also counts. Open space has become a more important consideration in residential choice. Also, the bigger you are, the greater the possibilities of inserting attractions like a golf course or a lake and the markup that lots next to them afford. All these considerations are on display in the Villages at New Albany, suggesting that politics might not have been important. But coming as it did in the wake of the so-called Win-Win agreement on schools annexation, that was far from the case.

POLARIS

Polaris Centers of Commerce is a major mixed-use development of almost 1,300 acres over the county line in Delaware County—not in Franklin County, therefore—where the developers found themselves lacking some of the money they needed for supporting infrastructure. The original intent in 1989 had been to build a freeway interchange at their own expense to provide the necessary accessibility. They also needed money for connecting highways. Delaware County promised a significant chunk but was holding out for more from the developers. On the other hand, Delaware County was keen that Polaris should go ahead as the local school district, Olentangy, was under severe pressure from residential development in the southern part of the county, development that had been facilitated not by Columbus public utilities but by another utility, Delco. And this is where it gets interesting. For the developers smelled loot, and while they denied wanting a bidding war—and who wouldn't?—they certainly were happy to watch and take advantage of it. They needed money. And who should provide the water and sewer was up for grabs. So they were ardently pursued, both Columbus and Delaware County offering very, very substantial financial packages: almost $6.8 million from the latter and almost $9 million from Columbus, including, crucially, money for the interchange. But if they chose to go with Columbus, which they would, then they would have to allow annexation, which is what happened.

Prior to the annexation, there had been some interesting developer machinations. The developers were anxious. As it stood, since all the land to be annexed was in Delaware County, the annexation request would have to be heard by the Delaware County commissioners, and not those of Franklin County. And in Delaware County there was ill feeling about Columbus, partly as a result of its competing offer, partly on the basis of a past history of using the county as a site for its water reservoirs. On the other hand, the developers knew, or their lawyers did, that according to Ohio annexation law, where an annexation request overlaps two counties, it must be heard in that county where the land in question has the largest number of residents. The 1,286-acre site had no residents, but it directly abutted Franklin County. So to assure it would be heard by the Franklin County commissioners, the developers purchased options on two contiguous parcels in Franklin County where there were four residents.[9] Their request would then be heard by the Franklin County commissioners, who duly approved it.[10] Who says that development politics is not just one big comedy show? You cannot make this sort of thing up.

The Polaris development sheds additional light on the virtues, at least for Columbus, of the annexation policy. We know that the tendency has been for newer vintages of shopping centers, like Polaris, to supersede older ones closer in to the city center. But in the Polaris case, the zero-sum nature of the game became very evident. For once the development was up and running, it wanted a shopping center. It would get it. This would be something called Fashion Place. The major anchor stores at an older shopping center farther south, Northland, then moved out for the greener pastures at Polaris, and Northland was no more. But its loss as a revenue source for Columbus was at least offset by the new center at Fashion Place.

EASTON

Easton, on the east-northeast side of the city, would be a "town center in the suburbs": streets lined with stores, restaurants, and a cinema, served largely by parking garages, and with faux architectural touches and toponymy[11] that seemed attractive to the visitor. Each of these new developments was on the edge of the built-up area but in a position to benefit hugely from the ongoing expansion along the northern arc: a bet that has paid off. They would also enjoy immediate freeway access, and to top it all, the developers would incorporate strip malls into the

9. "Polaris Developers Make Annexation Move," *Columbus Dispatch,* October 4, 1990, p. 1C.

10. "Franklin County Commissioners OK Annexation of Polaris Development," *Columbus Dispatch,* August 8, 1990, p. B1.

11. For example: A pottery store in a building with a front that suggests that it was at one time a cinema, and given its Art Deco style, an old cinema, which, of course, it never was; a building called The Train Station, hosting a variety of shops, that looks like it might just have been a train station, but again, never was. And then the street names: Regent Street, New Bond Street, The Strand. A bit obvious, but not sufficiently deterring, apparently, for the sort of person who shops there.

overall shopping complex: huge advantages when compared with the earlier vintages of shopping center where developers had no control of development beyond the immediate perimeter of the mall (and its parking) itself, because now the developers pocketed the rent rather than seeing it drain off to someone else piggybacking on their original, access-creating, development. The old Northland shopping center on Morse Road, which was the first regional shopping center constructed in the area back in the early '60s, is an interesting contrast. People went to shop there, but as well as Sears and Lazarus, they might also want to visit a discount store or a supermarket. So while Northland brought shoppers into the area, other developers got the rents from off-site activities. In the economist's jargon, the developer of Northland failed to internalize the externalities that it generated. Others reaped where they had not sown.

The presiding genius behind Easton was one Leslie Wexner: at the time, chief executive officer of a number of retail chains that he had either founded or taken over, a person of immense wealth, whom we encountered in the last chapter. But to create the conditions for Easton's success, as he, at least, saw it, he had to fight for it. His money surely counted in this. It attracts powerful collaborators like bees to honey, whether it is the real estate developers and lawyers who helped ease the way for the New Albany project, as we will see, or politicians swayed by the money donated to political campaigns.

Major controversy would attach to the highway changes seen as necessary, at least by Wexner himself. For while the land abutted on its northeast corner a major highway intersection, Wexner wanted an intersection that, while not de jure exclusive to the Easton development since the roads there would connect to the city's highway system, were de facto. In short, the goal was an intersection dedicated to Easton.[12] This created problems since the intersection envisaged would be, according to the rules of the Federal Highway Adminis-

12. "But the developers worked with city and state officials to get something more: a new interchange that led right into the middle of the project, a grand entrance that featured the name of the project as part of its decorative fencing. 'That changed things, gave us the ability to control the experience,' Flatto [president of the Georgetown Company] said. 'With the bridge, the light fixtures, you instantly start to associate Easton with being the very best in its class. It's not dissimilar from New Albany with its white fences, which give you the notion as you're arriving that New Albany is a special place'" (Tim Feran, "The First 10 Years: Easton Town Center Has Become Such a Popular Fixture, It's Hard to Remember That Its Concept Was a Risky Decision," *Columbus Dispatch,* July 5, 2009).

tration, which had authority in these matters, too close to the existing one (to the north). In practical terms, the problem was what is known as weave: cars trying to get on the freeway making way—or not—for those trying to get off. The only way to solve the problem would be an extremely expensive ensemble of parallel highways. But by 1992, the roadblocks had been cleared away. The Federal Highway Administration had given its blessing, and funding from the state was lined up.[13]

A major item of public disquiet was that at a time when there were a number of other highway projects demanding attention and very limited state funds, Wexner seemed to have jumped the queue, though this was later justified by reference to the jobs that the Easton project was to create. In the wake of expanding residential development on the north side and office development around interchanges on the northern Outerbelt, traffic congestion had emerged as a major issue. Another project that had been lined up for funding for some time had been the reconstruction of the Spring-Sandusky interchange in downtown Columbus. In fact, the Mid-Ohio Regional Planning Commission (MORPC), in charge of ranking projects, had put both of these ahead of the Easton request,[14] only to be overridden by the Ohio Department of Transportation.[15] But as a headline in *The Other Paper* put it, "I-270 Widening Stalls; Wexner's Projects Sail."[16] The same article went on to suggest that what had been important in getting state support for the project were Wexner's connections with the state governor at that time, George Voinovich, in particular donations amounting to $55,000 over the period 1990–94 and hosting a $25,000-per-plate fundraiser for him in 1993, a thesis that would be given additional corroboration.[17]

13. The original cost as of 1996 was $232 million, including $18 million advanced by The Limited for planning. See "Business Urged to Help Get Funding," *Columbus Dispatch,* June 21, 1996, p. 1B.

14. The "projects" included not just the Easton intersection but also a bypass around New Albany designed to service Wexner's other major development project, the Villages at New Albany, but this had been on the books for some decades and did not attract the same opprobrium, even while it probably should have.

15. "Business Urged to Help Get Funding," *Columbus Dispatch,* June 21, 1996, p. 1B.

16. November 3–9, 1994, p. 10.

17. See Margaret Newkirk, "Where the Road Money Went," *Columbus Monthly,* March 1995, pp. 35–40.

THE VILLAGES AT NEW ALBANY

Soon after the conclusion of the Win-Win agreement on schools annexation, which made Columbus water and sewer contingent on annexation by the Columbus school district, an interesting test case emerged, and one that would highlight just how important schools are in developer calculations. The occasion would be the issue of supplying water and sewage disposal to a highly ambitious development, largely of expensive housing, planned for the northeast of the county, and close to the very small village of New Albany in Plain Township. The name chosen for it by the developers was The Villages at Rocky Fork—nice and resonant of the rural, close-to-nature life and to be underlined by evocations of Virginia horse country, as in the proliferation of white fences. The *Columbus Dispatch,* however, chose to ignore this and to give it its own, evidently preferred, label, "Wexley."[18] The major developers were Leslie Wexner, who up to that point had made his money through his various clothing chains going under the umbrella name Limited Brands, and John Kessler, a developer who knew his way around the land-development scene in Columbus: a marriage of big money looking for an outlet and the sort of hands-on knowledge necessary for a big development. Others involved and who feature later on in discussions of recent development history in Columbus included Harrison Smith,[19] a local zoning and annexation attorney and bane of citizen groups, and the Don Casto Organization, a shopping center developer.

How, therefore, to get the necessary water and sewer? The developers were well aware of the provisions of the Win-Win agreement. Their development was meant to cater to, among others, families with children. The last thing they wanted was annexation to the City of Columbus since this would have meant, horror of horrors, Columbus schools. They thought, though, that they had found a way around it. This is

18. One can only speculate on why that was. A principal developer, in fact the major force behind it, was Leslie Wexner. As for the "exley" bit, well the longtime Columbus suburb of Bexley was known to have a Jewish minority of some size and Wexner was Jewish. So was this a casual bit of anti-Semitism? Or was the Wolfe family, owners of the *Dispatch,* irritated at this upstart coming in and messing around in their backyard and wishing he would go back to Dayton, where he was born? Or, of course, both? Ultimately, not very subtle.

19. An urbane, calmly spoken guy who chose his words carefully, was hard to irritate, and whom it was difficult to dislike, even while he was paving the way for all manner of developer disruption for those unlucky to be in the way of further development. But from the standpoint of the "Wexley" developers, an indispensable ally.

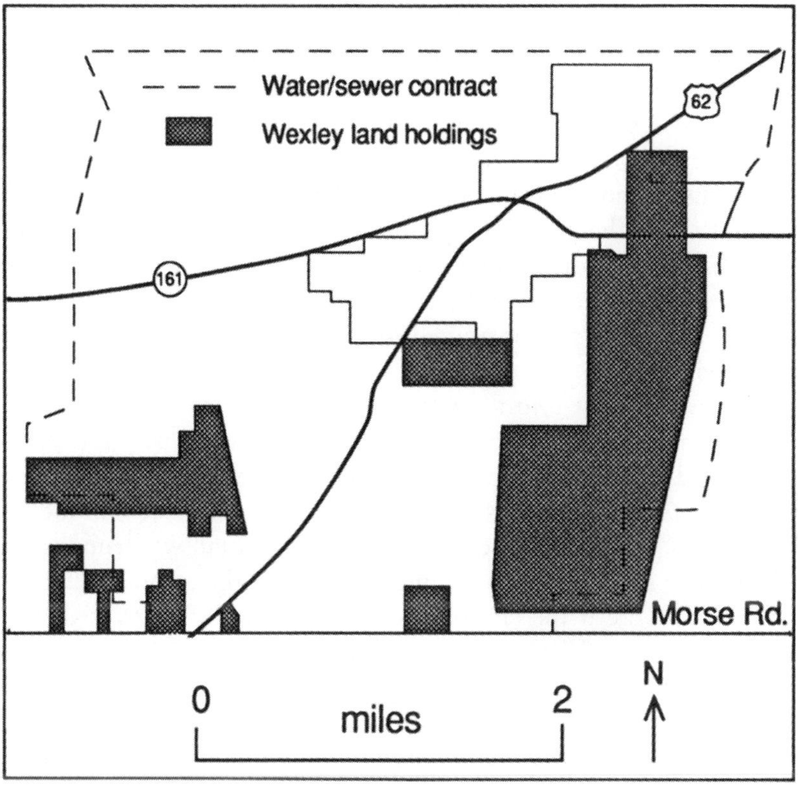

FIGURE 5.1. "Wexley" land holdings and their relation to the cancelled water–sewer contract. Source: Figure 3 in Cox and Jonas 1993, 26. By permission.

because of the strategic way in which the land had been assembled (see figure 5.1). They were aware that since 1973 there had been an agreement between Columbus and Franklin County to provide water and sewage disposal to a very significant area of the township and without requiring annexation to the City of Columbus: a present from heaven for those, like Wexner and his associates, seeking the necessary services without the tedious albatross of Columbus schools. So they were very careful. The problem was, they were not careful enough. If they had been, they would have tried to intervene in the unfortunate events occurring just prior to the date they had set for announcing their plans for the area. For in the summer of 1987, the city and the county had discussions, the result of which was the rescinding of the agreement.[20]

---

20. This was in exchange for the agreement of the city to take charge of various package sewage plants scattered across the unincorporated parts of the county.

So they were caught, in effect, in flagrante delicto and faced with a big problem.[21] Initially all seemed under control, once more courtesy of the city of Columbus. The plan was that the city would enter into a water-sewer agreement with the Village of New Albany and allow it to service a fairly generous expansion area that it would annex (figure 5.2). This included most of the land that had been assembled by what would later be called The New Albany Company. This would be the eventual "solution," but before it could be achieved, the way would be a rocky one. For unfortunately for the city, the Columbus City School Board did not see it that way. It wanted to see annexation of the whole area by the city since in accordance with the provisions of Win-Win, this would also bring it into the city school district, with all its implications for property tax revenues, as well as helping stabilize pupil enrollments and their racial composition. In this they had the support of the teachers, through the Columbus Education Association[22] and the local NAACP branch.[23] The pro-annexation position was hardened by the entry of the Apple Alliance into the picture, threatening a citywide referendum vote if the city offered the water-sewer contract to New Albany that would be the salvation of the developers. This was supported by the NAACP, which also proposed a recall movement against the mayor of the city and unnamed councilors if there was no resolution that it would regard as satisfactory. In other words: The conflict over municipal and school annexation had not gone away; it had just resurfaced in a different form.

The developers were then able to take advantage of something quite unexpected. Luckily for them, there were others also trying to avoid annexation of their land by the city of Columbus. For if the agreement went through as the city wanted, the expansion area would still leave large parts of the township vulnerable to annexation by the city of Columbus and hence incorporation into Columbus schools. But a merger of the township and the village would avoid this, as well as posing a problem for Columbus expansion through what it called "a

21. As John Kessler remarked in an interview, "The debate over who will serve Wexley would not have occurred if things had gone as the developers envisioned. When we started buying the property there was a water and sewer contract in effect. We were aware of that" ("Septic Tanks May Service Exclusive Wexley Sites," *Columbus Dispatch,* January 30, 1988, p. 1A).

22. "Council Tables Espy's Call for Wexley Annexation," *Columbus Dispatch,* December 22, 1987, p. 1D.

23. "NAACP Wants All of Wexley in City," *Columbus Dispatch,* December 12, 1987, p. 4B.

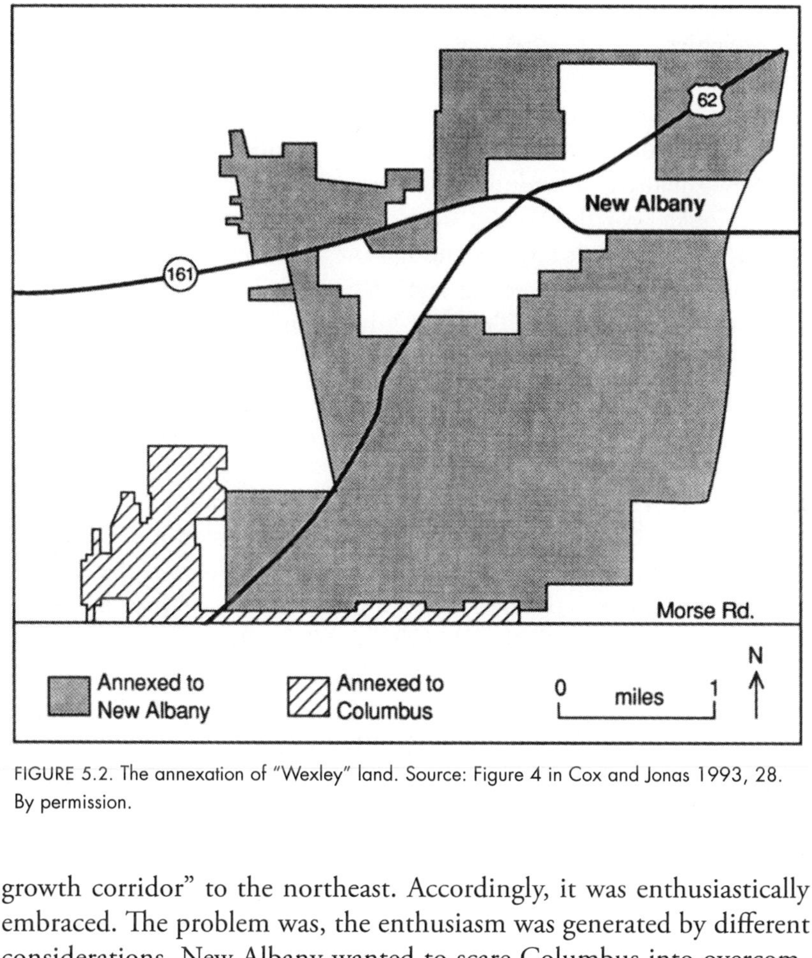

FIGURE 5.2. The annexation of "Wexley" land. Source: Figure 4 in Cox and Jonas 1993, 28. By permission.

growth corridor" to the northeast. Accordingly, it was enthusiastically embraced. The problem was, the enthusiasm was generated by different considerations. New Albany wanted to scare Columbus into overcoming the opposition of the Columbus school board and doing a deal as originally intended, and the developers were happy for them to go ahead. The rump of the township, though, which would be left high and dry by the agreement, wasn't trying to scare; it was scared.

For a while, it seemed feasible. If the merger was to succeed and provide a happy hunting ground for the New Albany Company, though, there had to be a source of water and sewage disposal alternative to Columbus. Again, fortune smiled on the plotters since this was not infeasible. Just to the north of Plain Township, over the county lines, was a rural water and sewer utility known as Delco. And just adjacent in Jefferson Township, the township trustees were planning their own water and sewer district and there was talk of contracting with them. But the township and New Albany were only bedfellows of convenience. As soon as Columbus offered a contract and an expansion area that would embrace the vast proportion of the Wexley land holdings, the merger idea was dead, leaving a lot of bitterness among the residents of the township, for part of the deal with Columbus was for New Albany to abandon the merger proposal. Hence the columnist Herb Cook: "For the Wexley developers, the merger commission has served its purpose. It applied enough pressure to prod Columbus into offering New Albany a sewer and water contract, despite the feeble protests of the Columbus Board of Education."[24]

Big question: Why did the city cave in to the demands for a water-sewer contract with a generous expansion area? In the quote above, Herb Cook refers to the protests of the Columbus Board of Education as "feeble," and that might be, though the protests of African American groups were a good deal stronger than that. One allegation was that the support of the then council president, Jerry Hammond, himself African American, had, in essence, been bought. This was the claim of a lawsuit charging improper influence brought by Bill Moss, a member of the Columbus School Board at that time. The basis for it was investments made around about the same time as the decision was being made, in Hammond's jazz club, the Major Chord, by leading figures in the Wexley development group. These included Wexner himself, Kessler, the development attorney Ben Hale, and the wife of Harrison Smith. Wexner, Kessler, Hale, and Smith had also been generous in financial support of Hammond and fellow Democratic council members in 1987, to the tune of $25,700 in campaign finance.[25] That may very well be; as we will see later, there is a pattern in Columbus of developers smoothing the way through campaign donations.

My suspicion is that what may have been at work was the economics of utility provision and hence the position of the Columbus Department of Public Utilities. They wanted a deal because they wanted to supply the water and sewage disposal service, and they wanted these because of their capital costs. There has never been a shortage of water and sewer service in the Columbus area because the department has always speculated on future growth and so expanded ahead of demand. But once that expansion has occurred, the demand has to be there so that the bond holders can be paid off—hence the desire to preserve

24. "Sorry, Plain Township," *Worthington Suburbia News,* July 13, 1988, p. 4.

25. "Bias Suit Revisits '87 Dispute over Nightclub," *Columbus Dispatch,* December 12, 2000, p. C2.

a monopoly of provision in Franklin County, as outlined in chapter 2. If schools had been a municipal responsibility, things might have played out differently as the conflict would have been brought into the city administration. But judging from the way in which the annexation policy has historically been pursued as the highest good, leaving behind it police and fire safety and highway departments struggling to keep up, one has to be skeptical. And this, I think, factored into the repercussions of "Wexley" as other suburbs sought to take advantage and Columbus found itself on the back foot.[26]

•

All this is to emphasize five major points. The first is the way in which the developers provided some novelty: obvious in the case of Easton's "town center" in the suburbs and its utter and complete faux-ness, and also in the Villages at New Albany. with its combination of golf courses, horse trails, a country club, a lake, Virginia horse country fences, and architectural designs supposed to muster up Jane Austen nostalgia. This aspect is less apparent in the case of Polaris; what is interesting there is a site that clearly sniffed out where the development frontier in Central Ohio was pushing, as the later and dramatic growth of Delaware County would confirm.

The second point is that these are all big-acreage developments. Polaris covers 1,200 acres and Easton 1,300. The Villages at the inception of the development amounted to just short of 4,000 acres, or a quite massive six square miles. In each instance, the acreage was needed because a major goal was to develop on such a large scale that it could allow for complementary land uses—all mixed use to varying degrees. The Villages started out less so but always had some retail in mind, and recent land purchases have allowed other, employment-generating uses. To achieve this goal, the developments had to be on the urban periphery. It is not just that land is so much more expensive farther in. It is also that property ownership is so much more fragmented, making land assembly quite difficult. On the edge of the city, and in contrast, acquiring a few farms might do the trick.[27]

---

26. Cox and Jonas 1993, 27–32.

27. This is not to minimize the challenge there. It is well known that when the Villages were being planned, in the land acquisition process, dissimulation was the watchword and different company names were used in making the deals. If the news

Third, we should note how significant politics is to all this. Both the Polaris developers and Easton had to fight for the accessibility advantages they needed. Polaris played Columbus off against Delaware County to get an interchange. In the case of Easton, donor dollars counted in getting the governor of Ohio to whisper a word in the president's ear to get the federal Department of Transportation on board, and then in loosening up state highway dollars. The Villages got a freeway too, though that had been planned for some years; it was just brought forward. The major issue at the Villages was schools. The development came in the wake of the Win-Win decision that made the provision of water and sewage disposal by Columbus, sans, as we have seen an agreement with an existing local government, contingent not just on annexation to the city but also on annexation by the city school district, which would have rather spoiled things from the standpoint of would-be residents. So pressures had to be brought to make the city yield.

Fourth, one cannot exaggerate the degree of detail that has to go into negotiating the politics of major developments like these. The New Albany developers thought they had avoided school problems by acquiring land that would not be subject to the provision of Win-Win. The land would have to be annexed to get Columbus water and sewer, but there had been an agreement between the city and the county exempting a large area in Plain Township. The county had wanted, or so it said, to get sanitary sewers into the area, and mitigate a problem of leakage from septic tanks. The New Albany Company had clever lawyers; how else to explain the fact that they were aware of this provision in the land acquisition process? But they were clearly outside the loop when it came to negotiations between the city and the county about rescinding this agreement. In the Polaris case, an annexation to Columbus had to be negotiated. There was anxiety that since the land was in Delaware County and nobody lived there, it would have to be decided by the Delaware county commissioners, judged a hostile body. But by negotiating with some property owners just over the county line in Franklin County to come in on the annexation deal, it would have to be heard by the, hopefully more neutral, Franklin county commissioners.

had escaped that a major land assembly project was underway, someone, and perhaps more, would have held out for more money.

Finally, we should note the significance of fragmentation in public provision and how it is exploited by developers to get what they want. The New Albany Company wanted Columbus water and sewer but not the schools annexation that the Win-Win agreement mandated. So it played off the Columbus Department of Public Utilities against the possibility of getting water and sewer either from Delco, a utility to the north in Delaware County, or from adjacent Jefferson Township. Polaris wanted someone to pay for their freeway interchange, and Columbus and Delaware County, on account of the fiscal advantages of the Polaris development, were more than happy to engage in a bidding war.

This, though, is only part of the story. Developers struggle to enhance their revenues not just through their individual developments, but by ensuring a more friendly development climate in the area as a whole: one that helps them keep down their costs and provides for more flexibility, as we saw in chapter 2 when the city of Columbus decided to engage in a bit of serious land-use planning. There is also a hidden hand: Developers develop in a way, most notably through their innovations, that also works to their collective advantage, even if that was not their intent. For that part of the story, we now turn to chapter 6.

CHAPTER 6

Scorched Earth

A Welfare State—for Developers

Some years ago in a discussion of what he called "urban regimes," the political scientist Clarence Stone argued for a distinction between the "progressive" and the "corporate."[1] Whether it was one or the other would determine its distributional consequences: who would get what. In a corporate regime, it was the developers who tended to benefit. Tax abatements, TIFs, the shouldering of infrastructural costs by local government, the rejection of impact fees, tended to be dominant practices. Under progressive regimes, the balance of advantage was otherwise: minimal resort to tax abatements, formidable impact fees, and also linkage fees in which developers have to pick up the less obvious of the external costs of their developments, so office developers in tight housing markets might be asked to provide some housing. San Francisco is often cited as a case of this. But by and large, as Stone observed, regimes tend to the corporate end of the spectrum, which is not surprising given the way in which the American state is structured, the resultant thirst for tax revenues, and the powers that reside in local government to promote development, powers that developers have been only too eager to harness to their own agendas.

1. Stone 1987.

Clearly, the Columbus instance nicely matches the corporate end. The city itself has bent over backward to accommodate the developers, and the suburbs have followed the lead, if often in a somewhat more discriminatory fashion, anxious to cement more exclusive forms of development. And if the city should in a fit of absentmindedness side with more popular forces, the *Columbus Dispatch* has been more than willing to remind them not to engage in policy it has deemed "unwise": a favorite word of its editorial writers, to the point of cliché.

The way in which advantages have been showered on developers by city government has already been referred to in chapter 2. This was in discussion of the Polaris deal, where Columbus provided a pot of money amounting to $9 million[2] in exchange for annexation to the city. An issue that continues to rile in certain quarters was the 1975 decision to grant tax increment financing to Nationwide as an incentive to build a new headquarters north of the downtown and just to the south of what is now the Arena District. Supposedly the alternative for Nationwide was to relocate to the north of the city, though there can be reasonable doubt about whether or not that was a realistic possibility.[3] According to the package, taxes would go into a special fund to embellish the area surrounding the new office tower. Money left over was then to be allocated in a prioritized order to eight different projects. One of these was a $20 million staff development center for the school district. This had been an important part of the deal since otherwise the school district was reluctant to see itself deprived of the tax revenues that would then have accrued to it. But it failed to happen. Seven of the eight projects were completed, but then the money ran out. There was a claim that the city had shifted its priorities: City documents show that the center was the seventh on the list rather than

2. Or $16.5 million in today's dollars.

3. A problem with the Green Meadows site, as it was called, was that it would make it hard for Nationwide to meet the racial quotas in hiring that the federal government required if it was to give insurance business to the company. For many white employees, the relocation would not have been that problematic since many lived in the northern part of the city anyway, but for African Americans, most of whom were tucked in on the near east side, it would have been quite a bit more difficult (personal communication, former Nationwide underwriter). Just how significant this was in the final decision is unclear. The lure of the tax abatements and other city incentives to stay downtown has been cited ("Nationwide on Every Side," *Columbus Dispatch,* July 11, 2004, p. F1).

Reaping Where They Have Not Sown

The vaster portion of public generosity to developers, putting money in their purses, is inadvertent. A headline in the *Dispatch* for October 26, 2017, referred to the Columbus Commons: what replaced the old Columbus City Center. This is an area of green space, with a café and stage for outdoor events. The headline posed the question: "Columbus Commons: Hero of Downtown or Pesky Rent Raiser?" For it then attracted investments in surrounding property, converting it to apartments or condos, and up went the rents: a nice public subsidy, therefore. One can retort that the properties pay property taxes—well, maybe, but given the city's history of granting tax abatements, there has to be some doubt about that. But that puts the focus on the nature of the tax. What developers gain from is rent but for downtown properties, much of that rent is owing to a favorable location; that is, where the land is located; what is next to it; and its proximity to various amenities, like the promenade along the river and "next to the Commons." The property tax as it is currently formulated is only in part a tax on land rent. So one can say that a decent chunk is tax-free. Henry George in his *Poverty and Progress* argued many, many years ago for an exclusively land tax that would tax away what had been reaped but not sown; rather, it had been sown by others. And if the city is "sowing" by giving you a nice amenity to help sell your apartments, might that not be a case of, and to put it politely, "reaping where you have not sown"?

the eighth.[4] This was rebuffed with an entirely spurious argument on the part of the city mayor: "'Unfortunately this has cast a bad light on Nationwide, one of our outstanding corporate citizens,' Lashutka [the mayor] said. He listed Nationwide's help in Operation Feed, United Way, and school partnerships. Nationwide received no tax break."[5] As an interesting follow-up, Lashutka moved from the mayor's office in January 2000 to take up a senior VP position with the corporation in question.[6] Enough said.

A final instance of city generosity to developers was discussed in chapter 3. This was the Arena District case: the abatements, the penitentiary land as part of the deal that secured willingness to build the arena, and the public bailout of the franchise renting it—a bailout that secured the tenancy when the team was threatening to leave town. The

4. "Moss: Nationwide Still Owes District a Development Center," *Worthington News,* July 7, 1999, p. 37.

5. Ibid.

6. He has since left.

developers have had the occasional reverse, but typically a way has been found, as indeed it was with the Arena. The public refused to have it built at public expense—no less than five times!—but now taxes from the casino, taxes promised for other purposes, have been diverted to make the public the unwilling owner. Brilliant! And it is called democracy (see "Reaping Where They Have Not Sown").

The Struggle Over Impact Fees

New development can impose very significant burdens on the public purse: Highways may have to be widened, which can mean the cost not just of construction but also of land acquisition; new schools have to be built to handle the children of incoming families; and provision must be made for recreational facilities for the newcomers. And to add insult to injury, local government typically has to pay over the odds as a result of the increase in land values subsequent to development and the identification of an area as a hot market. One of the solutions proposed in order to raise the necessary money is the impact fee: For every house built, the developer pays a certain amount that will go toward, say, the provision of new schools, or the shopping center developer pays a fee per square foot to help pay for highway improvements.[7]

In the Columbus area, anyone who was unaware of the idea before the mid-'80s could not avoid at least hearing about them as they rose to the top of the public agenda. The background was a perfect storm of events: a convergence of a spike in demand for capital improvements coinciding with a drop in the ability of the city to meet that demand—at least to the degree that the sudden increase in demand was within the city of Columbus, and much of it was, which takes us back to the annexation policy. So on the one hand, there was rising frustration with congestion issues, particularly in the burgeoning northern arc through which the Outerbelt threads, from Hilliard in

7. Currently, there is enabling legislation for impact fees in twenty-six states, but others allow it through what are called home rule provisions. As a result, impact fees can be levied in a clear majority of states. But, and remarkably, the vast majority of cities, including some of the larger, expanding ones, like Columbus, Dallas, Denver, Houston, Indianapolis, Minneapolis, Portland (Oregon), San Jose, and Seattle, do not. Likewise, allowing impact fees to go toward the provision of new schools—a major burden on existing residents and a critical issue in development fights—is allowed in only seven states (Evans-Cowley 2006).

the west, via Dublin, Worthington, and Westerville to Gahanna, taking in large areas of the city of Columbus. Rush hour on the Outerbelt had quickly deteriorated into a nightmare. Subsequent to the busing decision of 1977, there was a housing boom, much of it in areas that by virtue of being in the city of Columbus had access to water and sewer, but that were also in suburban school districts (see chapter 2). New schools had to be built, and the families moving in were not the only ones who were being called on to foot the bill. And on top of that, as developers rushed to take advantage of the surge in demand, the provision of other forms of public infrastructure lagged. New shopping centers sprang up without the highways to handle them. A stretch of Sawmill Road to the south of the Outerbelt became a metaphor for how not to plan.[8]

The demand for infrastructural investment, therefore, had drastically increased, but the money available to meet it had shrunk. Federal money had dried up and there was a squeeze on the city's bonding capacity and the monies available from the city's general fund.[9] This was owing in part to an expensive venture undertaken in the 1970s: the construction of the trash-burning power plant, aka the *cash*-burning power plant. Issues with landfills resulting from federal regulation, and a shortage of supply for the city's municipal electricity system led to the construction of a power plant that would burn garbage along with coal. Construction costs were significantly higher than anticipated ($200 million vs. $118 million), and interest rates soared toward the end of the decade. The debt burden was onerous and revenues fell below costs of operation and debt service. The city had to subsidize it. The resultant costs bit into the money available for other public projects.[10]

---

8. But kudos for candor: '"Development comes first and the infrastructure later,' explained David Younger, transportation planning engineer for the Columbus Public Service Department, division of Traffic Engineering and parking. 'It is not the ideal situation, but it's the way it is done in Central Ohio"' ("Taming the Traffic Monster," *New North This Week,* November 6, 1989, p. 1).

9. "Developers Have Chipped in on Roads, Sewers for Twenty Years," *Columbus Dispatch,* July 26, 1987, p. 2B.

10. "The trash plant was envisioned a decade ago as a moneymaker for the city. It was to pay its own debt, provide maintenance money and power for street lighting, and produce enough extra money to pay tipping fees for residual ash and noncombustible materials, which must go to the Franklin County landfill. Reality has been far from the dream. . . . Subsidies for the plant come from the 25% of city income tax revenue earmarked for capital improvements. The income tax is 2%. The trash plant will eat up about 40% of the $45M put into the fund this year" ("Capital

For the mitigation of highway congestion problems, part of the difficulty was their multijurisdictional nature; it was pointless widening a highway if, when it reached the boundary of another suburb, it suddenly narrowed again. But it was also that the developers, whose projects were overloading the highways, dragged their feet in making a financial contribution. In the decade starting in 1986 there were at least three attempts of cities, counties, private businesses, and developers, two of them coordinated by the umbrella planning agency, the Mid-Ohio Regional Planning Commission, or MORPC, to come up with solutions. A lot of attention focused on finding the money to fund various connectors, underpasses, overpasses, possibly a new freeway interchange, to take some of the pressure off the Outerbelt. There was support for a public-private solution, but when it actually came to putting money on the table, procrastination took over (see "Trying to Get the Developers to Cough up to Mitigate the Congestion That They Create").

This was the context within which the demand for impact fees emerged. Initially it was about highways.[11] The city had started things off by appointing something called the Northwest Columbus Development Task Force. This was in 1986 and concentrated on an area where the congestion problems were particularly bad, including the, at that time, notorious Sawmill Road. The task recommended impact fees. The developer response was to cry foul since the task force had included no developers, though it was revealed later that their input had been invited but they did not take it seriously![12] The then mayor, Dana Rinehart, had initially endorsed the idea of impact fees on developers. As developers reacted adversely to the task force report, he withdrew it on grounds that it would "chase retailers out of the Columbus market."[13] The immediate opposition was not so much from housing developers as it was the shopping center people. This

Improvement Funds Hurt Due to Trash-Plant Debt," *Columbus Dispatch,* February 3, 1986, p. 4D).

11. "The city [of Columbus] is looking for ways to squeeze money out of developers to pay for roads which their developments make necessary. Some kind of assessments based on impact will be levied against developers. That is certain. It is also logical, since developers make most of the money" (David Smigelski, "Who'll Pay for the Roads? Chances Are, We Will," *Worthington Suburbia News,* April 23, 1986 p. 4A).

12. *Worthington Suburbia News,* August 19, 1987, p. 6A.

13. *Columbus Dispatch,* June 17, 1987. There is in fact in Columbus a pattern of mayors either making or endorsing bold, progressive proposals and then, under developer pressure, having to withdraw them, or simply waiting to see what the developer

Trying to Get the Developers to Cough up to Mitigate the Congestion That They Create

In 1986, in order to study ways of pooling resources to carry out highway improvements, the Mid-Ohio Regional Planning Commission created something called the North Task Force. It included developers active in the area and major employers located there, like Worthington Industries and Liebert Corporation. Also part of the task force were representatives from Columbus, Worthington, Franklin, and Delaware Counties and three townships.[1] In 1988, MORPC tried again, with strong developer representation.[2] This would be followed in 1990 by something called the North Outerbelt Transportation Management Association: "The group wants to create public awareness and corporate cooperation with the public sector, and get area businesses together to work out an agreement with city, municipal and county governments regarding a traffic solution."[3] Projects for alleviating congestion were defined, but they always stumbled on an unwillingness to put money forward: "Ridgeway [Columbus city engineer] won't mention which developers have committed to help finance the project and how much each developer will pay until everything is finalized. 'We're still negotiating,' he said. 'If we say somebody hasn't signed we have a problem because someone else could say "if that person hasn't committed, why should I?"' 'It's a pretty touchy subject,' Ridgeway added."[4] And then: "Money from developers is the missing link holding up a railroad overpass to connect Campus View and Worthington Woods Boulevards, city Service Director Joe Ridgeway told Far North Side residents last week. The City of Columbus had already committed its agreed share."[5]

1. "Plan Seeks to Solve Boom-Area Traffic," *Columbus Dispatch*, June 19, 1986, p. 1E.
2. "Quick Fix Sought for I-270 Snarl," *Neighborhood News Northwest*, November 2, 1988.
3. "Worthington Coalition Forms to Fight Traffic Congestion," *Worthington This Week*, March 5, 1990, p. 2.
4. "Underpass Agreement Expected by End of Year," *Worthington Suburbia News*, October 21, 1987, p. 6A.
5. "Need for Private Cash Stalls Overpass Project," *Neighborhood News Northwest*, June 28, 1989, p. 1.

was the Columbus Retail Developers Group, which, in response to its failure to participate in the Northwest Columbus Development Task Force, asked the mayor to form another committee that would include development interests. Top marks for chutzpah, therefore, but this is

position would be before committing themselves, as in the casino/Arena District case reviewed in chapter 7.

Columbus, so it worked, and a committee heavily larded with development interests was duly formed.[14] And, you guessed it, other than a bunch of rhetoric, nothing happened.[15]

The prevailing claim was that impact fees were not the answer since they would be simply passed on to shopping center tenants, renters, and home buyers (crucial), and this became an ongoing assumption (even though outside observers were skeptical). They were wrong about this, but for utterly self-serving purposes, meanwhile shedding profuse crocodile tears for all those poor consumers who were going to be adversely affected. A letter to the editor of the *Dispatch*[16] from Steve Potter, president of the Central Ohio Building Industries Association, is indicative and worth a close scrutiny: "The truth is, anytime it costs more to build a house, the buyer of the house pays for it. Each time the cost increases, fewer people can afford them. First-time buyers, low-income families and senior citizens are the ones left out. That does not sound fair to me." He continued along that line to show how banks would profit from the increase in the mortgage that would be needed to pay for a house. But he then added, in a highly self-contradictory move, that impact fees would drive developers away from Columbus, implying that they would *not* be able to pass the impact fee on and that it was indeed their profits that were at stake. The idea of repelling developers was reiterated throughout the debate, and most notably in an editorial in the *Columbus Dispatch*:[17] "At a time when other communities are offering tax incentives to new development, impact fees might be seen as a penalty to a developer for developing his land—a punishment that will encourage him to invest elsewhere." Please.

The absolutely crucial point here is that impact fees are not necessarily passed on to the consumer, and in Columbus they would not have been; the developers were either misled or trying to mislead. Only where demand is intense relative to the supply of housing, retail space,

14. Seven out of eighteen members in toto: *Worthington Suburbia North,* August 19, 1987, p. 6A.

15. One has to pause and consider the deeply undemocratic nature of what happened. It is like holding a referendum in which a particular group decides to sit it out because they think that their view will prevail anyway. And when they find that that was not the case, they ask for a new referendum in the hope that they will then get the result that they want. But that is the point. Business everywhere is utterly amoral (note: not necessarily *im*moral); it is only interested in what will work from its particular viewpoint of making money.

16. "Impact Fees Not Way to Go," *Columbus Dispatch,* July 24, 1987, p. 10A.

17. "Impact of Impact Fees," *Columbus Dispatch,* June 25, 1987, p. 14A.

or whatever is that going to happen. The Columbus area did not and still does not fall into that category.[18] As noted earlier, as far as housing is concerned, the price elasticity of demand there is extraordinarily high,[19] which means in turn that competition is intense, and this counters the sort of market power that developers have in markets, like that of Southern California, where supply greatly lags increasing demand.

This does not mean that developers were getting away entirely scot-free. Some of the public costs of development *were* being funded. Cities, including Columbus, used the leverage of rezonings to extract the donation of land for parks or even for new schools, though not for their construction—a major expense. Significantly, though, some developers disliked the bargaining process and expressed a preference for knowing ahead of time what they would have to pay.[20] Their voice would not be the dominant one, and the attempt to introduce impact fees foundered.

And it would founder again. The debate revived in 1996 with a House bill that would allow school boards to collect a fee of up to $2,000 on every new house, with a view to alleviating the problem of finding money for new schools in rapidly growing districts, including ones in the Columbus area.[21] But, and predictably, it was opposed on the same grounds of increasing housing costs (i.e., reducing profits), though with the added complaint that not everyone buying a new home has children who will attend local schools.[22]

•

18. As indeed was noted by the then city attorney, Ron O'Brien: "Places where they're using [impact fees] are very hot markets. . . . I think you have to look at the market you're in, what the market will bear" ("O'Brien: Impact Fees Must Relate to City Needs," *Worthington Suburbia News,* October 7, 1987, p. 36A).

19. Green, Malpezzi, and Mayo 2005, 336.

20. "Developers Have Mixed Opinions on Impact Fees," *Worthington Suburbia News,* October 28 1987, p. 35A.

21. The bill sponsor "said the one-time assessment would help alleviate growing pains in rapidly developing districts such as Olentangy in southern Delaware County." See "Schools Hail, Builders Rip Impact-Fee Bill." *Columbus Dispatch,* February 19, 1996, p.1C).

22. Equally predictable was the position of the *Dispatch* in an editorial ("Drop Impact Fees: Tax on New Homes Is Unfair and Unwise," *Columbus Dispatch,* March 7, 1996).

In review, the arguments drawn on by the developer lobby in Columbus when opposing impact fees were utterly self-serving and, knowing what we do about the development industry and real estate markets, indefensible. Much was made of their implications for the consumer. It was claimed that passing on the fee to the buyer would squeeze out the first-time buyer. Impact fees were regressive for home buyers since low- and moderate-income families would have to pay a higher share of their income toward them. They would be unfair to new buyers since old buyers did not have to pay them (again, the assumption that the fees would be passed on). And finally, impact fees were exclusionary and a "no growth" ploy on the part of municipalities. In other words, in the impact fee debate the developers, by and large, presented themselves as the consumers' friend, white knights who would protect them against additional costs as well as being on the side of political correctness. In fact, though, it was otherwise since given the circumstances of the housing market in the Columbus area, passing the fees on would have been very difficult. Far from the well-being of the consumer being at stake, it was, as per usual in these arguments, that of the developer.

The claim that developers would decamp for elsewhere can also be questioned. At first blush it is not entirely unpersuasive. One can certainly imagine that impact fees on shopping centers in Columbus might drive their developers into neighboring suburbs that did not impose them. Or housing developers would put their developments in suburbs where the consumer would not be deterred by a fee to help cover the cost of new schools simply because it was not required. But this again calls into question the argument that the fee would be passed on to the consumer, for if it was easy enough, by virtue of market conditions, to pass on the fee, why would profits be in question so that shifting investment to other jurisdictions in the same metropolitan area appeared attractive? In Southern California, there is a similar fragmentation, but fees are almost universal and this because the shortage of housing is itself universal. The developers in the Columbus area did not enjoy that luxury, which is why they were so bitterly opposed to impact fees.

So they were able to bolster their profits by reducing their costs. This was intended. They have also been able to keep the profit engine humming nicely by effects that have been quite unintended. Speculating on the growth of future demand, developers have to innovate. This places them at an advantage with respect to existing owners of housing and shopping centers. If there are tendencies to overproduction, as there seem to be in the Columbus area, it is the older properties that go to the wall. Housing is devalued, neighborhoods are redlined, and eventually the structures are abandoned; the landlords walk away from them, leaving the city to take them over in lieu of property taxes unpaid.[23] Something similar happens to shopping centers that, while economically obsolete, are still physically sound. As they are subtracted from the market, so the profits of the developers are sustained. In other words, this is a developer's version of Schumpeter's (1942) creative destruction.

Scorched Earth: Onward and Outward

THE SHOPPING CENTER STORY

Shopping centers have a long history in Columbus. The initial form was the strip shopping center, the first of which appeared in 1928 in the, now older, suburb of Grandview. These could be set back in a line from the highway or, more ambitiously, surround a large parking area on several sides. There were numerous cases of this prior to the emergence of the mall type of shopping center,[24] which made its first appearance in Columbus with Northland in 1964. Later enclosed, it was followed by clones at the other three points of the compass (so, Eastland, Westland and Southland). This pattern, along with the addition of other, less ambitious malls,[25] remained in place until 1989, when there was a belated attempt to revive the downtown as a shopping destination. This would be the highly ambitious City Center, promoted by city government through one of its redevelopment arms, empowered with rights of eminent domain to enable land assembly, Capitol City South. In floor space, it would exceed the existing major suburban malls by at least 30 percent, it would have almost double the number of stores of any of its rivals, and it was served by some very large parking garages directly attached to it.

---

23. There is a five-year grace period in the payment of property taxes.

24. They included Town and Country (1949), Lane Avenue (1953), Northern Lights Shopping Center (1954), Great Western (1955), Graceland (1955), and Great Southern Shopper's City (1957). See "Columbus Retail History Part 2: Shopping Centers." *All Columbus Data,* January 22, 2013.

25. Westerville Mall (1975) and New Market Mall (1985) were enclosed, but the Continent (1977) was not.

The window of opportunity, though, would be relatively brief. By 1997, a still newer center, Tuttle, located strategically with respect to the wealthy northwest of the urban area, had opened. This would be followed quickly by two others, also serving the booming residential arc stretching from the northwest to the northeast of the city. The first of these represented a revolution in the shopping center idea. Easton, on the east-northeast side of the city, would be a "town center in the suburbs," as discussed earlier. Polaris Fashion Place, opened in 2002, would be part of the mixed-use Polaris development described in the last chapter, and on the far north side of the urban area. It had six anchor stores representing nationally visible chains. Each of these new developments was on the edge of the built-up area but in a position to benefit hugely from the ongoing expansion along the northern arc: a bet that has paid off. They would also enjoy immediate freeway access, and to top it all, the developers would incorporate strip malls into the overall shopping complex: huge advantages when compared with the earlier vintages of shopping center where developers had no control of development beyond the immediate perimeter of the mall (and its parking) itself, because now the developers pocketed the rent rather than seeing it drain off to someone else piggybacking on their original, access-creating, development. Not surprisingly, these three new centers would be the doom of the earlier majors. Northland would close in 2002 and City Center in 2009. At least Northland would have had almost forty years of profitability, but City Center had just twenty: utterly remarkable.[26] It is to these cases that we now turn.

City Center: The background to the development of City Center was a little more complex than simply a matter of countering the suburban drift of retailing, significant as that was. Capitol South Community Urban Redevelopment Corporation, which would be the landlord for City Center, had been set up in 1974 by the city as a private, nonprofit agency tasked with redevelopment of a three-block area south of the symbolic center of the city, the Statehouse. It leases land from the city and then leases it to developers, including eventually the developer

26. Still other, smaller centers have fallen by the wayside. Such has been the story of the Continent, a mixed-use development that included an unusual, French-inspired, outdoor shopping walkway, along with movie theaters, restaurants, and dance clubs. Hugely popular during the '70s and '80s, as population expanded to its north, along with still newer centers, it stumbled into the '90s with little retail left at all ("Aging Continent Was a Victim of Changing Trends," *Columbus Dispatch,* March 11, 2001, p. D1).

of City Center, Taubman Associates. There was nothing in its original brief, though, suggesting a downtown shopping mall, which is where the complexity comes in.

Prior to the construction of the convention center and the City Center, the major corporate players in downtown Columbus, the most actively involved in growth coalition activities, had been Nationwide Insurance Corporation and Lazarus. Lazarus was *the* department store in Columbus, locally owned and operated, with a very large seven-story building one block from the historic heart of the city and within easy, one- or two-block walking distance of the major banks and state offices—with a considerable lunchtime and late afternoon market, therefore. However, and for whatever reasons, the decision was made to locate the convention center some three-quarters of a mile to the north at a site virtually opposite the headquarters of Nationwide. This worked, and has continued to work, to Nationwide's advantage for a very simple reason. For many, many years, going back at least to the late '60s, its real estate development branch had been purchasing and stockpiling land in the vicinity of what is now its headquarters.[27] The convention center helped spark the emergence of a nearby entertainment district. Later there was to be the ice hockey arena, multistory car parks, and extensive office development. This has become a major downtown development node and Nationwide has benefited hugely as a result of its land and property ownership in the area, including, at one time, an 80 percent stake in the arena itself. It also stood to gain from the relocation of the city's minor league baseball team's stadium from a somewhat outlying location into what has become known as the Arena District.

At the time that the convention center location was being considered—clearly crucial from the standpoint of what was to unfold—the City Center project was seen in part as a way of getting Lazarus "on board" with a location that was adverse to its own interests. This was because the City Center would be located directly opposite Lazarus's downtown anchor store and connected to it by a covered walkway at the second-story level, incorporating it, in effect, into the City Center experience. In this way, it was thought, Lazarus would benefit, as indeed would the City Center mall. In the event, and over the long term, things have not worked out quite so neatly, and the synergy issue

27. "Nationwide on Every Side," *Columbus Dispatch,* July 11, 2004, p. F2.

raised by Leslie Wexner in his critique of downtown planning (see p. 87), has come home to roost.

Opening in 1989, City Center got off to a promising start. In fact, the numbers of buyers exceeded expectations.[28] It was built around a three-story atrium, with a sunken stage for concerts, fashion shows, and other promotional events. To offset the attraction of free parking in the suburban centers, customers could park for $1 for a three-hour stay at Center parking facilities, assuming, of course, that they bought something. The Center offered specialty stores, like a Metropolitan Museum of Art store, and more expensive department stores hitherto unrepresented in Columbus, like Jacobson's and Marshall Field. It was seen as filling a void in the Columbus retail market, particularly at the upper end of the merchandising scale.[29]

Initially it was indeed a huge success, attracting unexpected numbers of buyers.[30] But by 2000, things were beginning to look quite a bit less rosy.[31] Although an article in early 2000[32] was optimistically headlined "As Mall Wars Loom Again, City Center Battle-Tested," it also listed some of the challenges. The Tuttle mall had opened in 1998 and Fashion Place would open in 2001. Earlier, glitzy third-floor stores had closed and the spaces recast a bit down-market. Lazarus would close in 2004, further diminishing the reasons why one might want to shop at the walkway-connected City Center. And by 2009, the City Center itself was no more.

---

28. "City Center Is Exceeding Expectations," *Columbus Dispatch,* March 23, 1990, p. 1C.

29. According to one local analyst, "The mall gives shoppers from Ohio, Indiana, Michigan, Kentucky and West Virginia a mix of stores usually found only in places like New York, Los Angeles or Chicago" ("City Center Going Strong Despite Two Closings," *Business First of Greater Columbus,* July 30, 1990, p. 4). And "Roger Blackwell, professor of marketing at The Ohio State University, said the warm reception from consumers can be based in part on the fact that other shopping centers in Columbus were behind the times. 'Opening City Center was like throwing fresh meat to hungry dogs,' he said" ("Mall Demands Second Look," *Columbus Dispatch,* August 12, 1990, p. 1H).

30. "City Center is Exceeding Expectations," *Columbus Dispatch,* March 23, 1990, p. 1C.

31. This was just a year after the tax abatements granted to the owners of the City Center expired and the city and the school district started receiving something for their patience. See "Capitol South Developments to Start Paying Taxes," *Columbus Dispatch,* March 13, 1998, p. 3B.

32. *Columbus Dispatch,* January 28, 2000, p. 1D.

Polaris vs. Northland: On the front page of the *Columbus Dispatch* for March 24, 1998, appeared a headline, "Polaris Mall in Works." Among the highlights: "A six-anchor, upscale mall . . . and a 200,000 square foot theater entertainment complex is coming to Polaris Centers of Commerce. . . . Glimcher, Ovitz and Polaris owners NP Limited plan the biggest mall in central Ohio, and the most upscale . . . and 'Glimcher said all six department stores planned for the mall will be new to central Ohio.'" In fact, though, three of the six department stores were *not* new, and in that lay one of the keys to a process that would cast light on the details by which one mall with advantages of consumer access and newer ideas drives another out of business. For three of the anchor stores of the older Northland Mall—Sears, Penney's, and Lazarus—would decide to close their stores there and open new ones at, as it would be called, Fashion Place. Even then, all might have proceeded uneventfully if it had not been for a Tax Increment Financing District (TIF) that the developers of Fashion Place hoped to draw on to provide improved highway access. This provided an opportunity for the owner of the Northland Mall to galvanize nearby residents, who had their own fears about closure, to organize a petition drive to put the TIF to a citywide vote. In other words, this case sheds useful light on how newer malls drive older versions out of business.

The initial reaction of the owner of Northland Mall to the announcement, one Richard Jacobs, based in Cleveland, was to plan an upgrading, but only if what he called "tax incentives" were withheld from the developers of Fashion Place and his three anchor stores remained at Northland. What he was referring to was the TIF that the city of Columbus, along with Delaware County, had set up in the Polaris area three years earlier (1996) to facilitate the funding of infrastructural improvements to cover the 1,125 acres surrounding the Polaris freeway interchange. Glimcher wanted to take advantage of this and in fact had made his project contingent on it. '"It is the policy of this company that if there is no TIF, there will be no mall," said Michael P Glimcher, executive vice president. "We do not build roads; we build malls."'[33] Even so, by August 3 this position had changed.[34] Fashion Place would go ahead anyway. How the highway improve-

33. "City Wants to Help Polaris," *Columbus Dispatch,* July 8, 1999, p. 1A. No mention, of course, of who should pay for the roads, just who should build them, so a quite vigorous desire on the part of Glimcher to draw a line in the sand between what he at least regarded as a legitimate division between public and private.

34. "Work on Mall Set to Go Forward," *Columbus Dispatch,* August 3, 1999, p. 1A.

ments would be paid for remained, at that point, unclear, but the fact that they might not be there was used as ammunition in arguing the necessity of the TIF; without it, there would be congestion, and evidently the developers did not give a damn.

In trying to turn back the challenge, Jacobs was able to call on strong neighborhood support, and in fact, the neighborhood organization would work with Jacobs in putting the petition drive together so as to get the issue on the ballot. What seems to have been at stake here was a particular spatial imaginary. Most of the housing in the Northland area was fairly modest and largely white in racial composition. To the south of Northland Mall, though, there had been racial change, and it was extending northward. This was undoubtedly part of the mix of considerations. The mall and the prosperous retail strip that it anchored along the east-west Morse Road was seen as a barrier to this change.[35]

The initial position of city council and of those who were candidates for mayor later that year was to support rescinding the agreement. This was also the position of the *Columbus Dispatch.* In an editorial, it gave credence to the property tax revenue arguments being put forth by the developers of Fashion Place and Polaris, revenues that would go to the benefit of two school districts, but it nevertheless had serious reservations:

> Olentangy schools would get $194.5m. Columbus' share would be $175.6m—but Northland, the City Center mall, Easton, Tuttle Crossing and other shopping areas would suffer as a result. Each of these malls currently generate significant income, sales and property taxes for Columbus and Franklin County. The net effect of a Polaris development, therefore, is likely to be a loss, not a gain, for Columbus.[36]

In other words, it recognized the shortsightedness of policies that would simply enhance the rolling carpet effect. This position, though, would change.

This might have been in response to a view among the Columbus business class that rescinding the agreement would have deleterious effects on the area's "business climate"; in short, could the city

35. This also helps to explain the support of Northland residents for the so-called Bethel–Morse connector, a new highway that would have greatly expanded the market area for Northland Mall. See pp. 162–63.

36. "Worth the Weight," *Columbus Dispatch,* August 11, 1999, p. 2B.

be trusted to keep its word? This was the publicly stated reason given by city officials for their opposition to rescinding. It was given added effect by a speech of John McCoy, the CEO of Bank One, before the Metropolitan Club in Columbus arguing for the TIF and how its reversal would harm Columbus's ability to attract investment[37]—this from the person who not only had presided over the movement of Bank One's headquarters to Chicago but had a vested interest in the TIF himself since Bank One still had a very large office building within its boundaries and with plans for more. Talk about having your cake and eating it too!

By October, city officials had added a new argument: that regardless of the outcome of the referendum, Fashion Place would go ahead, creating a need for highway expansion in the area, and this would mean using tax dollars (so the assumption was that the city would have to come to the rescue, while, and ironically, elsewhere in Columbus, at Tuttle, the necessary highway improvements had been provided by the developer). One could argue that the city would be receiving tax dollars from Fashion Place regardless; it was just that those dollars would not be earmarked for infrastructural improvements in the area. But as the *Dispatch* opined in an editorial:

> If the TIF is repealed, improvements in the Polaris region still would have to be built as population and infrastructure use grows, but the money to pay for them would come from the pot of city money earmarked for neighborhood improvements instead of from Polaris-area property owners' pockets. Money that might have gone for the likes of roads, playgrounds and fire stations—perhaps in your neighborhood—instead may be used to ease congestion in the Polaris area.[38]

The assumption here is that the money would have to be public. But that was to conveniently ignore the fact that the highway interchange for the Tuttle Mall had been built at developer expense, and before its annexation to Columbus, the developers of Polaris had had similar plans of their own.

There were other spurious arguments. Just as the "outsider" claim would be wheeled out to beat off the threat of a casino in the Arena

---

37. "Bank One Exec Defends Tax Break," *Columbus Dispatch,* September 30, 1999, p. 1B.

38. "No on Issue 33—Repealing TIF Would Hurt All of Columbus," *Columbus Dispatch,* October 24, 1999, p. 2D.

District, so too would Jacobs be so designated. An initial reaction of one of the Polaris developers, Robert Weiler, was to castigate him in exactly this way: "Bob Weiler, a partner in NP Limited, which owns much of the land at Polaris, said after [a] council meeting that Jacobs was to blame. 'Mr. Jacobs came down here and played on the insecurities of the Northland people,' Weiler said."[39] Later on, the *Dispatch* would throw in its two-halfpenny worth in an editorial: "Don't be fooled by slick campaign commercials funded by out-of-town interests to protect their own backsides by deflecting competition for Northland Mall."[40] So "came down here," "out-of-town interests," and later on "absentee landlord":[41] just as if a local developer would be more caring of wider community interests—as if.

There is also the embrace of "competition" as a counterargument to the Northland camp: "A new mall at Polaris could cut into Northland's business, but complacency and a failure to offer shoppers an attractive, safe [nice code word, *Dispatch*!] and competitive shopping venue have done worse damage."[42] This support for the TIF was reiterated six days later in yet another editorial,[43] with the title "Ad Nauseum" [*sic*], arguing that rather than invest in Northland to keep it competitive, Jacobs had opted for the cheaper option of keeping out the competition.

A late development in the campaign was a pro-issue commercial suggesting that the TIF money would help "a wealthy developer" build the mall. This was seized on by opponents as misleading since money would not change hands in that direct way. In economic terms, of course, the commercial was spot on: The highway improvements were in fact going to put money in Glimcher's pocket by enhancing the payoff to his investment. But the opponents ignored that, giving the statement a literal gloss that was almost certainly unintended and bringing the matter to the attention of the Ohio Elections Commission. It was something that the *Dispatch* would gleefully exploit in its editorials on the referendum issue. As usual, the newspaper rose to the occasion in a

39. "Polaris Plan to Go to Ballot," *Columbus Dispatch,* July 27, 1999, p. 1A.

40. "No on Issue 33—Repealing TIF Would Hurt All of Columbus," *Columbus Dispatch,* October 24, 1999, p. 2D.

41. That the *Dispatch* should editorialize thus is a bit strange, since at one time even the Wolfe family, the then-owners of the *Dispatch,* had been newcomers to the city.

42. "No on Issue 33—Repealing TIF Would Hurt All of Columbus," *Columbus Dispatch,* October 24, 1999, p. 2D.

43. *Columbus Dispatch,* October 30, 1999, p. 14A.

way that has been a hallmark of its history—always for the developer, it would seem.[44]

The issue would be defeated 56.5 percent to 43.5 percent. What impresses is the way the developers were able to refashion highly plausible claims to suit their purpose, and drawing implicitly on some very dubious assumptions. This was the case in the rebuff given to the pro-Northland publicity that the TIF money was going to ultimately work to the advantage of the developer. Taken literally, it was incorrect; there was to be no *direct* transfer. But indirectly it was very clear that there would be, and that was why the developers had wanted the TIF in the first place. Seemingly, even defeat on the issue would not have phased them. If the TIF was abolished, it was of no interest to the developers. They would go ahead and congest local highways, and local government would ultimately have to respond, so it was local government's job even though, as pointed out above, the practice of some developers at least, as at Tuttle, had called that assumption into question.

Comments made after the result was announced refer less to guile and more to disingenuousness, but the same ability to turn the opposition's arguments around and to developer benefit is evident: dragging a sort of victory out of abject moral defeat. Robert Weiler, one of the Polaris developers, was especially prominent in trashing those who had dared to challenge their plans. He targeted the quite powerful and entirely legitimate argument that if Fashion Place went ahead and Northland closed down, Columbus school district would be the loser since Fashion Place was not within its boundaries: '"I don't know how that affected the vote, but the way they used the Columbus schoolkids was shameful—that was beyond reasonable campaigning," he said of ads that claimed school-tax dollars were at stake if Issue 33 failed,"[45] which, of course, they were. He would expand on his seeming disingenuousness by stating, again after the result: "I credit the intelligence of the electorate who saw through what Mr. Jacobs was trying to do," said Weiler . . ." He was trying to make this issue a mall war, when it had nothing to do with that at all. It was about creating adequate infrastructure, not for one individual. It was to alleviate traffic conges-

44. Unless, of course, the development was something that would work counter to its own quite extensive real estate interests, as would occur in the case of the casino.

45. "Tax Deal Secure, Mall Construction to Start," *Columbus Dispatch,* November 3, 1999, p. 1A.

tion, nothing more.'"[46] Nothing more? Really? And not a mall war? Even if you were stone drunk, how could you come to that conclusion?

And the Housing Too

The competition of developers, each one thinking—hoping?—that they have stolen a march on their rivals, encourages oversupply: too many shopping centers, too much housing. In consequence, if developer profits and rents are to be sustained, something from the existing stock needs to be withdrawn, and, as Columbus experience shows, there are no prizes for guessing where that is going to happen. It is not inevitable. Northland closed when confronted by the competition of Polaris and Easton. But some of the centers closer to the downtown, like Kingsdale in Upper Arlington, have managed to reinvent themselves with a different sort of mix: much less retail and more hospitality. Likewise, not all older housing is discarded. The fact of gentrification suggests that where the housing has some sort of visual attraction, it can be spared from the scrap heap. But poorer people have to live somewhere, and the evidence is that they live precisely where housing is most likely to be losing its value and where demand for it, as in vacancy rates, is lowest (figures 6.1 and 6.2). This is also the housing that tends to fall into the hands of small-time landlords, typically living elsewhere and ready, should the time come, to go tax delinquent and then walk away from the property, having milked it of its remaining value.[47]

The result mimics a sort of frontier movement in which the opportunities are exactly there, while behind lies a cut-over zone that might later be recolonized by the gentrifiers, but until then it can be left to stagnate and lose value. The newest forms of real estate development occur farther out, which devalues housing farther in; the hapless owners are left standing up, wondering what has happened, in a game of musical places. Eventually the properties may be abandoned, one residential property by one in a scattered sort of way. If the housing market in the area were tighter, as, say, in cases like Los Angeles or Boston,

46. "Issue 33 Fails; Polaris TIF Stands," *This Week in Worthington,* November 3, 1999, p. 9.

47. As pointed out earlier, housing can be delinquent on property taxes for up to five years before a local government moves to seize it. But five years of property taxes can be a significant addition to a landlord's revenue stream.

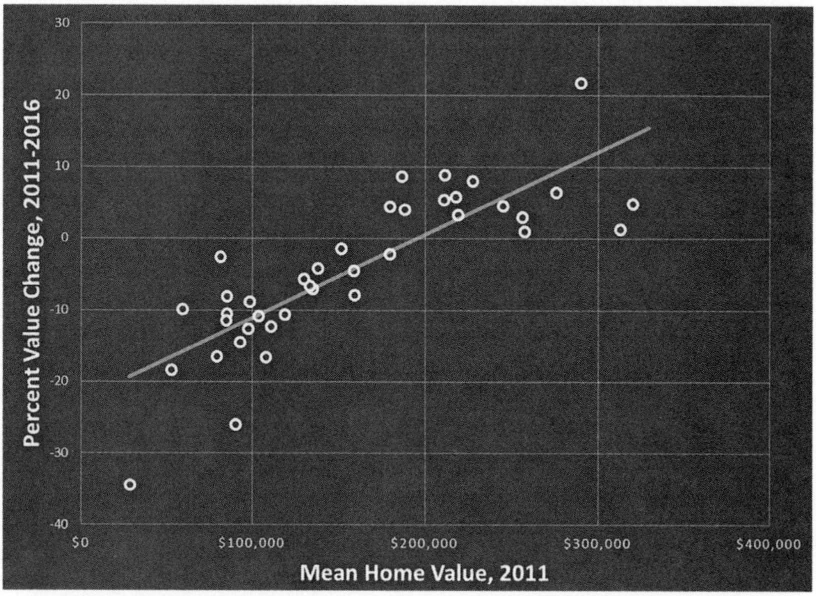

FIGURE 6.1. Housing values and changes in value. R = 0.753. Figure by Jamie Valdinger.

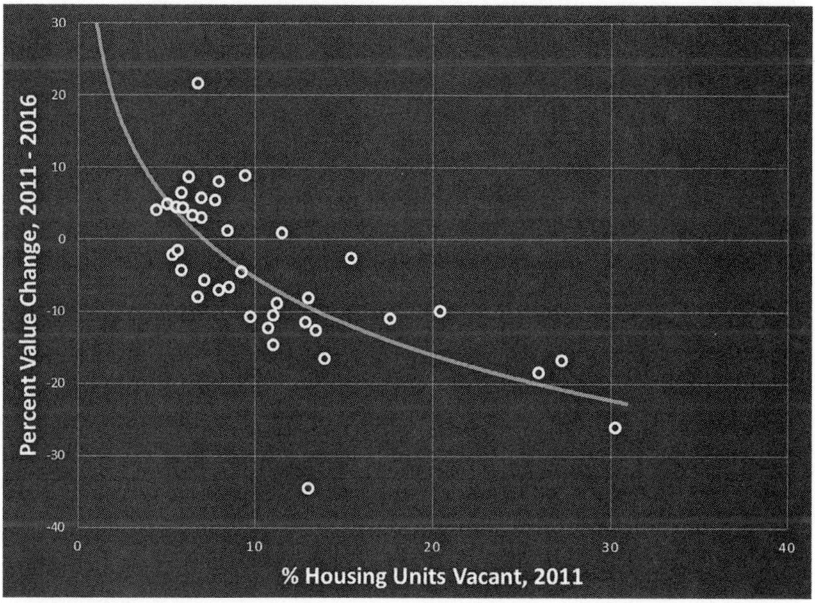

FIGURE 6.2. Vacancies and value change. R = –0.707. Figure by Jamie Valdinger.

this would be less likely to happen: To secure housing, people would have less choice. This might be a bad thing in one respect, and the developers would certainly lead the charge in playing up the (now lost) virtues of choice, even while they no longer hold the vulnerable properties. In other regards, it would be to the city's advantage; rather than being abandoned, housing would continue to have residents, allowing some greater compactness. Lack of choice has other virtues. According to one study, among the larger metropolitan areas of the country, Columbus is the most segregated by social class.[48] The reason for this is plain. If there are numerous housing vacancies at any one time and only the slightest preference to live among the better-off, the better-off can and will cluster together.[49]

How it all works is pretty clear. Developers of new housing compete, and the way they compete is through innovation. In innovating, they, in effect, suggest the virtues of new housing features before their would-be customers had thought of them. These can range from features of the house, like the conversation pit (remember those?), the now-clichéd granite countertops, his and hers closets, and picture windows, to features of the neighborhood, like the tree-lined cul-de-sac, low-density housing, or putting the housing around a golf course—all of which were new in their time. Of course, these innovations have to resonate with the buyer, but they are also molding buyer tastes and preferences. No potential buyer thought of the mobile phone, but when it went on sale, all of a sudden people recognized its possibilities and were quickly hooked.

The logic continues to work itself out. As people move into the latest suburb, so some of the older, existing housing loses some of its attractions, its relative value falls, and it filters down to those who cannot afford the latest models elsewhere in the city, typically on the urban periphery. Meanwhile, as units are being added by the developers, who obviously depend on it for their business, there is a risk of oversupply. Some, not all, of the older housing will struggle to find buyers or

48. Richard Florida, "America's Most Economically Segregated Cities," *Bloomberg CityLab,* February 23, 2017. Available at https://www.citylab.com/life/2015/02/americas-most-economically-segregated-cities/385709/ (last accessed 10/25/20).

49. Schelling 1971. Racially, Columbus ranks a little more favorably: twenty-first most segregated compared with Cleveland at #8 and Cincinnati at #12: Rebecca Baird-Remba and Gus Lubin, "21 Maps of Highly Segregated Cities in America," *Business Insider,* April 25,2013. Available at https://www.businessinsider.com/most-segregated-cities-census-maps-2013-4 (last accessed 10/25.20).

renters and its value will start to go down. Older, working-class housing close to old industrial sites is extremely vulnerable; the same goes for housing that lacks the sorts of qualities that might make it attractive to the gentrifiers. Less susceptible, therefore, are indeed areas that appear to have some sort of architectural merit, like the big houses on Neil Avenue in Columbus, and that can be rescued, even after some period of decay. Likewise protected from the threat of declining values are areas like Upper Arlington or Bexley, with their often larger houses, status, and local governments keen to protect, through code enforcement and tight zoning restrictions, their middle-class character. The problem there is different—one of the intrusiveness of McMansions as people of wealth try to capitalize on a reputable school district but on their own terms as far as the housing itself is concerned. Even in Columbus, areas of larger, expensive housing, like Old Beechwold, have managed to remain just that, and the suburban developers be damned. But for areas like Hilltop, Columbus's South Side, or much of Franklinton, salvation from decline and ultimately abandonment is elusive. Moreover, as neighborhood deterioration sets in, as the vacant properties become the haunt of prostitutes, addicts, and drug traffickers, so residents seek to upgrade their situation by moving in to adjacent neighborhoods, only for the cycle to set in again.

It is, accordingly, in the less affluent parts of Columbus, where home values are lower, that the excess of supply over the metro area as a whole shows up in declining values and in vacant properties (figures 6.3 and 6.4). And for those who like to count dots, note that in figure 6.3 in a remarkable twenty-three out of forty zip code areas altogether, home values declined. As value decline commences, neighborhoods find themselves on a slippery slope. For a start, the banks are no longer so keen to offer mortgages for their purchase where the collateral is losing value. This is the so-called redlining process. At that stage, the only people with the money or collateral to buy them out are the bottom-feeders, aka the professional landlords operating as individuals or behind the cover of a limited liability company—in short, not those big, often private equity companies that own the large suburban apartment developments across the country.

This least desirable of all the housing in the city has now entered into its end stage. The investors sniffing an opportunity have paid money for the housing. The trick now is to convert a devaluing asset into a money producer. There is a market, but it is the poorest of the poor who have no alternatives. Since their effective demand is so weak,

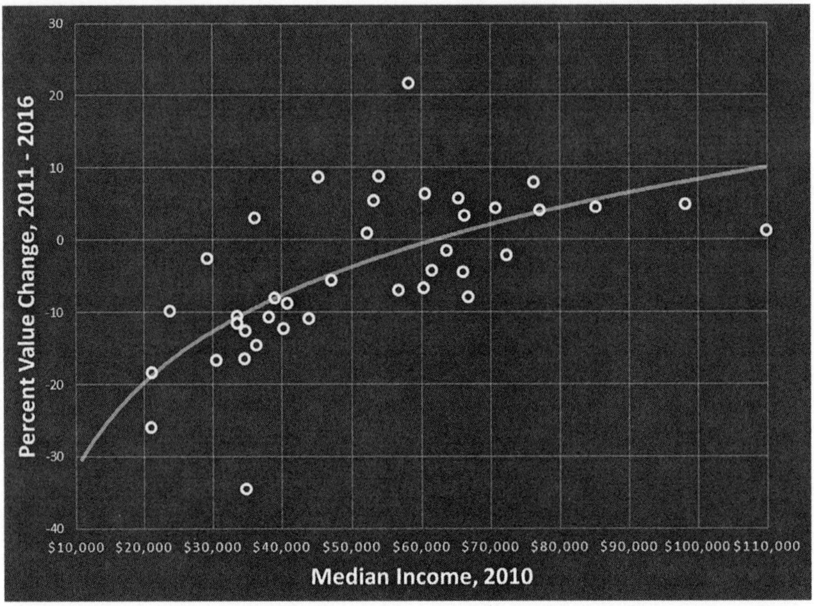

FIGURE 6.3. Median income and value change. R = 0.610. Figure by Jamie Valdinger.

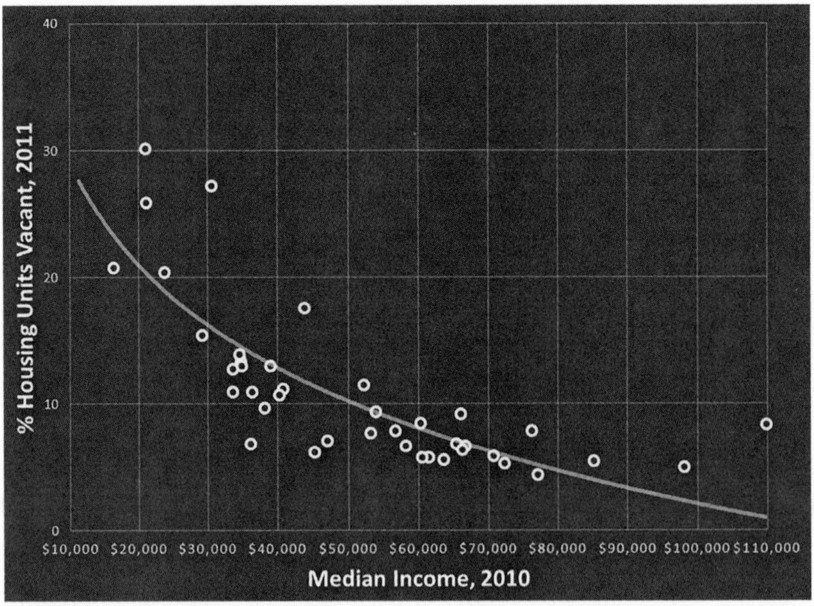

FIGURE 6.4. Median income and vacancies. R = –0.690. Figure by Jamie Valdinger.

money can be made by subdividing properties. Minimal expenditures will be made in maintenance. Property taxes may be paid initially, but as soon as the end is in sight, as soon as difficulty is encountered in filling vacancies, the landlord will go delinquent up to the legal limit of five years. They then walk away from the property, pocketing the property taxes they would otherwise have paid to the government. Of course, before this happens, the strategy of shorting on maintenance may get the landlord into trouble with the code inspectors, but they are typically understaffed, and Columbus is no exception.[50] And if they are called out by an irate tenant, a conference with the landlord, in which it is explained to the tenant that bringing up to code will require an increased rent, will often work its magic.

Of course, those purchasing properties in these areas may not start out seeking to milk them of their remaining value. There may be a speculative element in the purchase. Gentrification is the big hope: to have bought a property at rock bottom and then to sell it on at a big markup as the area becomes attractive once more to people with money. This, though, is a very limited market. A major reason for this is that families with children are put off by the poor reputation of the public schools. Meanwhile, to the extent that gentrification does occur, the displaced will move into areas that, for whatever reason, are impacted by the decline in housing values that has to occur somewhere when supply exceeds demand, as it does in Columbus. So as with the closure of manufacturing plants, the west side lost some of its residential allure, demand for housing in the Hilltop area went down, and the poorer people, like those displaced from the Little Appalachia that would become Harrison West and Victorian Village, would move in.

What has transpired to the northeast of the African American concentration on the east side is different in its details, but the underlying process of excess supply, value decline, and displacement is the same and recalls research that was done some years ago into housing markets in the St. Louis area. There, areas of dominantly African American settlement moved westward, displacing white populations. With the approach of what has been called, euphemistically, neighborhood change, areas close to the African American residential area would be

50. See, for example, the investigation that the *Dispatch* did into what it called "slumlords" back in 2013: "Legacy of Neglect: Slumlords Play the System," November 8, 2013; "Judge Hale's Court Stays Busy with Barking Dogs, Not Slumlords," November 10, 2013; "Landlords Cloaked from Citations, Prosecution," November 12, 2013; "Neighbors of Neglected Homes Feel Forgotten," November 13, 2013.

devalued, allowing the transfer of housing to those of lower income, in this case, African Americans. Something similar has happened on the northeast side of Columbus: first South Linden, then North Linden, and now the Northland area. This sounds like prejudice at work, and it certainly has been, but that would be to miss another crucial condition for what was happening and that helps explain displacement of the more affluent white by the less affluent white, and that is the fact that there were places to move to farther out. So, we are back to the imbalance between supply and demand, a supply constantly stimulated by the competitive activities of developers, always building something "improved" or "better" with a view to attracting the buyer from the older stuff and regardless of the consequences for housing values closer in, and a repeat of the cycle of redlining by the financial agencies and eventual abandonment.

Inner vs. Outer Suburbs

When it was formulated back in the late '50s, a major goal of Columbus's annexation policy was to make sure that the city would not be surrounded by independent suburbs and without any possibility of continuing to expand. One of the things that excited the attention of city officials at that time was what would come to be known as the central city suburban fiscal disparities problem. This was a bit of a mouthful, but the idea was quite simple: In a broad context of suburbanization of employment, retailing, and the wealthy, central cities risked a diminution of their tax base at the same time as the increasing concentration of the poor there increased the need for locally financed public services. Meanwhile the suburbs were getting off like bandits. What was happening in metropolitan areas like Cleveland was already clear. The view in Columbus was to avoid being Cleveland by making sure that, unlike in that instance, the city of Columbus could keep up with the suburbanizing wave by expanding in a suburban direction itself, which of course it did through its quasi-monopoly of sewer and water service in exchange for limits on the expansion of existing suburbs. So as the tax base migrated in a suburban direction, Columbus would corral it back in.

Meanwhile, as Columbus expanded, those existing suburbs, constrained in their geographic expansion, got surrounded and cut off from further possibilities of expansion. Elsewhere in the country, as in Cleveland, the older suburbs would be cut off anyway by a newer generation of suburbs still farther out. But in the Columbus case, the annexation policy has given this issue a particularity missing elsewhere. Not least, the newer suburbs have been keen to try to ensure continuing possibilities of their own expansion and have forever tried to push Columbus into more generous agreements on the areas into which they can expand. But bottom line: If a suburb is surrounded by other municipalities, as is the case with a number of them in the Columbus area, the balance between their tax base and expenditure needs can be an issue.

Fundamental to understanding this as a national problem has been a shift to space-extensive forms of all manner of new real estate developments, not to mention the demands for more space for industrial and office uses that had once found a home in the inner suburbs. Putting together those sorts of spaces in the older, often called first, suburbs is extremely difficult as a result of the patchwork of ownership, the paucity of large undeveloped spaces, and the time and expense of land assembly.

Ongoing change in the character of real estate products—housing, shopping centers, office parks—continually places older vintages at a disadvantage. Older, typically smaller, housing, perhaps without off-street parking and lacking modern insulation and contemporary design features, means, for existing residents at least, the danger that it will filter down to, horror of horrors, "them," and that the residential tax base will undergo some attrition. Inner suburbs often have their shopping centers, but they are usually on far too small a scale to compete with the newer mega malls appearing farther out. And their expansion possibilities are distinctly limited due to the fact that they are often already surrounded by other development. Small retailing/restaurant/coffee house clusters may succeed in converting themselves so as to occupy relatively unique niches in a wider geographic division of consumption. But parking, particularly when compared with the new entertainment complexes appearing farther out, is almost invariably an issue.

The responses on the part of local governments have been diverse. Shopping centers have been redeveloped. Support has been given to private initiatives that have coalesced in seemingly organic fashion around new niches in the wider spatial division of consumption: clusters of trendy restaurants along with an art cinema and cramped secondhand bookstores with a nice musty smell. Older industrial or warehouse sites may be redeveloped with offices and expensive apartments. But what is possible clearly depends on the wider legacy of the suburb: a particular built environment and social composition conducive to these transformations, perhaps a small liberal arts college. Blue-collar suburbs will struggle.

In a number of states, "first suburbs" have come together in coalition and formulated legislative programs for state consideration.[51] In Ohio, this has taken the form of something called the First Suburbs Consortium. This is a statewide group that emerged in the late 1990s seeking to mitigate through state policy what its members saw as a competitive disadvantage compared with the outer suburbs and including all the older, inner suburbs of the Columbus area: Bexley, Grandview Heights, Upper Arlington, Whitehall, and Worthington. They have had two major requests. One is the reallocation of highway money away from the periphery and in their direction—as in money for the construction of new freeway interchanges that can spark redevelopment. The second has been to join forces with an emergent agricultural land–preservation lobby spearheaded by farmers (who are not yet ready to sell but want the tax advantages that a preservation policy would bring, bless their hearts) and environmentalists. The intent here is to limit the advantage that outer suburbs enjoy from their relatively large acreages of undeveloped land and the annexing of still more of it. Change in annexation law was one of the things pushed for. Meanwhile, of course, the older suburbs disguise their intentions with high-minded talk of the dangers of urban sprawl and the need to rein it in.[52] Well, it does need reining in, but that is not what they are about.

In terms of employment, most inner suburbs have relatively weak economic bases; when they have a major employer, it is likely to be the only one. Employment is significant in that it generates income taxes. The premises themselves are a source of property taxes. An interesting contrast in the Columbus area is between Grandview Heights and Upper Arlington. With the closure of a large supermarket chain distribution center in 1997, Grandview Heights lost a major source of income taxes ($400,000 per year). Back property taxes were lost when the owner went bankrupt in 2004. Nothing happened until 2009, when it was bought by Nationwide Realty Investors, with ambitious plans for a mixed-use development including residential, office, and

---

51. Puentes 2006.

52. "Local Leaders Aim to Stop Urban Sprawl," *This Week in Worthington,* April 29, 1998, p. 19.

some retail and hospitality. Shortly thereafter, the parent company of Nationwide Realty, Nationwide Insurance, announced plans to bring together on the site 3,000 of its workers then mainly in Dublin and Westerville, an interesting transfer of fiscal benefits and hugely important for the relatively small suburb of Grandview Heights.

From one angle, something like the old Big Bear distribution center can be regarded as a windfall, the opportunity to maneuver a more tax-intensive land use into spaces that are rare in the inner suburbs. But while a space might exist, it may be hard to get agreement between all the parties. Such was the case with Upper Arlington in the '90s. A major source of income taxes for the suburb had been CompuServe, which, in 1993, had expansion plans. What it was looking at was almost thirty acres on the city's northwest side, and one of the very few opportunities available to it. This was the Zschach property, owned by a family of that name and living on part of it. Negotiations with the owners, though, broke down and there was also opposition from local resident groups.[53] Pressed for time, CompuServe opted for a site in a neighboring outer suburb with lots of developable land coming in large acreages: Hilliard. Staff numbers in the existing offices in Upper Arlington would not go down, but the city had lost 1,500 potential income tax payers.

This in effect was a wake-up call for the city, bringing to a head long-standing concerns about the city tax base, and led to a number of different initiatives. A Community Improvement Corporation was established in the same year, with the power to issue bonds and acquire property, if necessary through use of the power of eminent domain. Attention then returned, amidst considerable citizen angst, to the juicy Zschach property. And in fact the family did reach an agreement with a developer, but, alas from the city's standpoint, a *residential* developer—that is, no income taxes, unless residents just happened to work within city boundaries, which was unlikely, and in any case the number of homes planned was extremely modest. So there was deadlock again—a standoff over appropriate rezoning. Not until five years later would the city admit defeat.

Eventually the CompuServe saga would reappear in a different form. Even with the expansion in Hilliard, it had continued to be a major revenue contributor: more than $700,000 of the city's income

53. "Voters Seek Veto Power over Zoning Proposals," *Columbus Dispatch,* May 19, 1993, p. 1B.

tax revenues, and a sum amounting to half of the $3.6 million the school district received in personal property taxes.[54] But by 2000, the office had been closed. The city has since looked in vain for a replacement, and in the course of that search has had to defend the site—as in the case of the Zschach property—against purchasers far less promising from the fiscal standpoint. It is zoned for office, which means that schools are excluded, and purposefully, since they are property tax–exempt. That has not stopped a religious organization, Tree of Life, purchasing the site so as to consolidate its school operations in the Columbus area and then litigating up till the present time to overturn the zoning on constitutional grounds.[55] It is not easy being an older, inner suburb (see "Windfall Sites, Their Hazards, and How Local Governments Can Create Them").

In some contrast to the outer suburbs, where new development can often occur on sites relatively insulated from residential areas, in the older, inner suburbs, it is a matter of redeveloping existing sites, which are typically surrounded by people who are not about to be put out. This can make things tricky for local government, which then has to call on the supposed gains to the rest of the population in an attempt to push its plans through. Upper Arlington has been in the midst of a number of these conflicts. In 2011, keen to develop the sales tax income from restaurants, it seized on the apparent attraction of sites along Lane Avenue opposite the Lane Avenue Shopping Center to promote the area as what the state defines as 'a community entertainment district'; such a designation then allows a city to apply for an increase in the number of liquor license permits it is allowed by the state. The problem has been one of parking in adjacent residential streets.[56]

54. "Employees Await Result in Hilliard and Arlington," *Columbus Dispatch,* January 28, 1998.

55. The implication of tax exemption for educational institutions and how it can challenge the tax base prospects of land-locked suburbs was also highlighted in 2010 in the city of Bexley, when Capital University announced plans to buy a shopping center for purposes of university expansion. It was later retracted, though what role city opposition played—and it certainly existed—was unclear.

56. When it is a question of furthering the growth of the commercial tax base in the older suburbs, space for parking has been a continuing challenge. Lane Avenue Shopping Center has made a number of attempts over the years to try to solve its problem, ranging from purchasing adjacent residential properties so as to raze them and put in their place a multidecker parking garage to demolishing some of its own properties with the same end in view, but both encountered neighborhood opposition. No problems like this in the far suburbs.

Windfall Sites, Their Hazards, and How Local Governments Can Create Them

A classic instance of the politics of windfall sites has unfolded in Worthington, a suburb to the north of Columbus. The case there involved the site of the United Methodist Children's Home. In 2011, the church announced plans to vacate and sell the thirty-eight-acre site. But all the proposals for redevelopment have met with opposition from nearby residential areas. The initial one, for a supermarket along with, somewhat more vaguely, apartments, medical offices, and a gas station, was quickly shot down amidst the usual concerns of noise, traffic, and crime. It would not be until 2015, four years later, that another plan was brought forward, this time largely for a mix of owner-occupied and rental housing and some retail. Again, opposition was intense, leaving the impression that reversion to green space was the popular public option, and indeed, nine years later—that is right: nine years—there is still no resolution. Rather different has been the sequence of events in Whitehall. This came to light in 1999 when a lawsuit on the part of two motels and a trailer court in Whitehall claimed that the city had launched a crackdown on them in light of supposed crime and code violations. The two motels were subsequently demolished by the city on the grounds of being unsafe and used for drug sales. The lawsuit claimed that this was part of an effort to drive them out so as to facilitate redevelopment. At that time, Whitehall's redevelopment program offered financial incentives for new projects in former shopping centers and other unused properties along three major streets, including the one on which the two motels were located.

A year earlier, in 2010, the city had supported the owner of its major shopping center, Kingsdale, in his attempts to improve its accessibility by constructing a highway that would connect Ackerman Road to Zollinger; this would adversely affect not only people who would back on to the proposed connector but also those who fear increased traffic on the highway linking the connector to the shopping center. Again, a lot of neighborhood angst, and it is not yet off the table.

This recalls another "connector" issue in the Columbus area, but this time in the city itself. This might seem odd, but it underlines the dangers of forcing cities into a simple division between inner and outer. Columbus is both: It has the advantages of being able to annex large sites on its periphery—hence the major regional shopping centers with their lucrative sales taxes—as well as facing calls farther in from property owners for redevelopment or infrastructural projects that would boost sales. The latter was on display in the case of the "Morse-

Bethel" connector.[57] From the standpoint of circulation and reducing congestion, the case for it is a no-brainer. Columbus lacks east-west connections across the Olentangy River. Problems of emergency access to two major hospitals accessible from the west side of the river added to the case. But in 1998, a referendum took place, and the issue was soundly defeated: 63 percent to 37 percent. Pretty decisive.

The issue had been promoted not just on grounds of public accessibility but also by auto distributors along Morse Road in one of the city's automobile alleys, who saw the connector as a way of broadening their market and helping them in their struggle with distributors farther out. But opposition from residents in the area had been intense, particularly in an enclave of quite wealthy people in what was known as Old Beechwold. Many crocodile tears were shed about the impact of the connector on those who were to be displaced: nobody in Old Beechwold, incidentally. There was also a massive disparity in the funds raised for respective publicity campaigns: $62,400 for the case against and $8,900 for, over half of it from the auto dealers. The largest donation, $10,000, came from the Old Beechwold Residents Association—quite a chunk of change from an area that includes only 137 properties, for an average of over $70 per household.[58] But the Beechwold residents may just have gotten lucky. The issue got blurred as a result of the emergence of an alternative route prior to the vote that would have taken it through the Graceland Shopping Center. So were they voting for the alternative route, in which case, vote "No," or for the original one?

There have been numerous other cases where Columbus has found itself on both sides of the fence, trying to take advantage of expanding on the periphery while meeting the challenge of older neighborhoods and their businesses farther in. The assistance that the city gave to the Polaris developers in order to persuade them to annex to the city was met with dismay from the South Side and what it believed to be its superior claim to the money—but for redevelopment rather than development. A proposal for a new interchange on a freeway, east of Columbus, in Licking County, and pushed by local development advocates, put the city more clearly in the position of the inner sub-

57. For the geography of this issue, go to Google Street Scene and enter "Old Beechwold." Other things to look for on the map include: Bethel Road, Morse Road, and Worthington.

58. "Opponents of Connector Launch TV Ad Campaign," *Columbus Dispatch,* October 20, 1998, p. 1A.

urbs. Two Columbus city councilors expressed reservations to the state Department of Transportation director on the ground of the need for upgrading already existing interchanges closer in to the city.[59] The new interchange would not happen, though eventually there would be one even farther out.

•

The developer story is a remarkable one: costs dumped on the public in all manner of ways, ducking the moral imperatives of making good on a sorry story of racial segregation in schools, the premature obsolescence of vast swathes of housing, not to mention shopping centers, and this without mentioning the sprawl that is the hallmark of American urbanization. Columbus is by no means unusual in this. This is the common modus operandi. Nevertheless, we should resist claims that they are a self-serving bunch out of touch with what is right and wrong in the contemporary world. They *are* self-serving, but this is a result of the particular incentive structure that they face. On the one hand, they are in intense competition with one another and have to pay their bills, while keeping the banks and the shareholders happy. On the other, they live in a society where money is elevated as an ideal like nowhere else. Even so, one has to ask why regulation of the industry is so limited and why local government does not put its foot down more firmly. The next chapter tries to provide some answers.

---

59. "Boon or Threat? Opinions Split about Idea for I-70 Interchange," *Columbus Dispatch,* October 26, 1998, p. 4B.

CHAPTER 7

How the Developers Get Their Way

The Power of Developers

A central claim in the last chapter was the extraordinary power that developers wield in the Columbus area: their ability to get their way. Just why this is merits further investigation, though what has transpired in Columbus is typical of most American cities today; it is a game that virtually all local governments think that they need to play: giving away the farm on the dubious rationale that the local tax base will subsequently be bolstered. It does not have to be like this. Things are handled quite differently in the countries of Western Europe. Land-use planners, instead of being pawns of the developers, are much more powerful, and opposition to developers and their plans is more intense and seemingly more successful. Land speculation is discouraged. The sort of mushrooming of new commercial developments around new freeway interchanges is rare, as, consequently, are the gains that accrue to developers from reaping where they have not sown. There are costs. The responsiveness of property markets to shifts in demand is quite a bit weaker, so that rents are higher; property capitals gain but in a different way. In fact, they appear more parasitic than their US counterparts; at least in the US they put in a bit of effort. It might seem that you are damned if you do and damned if you don't, but that is another story and suggests that what is needed on both sides of the Atlantic is a dramatic change in land policy, possibly through a property tax that falls purely on land, as in Henry George's single tax proposal. But on that one, property developers in both the US and Western Europe would be united in their opposition.

How, therefore, to understand the peculiar sort of power that developers enjoy not just in Columbus, but in the US as a whole? Obviously since we are talking about a capitalist society, the power of money looms large. Just how it works, though, has to be placed in the context of a particular institutional framework and a discourse specific to the US, as well as the practices that emerge everywhere to negotiate the challenges of democracy to the social power of money and the particular features they assume in the US.

Jurisdictional Fragmentation

Like most metropolitan areas in the US, Columbus is divided into numerous local governments and then, on top of that, school districts: municipalities and school districts, to be precise. There again, as development has approached the boundaries of neighboring counties, they too have been incorporated into the developer's game, which in this particular instance is to get their way by playing one off against another.

It is, of course, not just a matter of proximity of one local government to another. Because of their heavy reliance on tax revenues from *within* their jurisdictional boundaries, taxes on incomes, sales, and property, they can be quite susceptible to the demands of developers. Also, by virtue of their small size, and therefore financial limits, aside from the city of Columbus itself, they do not have the resources to lavish on defending their land-use decisions against the lawsuits of the developers, on whatever grounds seem plausible.[1] This is in substantial contrast to Western Europe, where the fiscal redistribution of central governments limits the incentives to pursue tax base, and there again, central supervision of local land-use decisions makes it harder to connive with the developers.

As for how, in the US, developer interests can play one local government off against another, some classic instances were referred

1. Though one suspects that often enough, local governments use this as an excuse in order to reject popular demands around land-use decisions that would be against their own (pro-developer) wisdom.

to earlier in the book. The plans for the multiuse Polaris development, just to the north over the Franklin County line and in Delaware County, had included a freeway interchange to be financed by the developers: a necessary improvement to enhance the access of the development. But as discussed in chapter 2, those plans went awry, which meant turning to local government to bail them out. And there were indeed suitors. Delaware County wanted it, on behalf of one of its school districts, Olentangy, which had experienced significant residential growth without the taxes from commercial development to help support schools expansion. Columbus wanted it for its own revenue purposes, and, one suspects, the Columbus Department of Public Utilities was keen to snag it to increase *its* revenues and so offset the speculative expansions that it has always indulged in. So there was a bidding war: money for the interchange in exchange for either staying in Delaware County as a taxable entity or being annexed by Columbus.

Another outstanding instance of local governments being used in this way was the New Albany one. In New Albany, it will be recalled, the New Albany Company had assembled a considerable amount of land with a view to expensive residential development and had relied on an earlier agreement between the county and Columbus by which the latter would serve some parts of the area with water and sewage disposal without demanding annexation: important where, as a result of the Win-Win agreement over schools annexation, annexation into Columbus would be followed by annexation of the same area into the Columbus public school district. But then, just as a big announcement was to be made about the plans of the developers, the agreement was rescinded. This created a dilemma for the developers: how to get water and sewage disposal for the area without the dreaded schools annexation? As I pointed out earlier, Columbus was more than willing to negotiate a water and sewer contract with the Village of New Albany and a generous expansion area that the Village could annex. The problem was, Columbus Public Schools had other ideas and felt that this would be against the spirit of the Win-Win agreement. This put the city council in a dilemma as well as the New Albany Company. But as may be recalled, the latter saw a way out through playing other local governments off against the city and upping the stakes, as in all or nothing. The key move was a proposal for the Village to merge with the rest of the township (Plain Township) that included the land holdings in question and then to negotiate a water-sewer agreement with either Del-Co in contiguous Delaware County or with the equally contiguous Jefferson Township, which had its own water and sewage treatment plant. This got Columbus's attention. If this happened, its avenues of future expansion elsewhere in Plain Township or even over the county line into Licking County would be off-limits. So, regardless of the protests of the school board, Columbus negotiated a water and sewer agreement with New Albany along with the generous expansion area to include most of the land holdings of the New Albany Company. The price it demanded was the abandonment of the village-township merger so as to protect its future annexation interests in the area. So Plain Township was thoroughly used, just as Delaware County had been in the Polaris case.

This is to emphasize jurisdictions that are, geographically, mutually exclusive. But there can be considerable overlap, even coincidence. As we have seen, the city of Columbus does not coincide with any particular school district, though as a proportion of its total area, the Columbus school district is clearly the biggest. This might not be so significant if their sources of revenue were the same. But they are not. Municipalities, including Columbus and the independent suburbs, draw significantly on sales and income taxes, as well as property taxes. School districts, on the other hand, and in addition to any state aid that they receive, depend entirely on property taxes: no sales or income taxes in that instance. But it is municipalities that make the development decisions, and their incentives are quite different from those that a school board would face. For a city, offering tax abatements to developers—and we have seen that this has been a major part of at least the city of Columbus's development policy—means some loss of property taxes, but this gets to be at the very least offset by income taxes, and in the case of shopping centers, sales taxes. Meanwhile, school districts turn out to be the big losers, unless, as sometimes happens, particularly when the school board puts up a fuss, some transfer payment is arranged from municipal coffers.[2] But the arrangements are all very ad

2. The implications of the incentive structure confronting the city council were laid out well by Joe Motil, longtime observer and critic of city council tax abatements, in an address to the city council ("Nationwide Children's Spinoff Latest Stop on Columbus Gravy Train," *Columbus Dispatch,* September 18, 2017): "Your tax abatement policies have also recently shown to have a clear impact on our Columbus school teachers' salaries. Just last week our teachers reluctantly approved a mere 1.5% and 1% increase in a two year salary agreement. How unjust is that? If you were

hoc, and developers know it and will exploit the vulnerability of the cities. The Nationwide building and plaza story and its fallout, discussed in the last chapter, are well known.

It is not just the tax abatements, though. There are also the TIF provisions granted to developers that allow the taxes on value increases subsequent to a real estate investment to be diverted to improving the immediate public infrastructure. These have been an issue not just with the school district but also with the county.[3] What has also rankled is the way in which the favors go to developments in parts of the city that are booming and that should not require incentives. A particularly egregious case involved handouts to give the Georgetown Company, the codeveloper with Leslie Wexner at Easton, quite massive tax breaks (see "Welfare for the Wealthy").

In this regard, the Columbus metropolitan area is no different from other metropolitan areas in the country. Fragmentation of governmental authority, along with the desire of those local governments to enhance their revenues as well as that of elected officials to cozy up to developers for their own reasons, makes them extremely vulnerable when those same developers come calling. It is to the role of local government officials, particularly of the elective variety, that we turn next.

---

teachers, how many of you would find that to be an acceptable offer? It wasn't too long ago this City Council approved a 3 year contract to 2,500 city employees for a 2 year 3% increase and a one year 2% increase. One of the reasons for such disparity in these contracts is the fact that this City Council and our Mayor are more concerned about increasing the income tax revenue of our General Fund by using tax abatements (which contributes to about 75% of city's General Fund) than you are about reducing property tax revenues that pay for our children's education, teachers' salaries, children with developmental disabilities, libraries, seniors services and critical dollars to help address this communities opioid crisis."

3. "Franklin County's drug and alcohol agency could have served 100 additional clients last year if it had received its share of property axes diverted to pay for roads at Easton and the Arena District, and for other public improvements. Progress has a price, and Franklin County's social-service agencies and other organizations are paying it. Tax-increment financing in Franklin County since 1999 has diverted more than $37 million I property taxes, money that otherwise would have gone to social-service agencies, schools, libraries and the zoo" ("Developer Tax Deals Can Cost Agencies," *Columbus Dispatch,* September 19, 2004, p. A1). See also "Franklin County Casts Critical Eye over Tax Districts for Suburban Developments," *Columbus Dispatch,* July 21, 2019.

Welfare for the Wealthy

In 2017, it was announced that the city of Columbus would grant a ten-year, 100 percent property tax abatement to the Georgetown Company, which was planning to construct housing at Easton, the major multi-use development on the northeast side of the city. This would save the company about $6.8 million per year. As a sort of quid pro quo, the developer offered to give the city $5.75 million to stimulate development in Linden, a very deprived neighborhood. However, the company then lobbied the state for a special taxing district that would allow it to claw back $4.25 million of that grant. Amazing, no? It doesn't stop there. How to justify the abatement when they are usually granted for developments that generate jobs? In this case it was argued that without the houses, there would be no jobs. Very clever. Ever wonder where those kids in law school end up and why they want to go to law school and do the dirty work for the likes of the Georgetown Company, all in exchange for bloated salaries? And one more consequence: Since it is a matter of housing, and according to state law, the school district is not allowed to negotiate with the city for some relief from the fact that it is going to lose a lot of revenue as a result of the city's generosity.[1] No wonder the teachers get ticked off—which they did when they protested in the summer of 2017 on the occasion of another instance of tax abatements gone wild. This was CoverMyMeds, which wanted a tax break for a decision to build its headquarters in Columbus. The city was more than willing, citing the usual stuff about firms that are mobile: "Development officials in Columbus say tax incentives are critical to keeping companies such as CoverMyMeds, which are 'inherently portable," according to the city's development director, Steve Schoeny."[2] Well, if they are so mobile, what is to stop them moving once the tax abatement expires? The only insurance is the company's word: "Asked after the meeting if CoverMyMeds could simply relocate to a new headquarters in 15 years to avoid paying property taxes as part of its rent, Lenio [the site consultant hired by CoverMyMeds] said the firm has no intention of doing that."[3] And we are supposed to take that on trust?

1. "Columbus Schools Left out of Easton Tax-Break Deal," *Columbus Dispatch*, February 14, 2017; "Editorial: City Trying to Make Amends," *Columbus Dispatch*, February 27, 2017.

2. "When Midwest Startups Sell, Their Hometown Schools Often Lose," *Bloomberg Business Week*, August 12, 2019.

3. "CoverMyMeds Proposes 1,000 New HQ Jobs for Columbus in Return for Tax Deal," *Columbus Dispatch*, June 19, 2018.

Democracy and Its Limits

From its very birth, democracy in capitalist forms of society has confronted a major tension. On the one hand, wealth is very unevenly distributed, and the wealthy want to make more money by investing what they have, like the developers in Columbus. On the other hand, everybody has the right to vote, which can make those who monopolize the wealth very vulnerable to state actions that would either redistribute it or limit their ability to multiply it by putting it where it will make the most money for them, and the public be damned. So if you are wealthy, or in the particular case that we are discussing here, a developer, how do you get your way with city government? How do you manage the rezonings you need when people in the neighborhood are opposed to what you are planning? And how do you get those other favors from city government that are going to impose on the citizenry in general, like generous tax abatements or even using casino money to buy an arena and so subsidize an ice-hockey franchise? If you are a developer with an interest in maximizing profits from rents or sales, these are serious questions. And answers have been found.

In the Columbus case, one of the answers has been a mode of electing city councilors that has made them vulnerable to the buying of influence by developers. The ways in which city councils are elected in the US vary. At one extreme are those, like Los Angeles, where councilors each represent a geographically delimited area—a ward; only the people living in a particular ward get to say who will represent them. At the other extreme are ones like Columbus, where councilors are elected "at large." This means that at election time, regardless of where you live in Columbus, you are confronted with a list of several candidates and asked to select a smaller number to represent you. The preferences are tallied up, and those with the most votes are elected. In between Los Angeles and Columbus, there are various mixes of the two systems: some councilors are voted into office by wards and others at large, as in Austin, Texas, and Seattle.

The incentives that the two extremes set up are quite different. In a ward system, you need to be well known, have visibility and a reputation in the ward, but not in the city as a whole. In at-large systems, you need citywide visibility, which is a much tougher proposition. To make yourself visible, you need money, which is where the corporations and the developers come in, offering campaign finance. The argument is that this is less likely to happen in a ward system, though as we will see, there has to be some doubt about that. The more common case against wards has been that it puts one local group in opposition to another, resulting in horse trading and misallocation of municipal resources—something for everyone, which makes it harder to provide more concentrated infrastructural investments, say, that will allow thresholds to be reached beyond which development will be self-sustaining. Again, this is by no means clear-cut. Rather, as in the case of the jurisdictional fragmentation of the city, even without a ward system, developers can play different parts of the city off against one another in order to get what they want.

Nevertheless, the demand for elections by ward in Columbus is long-standing. One of the ways in which the city has responded, short of providing what was being asked for, has been the creation of area commissions that would act as intermediaries between, on the one hand, residents, and on the other, developers and city officials. This process started in the early 1970s. Establishment of a commission requires a petition from residents in the area in question. There are now seventeen of them, though with a notable absence in the far north. They cover a variety of areas, though interestingly not the gentrifying ones, except as parts of broader areas. Rather, German Village and Victorian Village have separate bodies, still named commissions, appointed by the mayor, and charged with historical and architectural preservation.

Each area commission has a board with members elected by area residents. Boards consider planning and development issues affecting the area in meetings open to the public and make requests of, and recommendations to, the city, but their functions are strictly advisory. These issues can include rezonings affecting the area, the closure of a shopping center, and highway changes, like new highways or expansions of existing ones. The boards are also the guardians of boundaries: an important consideration when trying to combat a dilution of neighborhood identity and, more important, property values.

However, this is no mere parish pump politics. The area commissions get involved in issues of significance for the city as a whole. Once the *Dispatch* had made the location of the casino next to the Arena District moot, at least three of them entered the fray to compete for it. The Morse-Bethel connector had serious implications for traffic circulation in the mid-north part of the city but stumbled on the intense opposition of the Clintonville Area Commission and particularly that of the Old Beechwold neighborhood, as we saw in the last chapter.

Even so, their effectiveness when coming up against the entrenched power of the developers in the city of Columbus has been seriously questioned. It is not just that the city council has the final say and that the area commissions can only recommend. There are other nonelected city agencies with which they must contend and on which development interests are grossly overrepresented under the fig leaf of "expertise." How a case unfolded in the area just to the north of Ohio State University is indicative. At issue was a request for a zoning variance for a development that would have been out of scale with a neighborhood of two-story buildings: a six-story and a three-story building to include 297 bedrooms and parking for 230 cars. This was vigorously opposed by the area commission in question—the University Area Commission. But what they would discover was that ultimate jurisdiction over the variance was held by something called the Board of Zoning Appeals. This is an appointive body where, according to the city code, at least three members have to be city residents and at least three have to be either an architect, lawyer, building contractor, professional engineer, real-estate broker, or mortgage banker: that is, "experts."

As if this developer defense apparatus was insufficient to keep the masses at bay, there is also something called the University Area Review Board, whose brief is "to preserve, protect and enhance the urban environment and neighborhood characteristics of the University Area." This is also appointive. Of the seven members, three must be registered architects, one from the Columbus Apartment Association, one from the University Community Business Association, one from the University Area Commission, and one at-large appointment.[4] No surprise, therefore, that it voted 4–0 in favor of the variance.[5] Meanwhile, the University Area Commission, poor sods, had voted 15–1 against. In the aftermath, it was pointed out that since the variance met the legal standards, it was hard to reject, which in turn put the spotlight on the whole business of requests for variances and

4. "Many of our board members are very familiar with the university area," said Ted Goodman, the architect who leads the board. But he said those who live outside the area bring "fresh perspective" ("Zoning Board Makeup an Issue in View on Pavey Square Project," *Columbus Dispatch,* August 29, 2016). That's right, Ted. But the question is: Whose perspective are they bringing?

5. Just why only four members voted is unclear, unless the others had to recuse themselves.

the subordination of planning to developer interests. One member of the University Area Commission, Aaron Marshall, underlined this by referring to the University District Plan that had been adopted by the city council: "We spent two years working on a university area blueprint for smart development," Marshall said. "It's not worth the paper it's printed on. Developers know they can get whatever they want from the BZA [Board of Zoning Appeals]."[6]

All this has contributed to the recent demand for some sort of ward representation. Columbus City Council has seven members, each of whom is elected at large. As noted above, a common view is that the at-large form increases the likelihood that a councilor will be in hock to developer interests.[7] The view is that what is needed to remedy this is a move to a ward system. In turn, this should be from more wards than just seven, since the city has grown enormously, area- and population-wise, since the original mandate for a seven-member council.

The way in which council members are elected is not a new issue. Columbus City Council *used* to be elected from wards.[8] In fact, from the date of the city's foundation in 1816 until 1914, city council elections were held according to that principle. One of the conditions prompting the change to at-large elections was an early incarnation of the red scare. In 1912, the Socialist Party presidential candidate Eugene V. Debs had polled 6 percent of the vote and seemed on an upward curve. In that same election, Columbus elected four Socialists to the city council out of a total possible twenty-two. From 1914 on, elections would be at large and for a mere seven councilors; this remains the case despite the fact that the city has grown in population by a quite massive 350 percent. As Fitrakis points out, this puts Columbus substantially out of step with its peers: "If you average the top 50 cities in America, the average city council has 1.9 council members elected at-large, to 11.2 members elected from Districts. Among the top 20 cities, the average council has 2 council members elected at-large, to 13.7 council members elected from Districts."[9]

6. "Does Columbus Zoning Board Bulldoze Area-Commission Decisions?" *Columbus Dispatch,* September 25, 2017.

7. "With the expense of running citywide campaigns with Columbus' all at-large Council format, competition is negligible. A candidate needs an estimated $250,000 to run a credible campaign citywide" (Bob Fitrakis, "Welcome to the Machine," *Columbus Free Press,* September 12, 2013).

8. I am relying heavily here on Bob Fitrakis's historical survey in "Welcome to the Machine" in the *Columbus Free Press,* September 12, 2013.

9. Ibid.

There have been numerous attempts to change this. In both 1968 and 1975, proposals to introduce mixed systems combining ward and at-large representation were endorsed by the council but failed the popular vote. By the 1990s, the interest in shifting to greater representation by area was clearly tied up with how development issues were impinging on the neighborhoods. There was a proposal from neighborhood organizations to abolish both the Development Commission, which made recommendations on zoning issues, and the city council's jurisdiction over zoning matters. Rather, the proposal was for a zoning board with members elected from each part of Columbus to determine land-use issues.[10] High hopes indeed!

Some twenty years later, in 2011, there was another proposal for wards, put forward by an organization calling itself the Columbus Coalition for Responsive Government. The call was for a shift to four at-large and seven councilors to be elected by ward, but the numbers required on the petition to force a referendum fell short. A further attempt to reduce what was seen as a developer lock on the city council was a proposal from the same group to limit campaign spending and use a neutral source to fund election campaigns for city council and mayor. This would be tax revenue from the casino. Rejected by the city council[11]—surprise, surprise—the coalition organized a petition for it to go to a popular vote, but while the petition drive succeeded, it was rejected by the Board of Elections on technical grounds (see "Beware the Board of Elections: Time to Look More Closely").

The hitherto crowning accomplishment of the Columbus Coalition would be to actually succeed in running the gauntlet of the petition process and the Board of Elections and get a vote for a reformed electoral system—ten elected by ward and three at large—in 2016. An impressive 39,000 people signed the petition. This would be Issue 1, brought to the public in August of that year. It would be decisively defeated—only about 28 percent "for"—but that does not make the campaign any less interesting. The position of the president of the

---

10. See "More Voices Joining Call to Change City Council," *Worthington Suburbia News,* December 16, 1992, p. 26A; "Activists Want City Zoning Role Curbed," *Columbus Dispatch,* December 8, 1992, p. 1D.

11. "Council President Andrew J. Ginther said the proposal is 'unnecessary, unconstitutional and diverts tax dollars from neighborhoods to fund political campaigns'" ("Columbus Council Rejects Tax-Paid Campaigns," *Columbus Dispatch,* December 3, 2013)—no mention of the good works developers could accomplish if they diverted funds otherwise sent to city council candidates to some public purpose.

Beware the Board of Elections: Time to Look More Closely

The headline was: "Elections Board Won't Place Nationwide Arena, Campaign-Finance Issues on May Ballot."[1] The grounds were that "the petitions to place the issues before voters contained misleading language that might have swayed people who signed them."[2] Well, this is an odd reason. "Misleading" from whose standpoint, and who stands to gain from declaring it "misleading"? And this, of course, raises quite serious issues about the gatekeeping role of the board and the way in which it is a happy hunting ground for lawyers. By law, an elections board has to have two Democratic and two Republican members, which is a bit weird in itself, since it assumes the two parties embrace all possible political views. There is also the fact that in this instance, the concerns about the petition wording were brought by the lawyer representing the county Democratic Party, and, of course, it was the Democratic Party that, under the at-large system, was monopolizing the city council, albeit to the advantage of the local political establishment as a whole, including the developers. Interestingly, the chair of the board at that time, Douglas Preisse, a Republican, had attracted adverse attention in 2011 when he responded to *Dispatch* questioning about early voting policy: "I guess I really actually feel we shouldn't contort the voting process to accommodate the urban—read African-American—voter turnout machine."[3] Conclusion: Time to put election boards, or at least this one, under more critical scrutiny.

1. *Columbus Dispatch,* February 3, 2014.
2. Ibid.
3. https://ballotpedia.org/Doug_Preisse.

council and the mayor was a predictable one: They feared that "wards would pit neighborhood against neighborhood and hurt the city's progress"[12] and that it would lead to "horse-trading."[13] The disparate funding thrown into the campaign was also predictable, as were its sources. The anti-ward campaign, under the banner of OneColumbus, was able to outspend Represent Columbus colossally: a total of $1.1

12. "Boundaries for Columbus Council Wards Would Be Set after Election," *Columbus Dispatch,* May 26, 2016.

13. "As Ward Vote Nears, Columbus Leader Plan Charter Review," *Columbus Dispatch,* July 6, 2016. But no mention of the horse-trading already entrenched in city council practice, as in the way the bone of the City Center was thrown to Lazarus to mitigate their chagrin at the support shown to Nationwide and development at some distance to the north.

million, as opposed to an almost trivial $17,000 available to the campaign pushing for the issue, or a ratio of almost sixty to one in a supposedly democratic process. Meanwhile, over half of the money for OneColumbus came from some of the city's biggest businesses, including American Electric Power Ohio, Nationwide, Wolfe Enterprises, and Huntington National Bank. The remainder came from developers, law firms, construction companies, and labor unions (see "The Publicity That Money Buys").[14] As the article continued, "Nearly all these donors do business with the city."[15] More particularly, though, it was the local development interests that were to the fore.[16] Probably *the* master stroke of the OneColumbus group, and testifying to the advantages that accrue to those defending the status quo, their ability to determine the field of battle, was the city's proposal at the beginning of July, with a month to go before the vote, to review the city charter, including, implicitly, the institutions governing elections to city council.[17] However, and so strategically, it was announced that the results of the review would not be known before the vote. Amidst the confusion thrown into the debate by this move and the disparity in funding, the result was almost foreseen, though the size of the majority was a surprise.

In retrospect, a major error on the part of the coalition was to ally itself with the Republican Party. All city councilors are Democrats, and the Republicans feel left out by the 'at large' form. A shift to wards would almost certainly bring some salvation, so it is far from surprising that they came out in favor. But it did not do the ultimate goal much good since it converted the issue into a partisan one in a city where Democrats outnumber Republicans by a considerable margin.[18]

14. The one labor union that came out publicly in support of the status quo was, and once more predictably, the construction workers represented by the Columbus/Central Ohio Building and Construction Trades Council ("Trades Council Opposes Issue 1" [letter to the editor], *Columbus Dispatch,* July 15, 2016).

15. "Follow the Money Flowing to Ward Initiative Campaigns in Columbus," *Columbus Dispatch,* July 22, 2016.

16. The development interests of Wolfe Enterprises and Nationwide are well known, and not just through their stakes in the Arena District. The Ohio branch of AEP is hugely dependent on the growth of the Columbus market. As for Huntington, one has to assume that it is heavily invested in lending money for the local development process.

17. "As Ward Vote Nears, Columbus Leader Plan Charter Review," *Columbus Dispatch,* July 6, 2016.

18. This is not easy to confirm quantitatively since mayoral and council elections are supposedly nonpartisan. However, campaign contributions to Democratic

The Publicity That Money Buys

The money in this particular instance funded some extremely dubious advertising. Even while the *Dispatch* opposed the issue, it had the decency to recognize how misleading the publicity was. As the newspaper editorialized, "Political advertising has never been noted for its fairness or accuracy, so it's important to point out when this advocacy engages in misdirection and distortion." A case in point is a mailer sent to Columbus households from One Columbus, the "Vote No on Issue 1" group. The group opposes the proposal to convert the seven-member at-large council into one with ten members elected from wards and three at large. The mailer asks, "Do YOU want to pay for a 25-member city council?" It shows a grid of twenty-five photos of these supposed council members—no faces, just white, male hands . . . adjusting silver cufflinks, conservative ties, dark suits, and burnished leather oxfords. The subliminal message: Vote for wards and the new council won't have women, blue-collar representatives, or people of color. That's rich, because as Democratic state representative Michael Curtin noted in a recent article for the *Dispatch*, after Columbus voters abandoned their ward system of government in 1914, "no African-American would be elected to the council for 55 years." So where does the twenty-five figure come from? The number of wards would increase as the city grows, with an upper limit of twenty-five members, but this would take years. This number is accurate, but misleading."[1]

1. "Political Mailer Takes Some Liberties," *Columbus Dispatch*, July 24, 2016, p. 5H; quoted in full with permission of the *Columbus Dispatch*.

But all was not lost. The latest news as of November 2017 was that the NAACP Legal Defense Fund, at the urging of a group calling itself Everyday People for Positive Change, was showing an interest in the situation on the grounds of the possibly racially discriminatory nature of the current system of electing city councilors, even while four of the current seven are, in fact, African American.[19]

candidates greatly outnumbered contributions to Republicans over the period of 2015–2018: 81 percent of contributions were to Democrats. See http://www.bestplaces.net/voting/city/ohio/columbus (last accessed October 25, 2020).

19. This may sound strange. The problem is that the vast majority of Democratic councilors are initially appointed by the existing party machine to replace resignations or those who have died or moved away. This then gives them an incumbent visibility that facilitates their later election. Apparently this practice is not confined to Columbus. See the letter to the editor from Gerald Dixon, "Political Entrenchment Grips Whitehall," *Columbus Dispatch*, December 11, 2017.

And the charter commission that provided a distraction to the referendum process did in fact come up with some proposals. These were approved by popular vote and went into effect in 2018, but the changes are a classic fudge. The council expands from seven to nine members and there *will* be representation by ward. But they will continue to be elected at large! Utterly staggering. That means that a person living in a particular ward might actually lose the vote there but be elected anyway because people elsewhere in the city voted in her favor. So the whole idea of having elections by ward is vitiated. Not a half-loaf; not even a hamburger bun.

Having said all this, though, would a shift to wards in fact make a difference in curbing developer power? Developers certainly showed their displeasure at its prospect in their campaign funding preferences. But judging from elsewhere, where ward systems prevail, one would hesitate to be optimistic, even setting aside the Chicago case,[20] noted for its corruption, and that includes development matters. Los Angeles, where the so-called pay-to-play system has recently been subject to critical scrutiny,[21] is a case in point. This suggests that developers will make a virtue of necessity; they are infinitely adaptable, and have to be if they are to make money. In the Columbus case, moving to a ward system would disrupt current modes of influencing government decisions—which I suspect explains their resistance—but once the dust had settled, they would find a way.

The case that the political establishment and the developers have always made against wards in Columbus has been that it would set one neighborhood against another to the disadvantage of the city as a whole: read, to the disadvantage of the developers. But setting one part of the city against another is nothing new in Columbus, and the developers have played a central role in the process, all with a view to getting what they want. The saga of Tuttle Mall is only the first item of evidence for the prosecution. In this instance, unfolding in 1993, the developers had already erected a number of office buildings around a

20. There is a lot of material on this. For one particular case, and to illustrate how it can work, see Ben Joravsky, "It Pays to Have an Alderman in Your Pocket," *Chicago Reader,* February 10, 2010 (https://www.chicagoreader.com/chicago/isaac-carothers-ike-carother-indictment-cloud-tif-corruption/Content?oid=1446540; last accessed April 30, 2020).

21. For example, and only for example, see "Pay to Play in the City of Los Angeles" (https://d3n8a8pro7vhmx.cloudfront.net/voteyesons/pages/19/attachments/original/1488665725/Special_Report_Final.pdf?1488665725; last accessed April 30, 2020).

freeway interchange that they themselves had financed. A considerable area of undeveloped land remained, and it was this that they planned for a major regional mall. The obstacle was a residential neighborhood that abutted the site. Resident opposition was all the more entrenched since they believed that they had been misled when they purchased housing from the same developers; rather, when they had moved in, a publicity brochure provided by the developer made no indication of any large-scale retail-commercial use nearby.

Negotiations resulted in concessions from the developer, but these were regarded by the residents' association in question as insufficient. The city proceeded to pass the necessary rezonings, opening the way to the development. But as discussed earlier on p. 43, there is provision for appeal: What you need to do is to organize a petition to rescind the ordinance in question. This has to have a minimum number of names. This the neighborhood organization—the Shannon Heights-Kilbannon-Kildare Civic Association—proceeded to do, through something that it called Families Against Forced Zoning.

What is significant here, though, is the way in which the developer, the Tuttle Road Limited Partnership, of which the Edwards Land Company was the general partner, and The Limited, keen to take advantage of a new shopping center for their various lines, then put together a pro-mall group to promote the issue. This would be Citizens for Columbus Jobs and Schools. The schools bit is crucial, for the developers would play up the implications of the development for school district revenues and so gain endorsements from not just the Columbus School Board but also the NAACP. In other words, it would be the area around the site of the projected mall against the rest of the city. Brilliant!

"Development" Speak

While the jurisdictional fragmentation of metropolitan areas and the pro-development disposition of city councils, and not just that of Columbus but also the suburbs, can be seen as the immediate conditions for the ability of developers to get their way, standing behind them, in a sense conditioning *them,* is something much more fundamental: This is the way in which development issues are imagined. There is no point spending millions of dollars on a referendum to thwart neighborhood or citizen groups unless people are primed in some way to accord you credibility, and that takes us back to the way in which American society is organized, for what it is organized, and how it is practiced. The practices of homeownership, the pursuit of the American dream, competition in all spheres of life, a suspicion of government, are taken utterly for granted, and in their turn they generate particular ways of viewing the world that are equally unquestioned: ways that are shared with the developers and the city councilors who are so willing to yield to their demands. In consequence, any progressive movement like the Coalition for Responsive Government or Yes We Can is bound to face an uphill struggle.

This does not mean that the dominant discourse goes uncontested. You can see it in the comments responding to articles and editorials in the local press: always a relief to those similarly provoked. You can also see it in the programmatic statements of oppositional movements. In this regard, the local media can play an important role in swinging the balance: emphasizing certain interpretations, neglecting others, and using an often skillfully developed rhetoric of an emotive sort. In other words, from the developer's standpoint it helps if the local media are on your side, and in Columbus that has historically been the case with the *Dispatch,* ever willing to enter the fray.

It has, of course, had its own material interests since in a variety of ways its owners had their own stake in local development. The Ohio Company, part of the Wolfe empire, was an important investor in Jack Nicklaus's Muirfield project, which then laid the foundation for the growth of Dublin. The Dispatch Printing Company has a 20 percent stake in Arena District developments. Through the Ohio Company, the Wolfe family was part owner of a commercial real estate firm, Ohio Equities, and is still associated with it through the Capitol Square Company. According to an article in *Columbus Monthly* in April 1986, they owned "hundreds of acres of prime commercial development land in northwestern Franklin County" and "more than 5,500 acres of farmland in Madison and Clark counties, just west of Columbus." One implication is that there has been an ongoing conflict of interest, and one not always acknowledged. Enough said.

What, therefore, is the dominant discourse drawn on by the developers when making their case, by the city council when justifying their support, and by the *Dispatch* when putting down challenges to it? Several related themes stand out. Some have already been touched on in the course of the earlier discussions, but they need emphasis. The first is the idea of "development" itself. It conveys the notion of something for everyone. Everybody is going to benefit and should, therefore, support it. There will be more jobs, increased tax revenues, improved property values, and, paradoxically, even less congestion as the developers add their bits and pieces to the highway network. And there will be things that we can all take pride in: hip hip hooray for Columbus.[22] Bottom line, development is a no-brainer. This is the drift of the attorneys for the developers as they make their case before zoning boards or the city council. City departments themselves make arguments along similar lines: how their infrastructural investments will enhance "development" and reduce electricity prices, as in the famous 'cash-burning' power plant. Sometimes, if the case is likely to be particularly controversial, it will be backed up by the reports of consultants: the supposedly "objective," technically informed experts, of which more later. But the arguments are invariably highly selective. A shopping center is going to create X number of jobs; there is no mention of the jobs lost elsewhere as competing centers implode, as in the Polaris/Northland instance. The addition of new housing is going to increase the supply so as to keep housing prices steady; there is no mention of the negative impact of the newer housing on the values of the older stuff or the abandonment that is very often its ultimate destiny. As for the trash-burning power plant, let's keep quiet about the carcinogens those chimneys are about to unleash on the unsuspecting public. In other words, lots and lots of what the economists call negative externalities or uncompensated costs imposed on others.

"Development" is a word of long standing, long accepted, and its wider implications protected by a lack of transparency. This is not the case with "gentrification," where people get displaced, where public housing projects are sold to developers for conversion to hotels, and it generates a lot of adverse publicity. So how to massage the problem away? Enter "neighborhood revitalization," and other soporifics like "neighborhood improvement." Something for everybody?

Defining the common interest as constituted by "development" is part of a broader framework of understanding brought to bear on development issues in a way that will advance a particular agenda. The people who share the interest are, of course, supposed to be us. And for an "us," apart from those obstinate people who just will never get

22. So an editorial singing the glories of the Arena District (Thursday, October 22, 2015) and how "once a scar on the city, old Pen is point of pride," and always celebrating growth: "High-End Hotels Signs of City's Growth," *Columbus Dispatch,* October 25, 2015.

it, there is often a corresponding and threatening "them." This gets defined in territorial terms: as in the NIMBY-ism of neighborhoods standing in the way of the developers, "Columbus versus other cities," or, to the extent that it affects Columbus, "Ohio versus other states." As discussed earlier in the chapter, impact fees were a topic of ferocious debate in the late '80s in the Columbus area and one from which their advocates would be forced into a bloody retreat. Part of the argument made, speciously, as I explained, was that if impact fees were imposed, developers would look elsewhere, where they did not have to pay them. Thus the *Dispatch*:

> Columbus developers should not be asked to commit substantially to street construction and utility extension in one community when those things are provided as no costs in another community nearby. Columbus City Center would not be under development today if impact fees had been in effect. Areas hungry for development today would be punished even more by impact fees.[23]

Of course, the threat from elsewhere can also assume the form of a dreaded intruder: an out-of-state contractor or company bringing in something defined as vile, like a casino, and illegitimate in part by virtue of being out of state. An issue in the provision of public infrastructure in the Columbus area has long been adherence to state minimum wage law, with the common effect of barring nonunion contractors, but:

> These shenanigans added hundreds of thousands of dollars to county-supervised construction projects, such as the Huntington Park ballfield, and even led to the hiring of *a questionable out-of-state contractor* whose workers nearly collapsed part of the stadium during construction.[24]

Ignoring the rhetorical flourish of "shenanigans," the message is that even when these out-of-staters are conniving in the heinous preference of the county commissioners for union contractors who can be expected to pay a decent wage, even a decent job is beyond them.

---

23. "Editorial: Impact of Impact Fees," *Columbus Dispatch,* June 25, 1987, p. 14A.

24. "Editorial: Enough Already: County Officials' Efforts to Steer Contracts Has Been an Expensive Mistake, *Columbus Dispatch,* June 14, 2010; my emphasis.

This particular angle on "development for the insiders"[25] reached something of a crescendo in the struggle to bring a casino to Columbus, which was referred to in chapter 3. In the state elections in Ohio in November of 2009, an issue appeared on the ballot regarding casino gambling. Hitherto it had not been permitted. Passage of Issue 3 would allow an amendment to the constitution permitting, in turn, the establishment of casinos in four of Ohio's major cities: Cincinnati, Cleveland, Columbus, and Toledo. The projected $600 million in state revenues would then be distributed to local governments and school districts. In the neighboring states of Indiana and Kentucky, casino gambling *was* permitted and attracting gamblers from Ohio. This meant, according to the arguments for casino gambling, that Ohio and the four cities in particular were losing out from the development gains that supposedly it would bring.

If Issue 3 passed, the casino in Columbus would be built next to the Arena District: an area, as discussed earlier, of new office developments, bars, and restaurants; home to major sports attractions, notably an ice hockey team, the Columbus Blue Jackets, and the minor league baseball team the Columbus Clippers; and above all, an area of booming real estate values. It should come as no surprise, therefore, that once the issue *did* pass, the principal landlords in the Arena District—Nationwide Insurance and the *Columbus Dispatch*—were quick to express their concerns and to mobilize others in their cause. Hence:

> Franklin County Commissioner John O'Grady best summed up this sentiment. The Arena District, he said, represents the most family-friendly Downtown development in decades. Why would anyone want to jeopardize that? Why would anyone side with an *out-of-state gambling mogul* over the express wishes of central Ohio's voters and its business community?[26]

> Penn National, *based in Wyomissing, Pa.*, did not consult with central Ohio leaders before *secretly negotiating* for the purchase of an 18.3-acre site just west of Huntington Park on Nationwide Boulevard.[27]

---

25. But it is always a selective gambit. There were no complaints when another "outsider," Hunt Sports Group, based in Kansas City, brought the Crew FC to the city, nor more recently when the *Dispatch* itself was sold to an outsider, Gatehouse Media, itself owned by, heaven forbid, a Japanese hedge fund.

26. "Mike Curtin Commentary: Casino Isn't Wanted So Columbus Leaders Should Just Say No," *Columbus Dispatch,* November 15, 2009.

27. "Editorial: Standing Firm," *Columbus Dispatch,* November 29, 2009.

And in reference to a group called Stand Up Columbus! to oppose the Arena District site, a county commissioner, Dewey Stokes,

> said in a news release that the group represents "neighborhood leaders, soccer moms, doctors, accountants, coaches, lawyers, business owners, union workers, elected officials, retirees, independents, Democrats and Republicans. But all of us *agree it's not right that an out-of-town casino operator—without any community input—gets to decide where a casino will be built in our city.*"[28]

The italics are mine. Why were the *Dispatch* and spokespeople like the two county commissioners so keen to underline the out-of-state origins of the casino company, engaging in "secret negotiations" and so breaking the local rules, and with the nerve to build the casino "in our city" unless they believed that that reduced the legitimacy of its desire to establish a casino in Columbus? And then the organization of an opposition group with the name Stand Up Columbus!, supposedly appealing to all people to come together to ward off this evil threat from the world beyond city limits. The implication is that if the casino company had been home-grown, things would have been different: It would not have engaged in secret negotiations and would have sought community input, though clearly that has to be in doubt; no mention of the secret negotiations through which developers assemble land from diverse buyers, as in the case of the Villages at New Albany. And aside from which, it all sounds so petty and provincial.

The third theme, even strategy, is simply historical amnesia: in discussing an issue carefully excluding reference to what actually did happen in the past so as to play up a particular contemporary interest and agenda. Such has been the case with the Win-Win agreements between Columbus City School District and suburban districts—agreements that, as discussed in chapter 2, are now in the course of dissolution. Thus the *Dispatch*'s take on the issue:

> The Win-Win agreement between Columbus City Schools and neighboring school districts has kept a nervous peace for three decades, glued together by an obvious threat: If the suburban districts don't fork over a share of their tax revenues, the big-city district might come after their tax-rich commercial areas and take their kids.[29]

28. "New Community Group Campaign on to Move Casino Site," *Columbus Dispatch,* December 27, 2009.

29. "Win-Win Pact Lacks Teeth," *Columbus Dispatch,* May 22, 2017.

Ignoring the rabble-rousing "forking over" and "taking their kids," the editorial goes on to say that for the suburban districts, "their predicament results from the city of Columbus having annexed, over decades, unincorporated areas of the county historically served by suburban school districts." This makes the city sound like an aggressor. But as I pointed out in chapter 2, it was a case of annexations in which suburban school districts at the time connived and from which the various cities whose populations they served gained immensely. What would then upset the suburban applecart was busing for racial balance in the Columbus public schools, white flight, and a subsequent push on the part of Columbus City School District to bring back into the city those parts of the city that had been left in the suburban districts and to which much of the flight had been directed. This was the background to Win-Win: The suburban school districts got to keep their districts intact, while the Columbus school district had to make do with a relative pittance—today, $5 million annually, as the editorial points out. Nice work if you can get it. There is a history here of white flight and suburban school districts conniving in it, therefore. It would seem that the latter have no shame about their past, that they benefited from people trying to escape policies designed to rectify decades of wrongs heaped on the most vulnerable sections of the population. It is well established that children from less privileged backgrounds—African American or white—benefit from social mix. But that was not allowed to happen. This is a history the editorial quietly airbrushes out.

Finally, there is strategy of appealing to so-called expertise. Experts are the ones who are to be trusted. I have already referred to how the consultant's reports are wheeled out to convince those making the ultimate decisions, parading statistics designed to play up the positives and silence the negatives,[30] and appealing to shady practices like cost-benefit analysis.[31] In other words, expertise is something that should be approached with some critical care. There are the "independent" consultants, but their business depends on providing the ammo their clients are looking for. Expertise is also often equated to experience: hence the way in which city commissions are packed with lawyers and businesspeople. They may indeed be highly knowledgeable, and conflict of interest in the narrow sense is typically not apparent; they are usually people who would loudly proclaim their integrity and, nar-

30. As in the old aphorism "Lies, damned lies, and statistics."

31. The academic journals are full of critical discussion of these; just Google "cost-benefit analysis critique."

rowly defined, rightly so too. But they cannot help being guided by frameworks of understanding that work to the advantage of the development process: a bias toward growth, an impatience with obstacles, a belief in the integrity of the law, and therefore an ability to identify the technicalities that can repel all boarders, and indeed lots of experience to draw on to justify their positions. And if you leave the experts out, you flirt with danger.

Such was the concern in 1993 when the Columbus city council decided to dispense with the experts in drawing up its design for future development, the Columbus Comprehensive Plan. Just what the bother was about was articulated once more by that guardian of developer interest, the *Columbus Dispatch.* In an editorial with the title "Handle with Care: Don't Let New City Laws Stifle Development," it opined:

> Although not hiring professionals in city management and development could save money in the short term, relying on community groups to write the rules for growth could cost the city in the long run.
>
> Those crafting the ordinances have to resist the pressures of those with a narrow agenda who would erect so many roadblocks to development that companies would look to the suburbs and other cities that are more accommodating. This could be disastrous for Columbus Public Schools and city residents, who benefit from expansion in the business community. The broader the tax base, the lighter each person's burden of paying for government services and schools.
>
> It is the economy—not a planning official or body—that drives development. Typically, a neighborhood's residents fight any construction project proposed for their backyard. Any changes in zoning and other regulations should not allow the interests of the few to take precedence over the needs of the many.[32]

I have quoted here at length because the editorial was so utterly exquisite in bringing together the different elements of "development" speak, and almost to the point of cliché: the idea that development will benefit everybody and that Columbus is engaged in competition for it with others, and the danger that "companies would look to the suburbs and other cities that are more accommodating." And reading between the lines, you can see why expertise is a defense of a particular agenda.

32. *Columbus Dispatch,* December 12, 1993.

The danger is that you'll rely on "community groups": a nicely coded expression. If experts are not brought into the game, you risk "the pressures of those with a narrow agenda"—as if, that is, the agenda of the developers was not narrow enough.

I do not want to dwell on the *Dispatch*: It has simply been the mouthpiece for assumptions and reactions that are common coinage in the development community. And it has been all the easier since, as I showed earlier, it has had its own stakes in development. Accordingly, one might have thought that with the transfer of ownership to Gatehouse Media in 2015, an organization with no particular stake in the "development" of Columbus, and now owned by a Japanese hedge fund, there might have been a change. There is some evidence for that. In its editorials, the *Dispatch* has spoken out against liberal tax abatement deals and the harm they inflict on the school district.[33] It has also been extremely critical of the deals that led to the Nationwide Arena being transferred from a private ownership that had become onerous to a county that then had to draw on tax revenues that could have been spent on more pressing needs of a social character.[34] But the honeymoon now seems to be over. In its editorial on the topic, it came out against Issue 1, which would have led to the introduction of wards. The reasoning was reminiscent of the good old days and the virtues of "expertise":

> If this sounds complicated, our point is made. If Columbus is to change its governing structure, it shouldn't be rushed, a flaw of Issue 1. The community's best minds—Democrats, Republicans, neighborhood representatives and experts on urban governance such as those at Ohio State University—should have time to examine alternatives, weigh the pros and cons and propose options vetted by the community.[35]

As John Hartmann commented on another negative editorial position, one regarding reining in drug prices, which would be Issue 2 in November of 2017, "The Japanese hedge fund-owned *Columbus Dispatch* is trying very hard to get back in touch with its old family-owned crazy. The experiment with being even-handed and rational in its news

33. "Editorial: City Trying to Make Amends," *Columbus Dispatch*, February 27, 2017.

34. "Editorial: Arena 'Profit' Is Accounting Fiction," *Columbus Dispatch*, June 27, 2016.

35. "Editorial: Vote No on Issue 1," *Columbus Dispatch*, July 10, 2016.

Building a Newspaper Monopoly

At one time there *was* an alternative daily newspaper in the Columbus. This was the *Citizen-Journal,* which closed down in 1985. Part of the reason for the closure—but only part—was decisions made by the *Dispatch.* The *Citizen-Journal* had a contract with the *Dispatch* whereby the *Dispatch* acted as its printer. Three years prior to the termination of the contract, the *Dispatch* informed the *Citizen-Journal* that it was no longer willing to print it. The *Citizen-Journal* was owned by the Scripps-Howard media conglomerate. It was profitable for them and could conceivably have invested in printing presses of its own. But as a result of the fact that it was in competition with the *Dispatch,* and Scripps-Howard preferred markets where it owned the sole newspaper, it was decided not to. But the *Dispatch* gave them a nudge. Something called *The Other Paper* provided an alternative until the *Dispatch* bought it out in 2011 and then closed it in 2013.[1] According to the same article, the rationale for this was that another *Dispatch* publication, *Columbus Alive!,* was preferred by advertisers and readers. Perhaps. But when it had been independent, *The Other Paper* had provided a critical counterpoint to stories in the *Dispatch.* So much for the democratic responsibility that the newspaper likes to argue for on other occasions.

1. "'The Other Paper' to Cease Publication Jan. 31," *Columbus Dispatch,* January 7, 2013.

and editorial page policies is apparently at an end."[36] It might have been somewhat different if the *Dispatch* had had some competition in the local newspaper market. But competition vanished a long while back, in part as a result of the *Dispatch*'s own actions (see "Building a Newspaper Monopoly").

The Power of Money

The final reason that developers are so powerful in politics in the Columbus area is that they have money, or at least access to it in the

36. As he elaborated: "The *Dispatch* editorialized against Issue 2, a proposal that shows promise of reining in soaring drug prices. Millions are being spent on TV advertising by both sides. The 'No' campaign is being funded largely by the big drug makers, aka Big Pharma. Large newspapers like the *Dispatch* rake in big bucks by printing advertisements for new and expensive drugs that are paid for by, guess who?, Big Pharma." See "ColumbusMediaInsider: Dispatch Takes Mandel to Woodshed, Goes Easy on Kasich's Tax $$ Waste," *Columbus Free Press,* November 4, 2017. Available at https://columbusfreepress.com/article/columbusmediainsider-dispatch-takes-mandel-woodshed-goes-easy-kasichs-tax-waste; last accessed October 25, 2020.

form of loan finance. This pays off in multiple ways. In referenda on land-use issues, they can spend on a scale denied to their opponents in the neighborhoods, engaging in a veritable barrage of media publicity and seemingly plausible promises of what their developments will bring to the population at large. Such was the case with the Tuttle Mall on the far northwest side of the city, referred to earlier. What I did not mention then was the stunning inequality in the resources brought to that particular battle. The curiously named Citizens for Columbus Jobs and Schools spent over half a million dollars on publicity, or about $13 per vote cast in their favor; the neighborhood at the center of the tussle, meanwhile, spent a miniscule $11,000 but still managed to harvest a third of the total votes cast. There were also some not-so-subtle appeals to employees of firms that stood to benefit from a decision favorable to the developers. These included letters from the president of The Limited and the CEO of Huntington National Bank encouraging employees to vote in favor of the issue. The Limited had plans for outlets in the planned mall, while one has to assume that Huntington National Bank had a financial stake. But again, big money was involved and keen to go for more.

At least in the Tuttle case, everything was in the open and exposed to the public. One knew of the disparity in funding the respective campaigns. But money also opens up for developers the prospect of more covert approaches to getting what they want, as was discussed in chapter 5 in the context of how Wexner managed to secure his own off-freeway entrance to the Easton Project. Campaign finance donations, a close relation with the Ohio governor of the time, George Voinovich, to all accounts, worked their magic. In other words, money, but money that can take advantage of an extremely supine state. The state of Ohio came over with a chunk of it, and the federal government stepped aside. Very nice.

Something not dissimilar played itself out more recently in the dispensing of favors to OhioHealth. In June of 2018, some investigative journalism by Bill Bush of the *Dispatch* brought to light something that Columbus had kept carefully closeted from public view for two years.[37] The issue was that of closing an exit ramp from the 315 freeway in order to make room for a parking garage for OhioHealth employees who would be housed in an adjacent building. The emphasis of the

37. "Public Kept in the Dark for 2 Years about Plans to Demolish Rt. 315 Ramp," *Columbus Dispatch,* June 9, 2018.

article was the secrecy with which the preparations were made and the phony narrative of a dangerous off-ramp used to justify the closure: in other words, nothing to do with a parking garage, and even while the ramp closure would commit the city to expensive highway works in the vicinity in order to make up for the loss of an exit. This is true. What got less emphasis, though, was state and federal connivance in something where the law was not on the side of Columbus.

Part of the land in question was owned by Columbus, who gave it free of charge. Another part was owned by the state. They too donated their share, claiming that state laws about vacating part of the state highway system did not apply in this case since part of the land was owned by Columbus. Yet while the state forfeited its land, it still owned the right of way, but nothing was said. State and federal governments that had originally combined to foot the bill for that part of the freeway were not reimbursed, even though there was a case for it. Moreover, the transfer of the exit ramp in question was already underway, despite the fact that under state law there can be no "significant changes" in state highways unless the state Department of Transportation makes an announcement to the public and provides for public participation in the decision-making process. Again, the state seems to have looked the other way. And likewise the federal government. If any section of highway is given away for free, it requires Federal Highway Administration approval, which was never received in this instance. In fact, the FHA seems to have been totally unaware of what was happening and in the situation of having to fabricate an explanation in order to get themselves off the hook.[38]

On the other hand, OhioHealth doled out tens of thousands of election finance dollars to local and state elected officials prior to the property transfer. According to the city, the ramp transfer was good for the city since it would result in bringing over 2,500 jobs to the area, including 1,311 new ones, though of course those promises are both easy to make and easy to break. And no mention of the office space

38. "The highway administration was never notified of the ramp's removal and granted no approval, spokeswoman Nancy Singer said. After investigating, Singer said it wasn't required because Route 315 is a state highway, even though records show ODOT officials were convinced that they needed federal approval. She directed questions concerning those rules back to ODOT" ("ODOT Raised Safety, Legal Concerns about Removing Rt. 315 Ramp," *Columbus Dispatch*, June 11, 2017).

vacated downtown by the move of staff to the new headquarters—more scorched earth, in other words.[39]

•

The Columbus metropolitan area is an *American* metropolitan area. As such, it bears the imprint of a highly distinctive social formation: a particular state form, particular values and discourses, so that it is in many ways an exemplar for urban development in the US as a whole. What I have described has its counterparts—and they would leap out on the most rudimentary of investigations—in other metropolitan areas. It is different in Western Europe. The jurisdictional fragmentation that allows developers to make hay by playing one local government against another, as in the tax abatement game, is missing. The discourse of competition for real estate investments is missing, and the power of money is nowhere near as blatant, reflecting historical inhibitions in countries with precapitalist pasts where quite different sets of values held sway.[40] The same goes for the all-too-easy acceptance of the expertise that businesspeople are supposed to have and that helps surmount the obstacles posed by supposedly democratic institutions to the task of piling up the wealth. In other words, the distinctiveness of Columbus in these matters is an American distinctiveness. So while it is indeed Ohio's "sunbelt" city, that is only one aspect of its distinctiveness in the world as a whole.

And to be sure, while Columbus works for developers, there might be another side to that coin. Does it work for everybody else? Some clearly gain, but others suffer from it, as has been apparent at various points in the previous chapters. Developers have been able to shuck off a lot of the social costs caused by their developments, not least financing the school and highway expansions that their developments entail. There again, as the metropolitan area has expanded at its edge, residential property closer in, and gentrifying areas notwithstanding, have tended to be devalued. In short, asking the question "Whose city?" might be illuminating, as we do in the chapter that follows.

39. "OhioHealth Move Creates Another Downtown Office Vacancy," *Columbus Dispatch*, June 2, 2019.

40. Cox 2016, chapter 8.

CHAPTER 8

Whose City?

Setting the Scene

The fundamental point about the US, the center of gravity around which all else there revolves, is that it is a class society. This will come as a surprise, even a shock, and possibly an insult, to many Americans. Class is something for Europeans; in the US, if you work hard enough, anyone can make it.[1] "Class" is a dirty word. People complain in letters to the editor about op-eds or other letters supposedly "bringing class into it." But alas, it is already there, and to understand contemporary dilemmas, whether in Columbus or in the country as a whole, it has to

1. But see S. M. Lipset and R. Bendix (1959) for a resounding rebuttal of this old claim. They were writing a long time ago, but there is no reason to believe that matters have changed. The simple fact of the division of labor and how positions in it are differentially rewarded is enough in itself: A society only needs so many lawyers, doctors, marketing executives, and so on, and it also needs garbage collectors, cab drivers, assembly workers, and lots more besides. But even allowing for that, and the possibility that the upwardly ascendant are matched by those moving downward, the evidence suggests an ossification of probabilities of upward mobility at very limited levels. See Richard V. Reeves and Eleanor Krause (2018) "Raj Chetty in 14 charts: Big findings on opportunity and mobility we should all know," *Brookings Institute,* January 11, 2018. Available at https://www.brookings.edu/blog/social-mobility-memos/2018/01/11/raj-chetty-in-14-charts-big-findings-on-opportunity-and-mobility-we-should-know/; last accessed October 26, 2020).

be brought to the surface. We encounter it—participate in it—all the time. The issues are all around us, and have to do with our employment, our neighborhoods, and lots more besides.

Unemployment benefits have long been a contention between employers and workers. The employers want to keep the unemployed hanging around so that they will be there when business experiences an uptick, but they want to make the benefits low enough so that workers will have an incentive to go back to work. The workers, though, know that unemployment benefits are not enough; they have commitments like mortgages and keeping children clothed that cannot wait for a possible resumption of paychecks in the future. So unemployment compensation remains a continuing point of tension, only relieved in boom times. There again, there are issues in where people live. Subprime mortgages were issued to make money but left a trail of devastation and anger behind them; meanwhile, the banks were kept alive on government money. Likewise, the talk now, particularly in Ohio, is of opioid addiction. But this is a class affliction, borne of desperation. Meanwhile the poor people get locked up and business makes money out of it through the construction of private prisons. To protect their investments, the owners then oppose early prisoner release. Ugly.

So the fundamental class division is that between those with the money to put others to work and those who are put to work, or between those with money to lend and those who, by virtue of their poverty, need it. But if you have money, you have to exploit or you lose it; such is the nature of competition, and it is the working class that pays the bill. This occurs in multiple ways, some more obvious than others. There is continual downward pressure on wages, even when, by virtue of a scarcity of labor, employers feel forced to raise them. One of their solutions will be to look elsewhere, to move to where the labor is cheaper, maybe China, or, far more common, if it is feasible, to replace the workers with machinery. These tendencies are obscured by the fact that while some sectors of the economy are declining, others are growing: Employment and wages are declining in some branches and in the places dominated by them, and increasing in others and in places like Silicon Valley, where the new sectors are so strongly in evidence. But even while in those growth sectors employers are more willing to grant wage increases to avoid strikes and take advantage of booming markets, they are also looking to curb their wage bills in any way they can, like decanting some of their operations to places where wage rates are lower. Certainly the general tendency over many decades has been for wages to increase, even while there has been wage stagnation since the early '70s. Nevertheless, there is always unemployment somewhere and for some people, as well as struggles to pay the bills.

And particularly for some since the working class too is divided. It could not be otherwise where, on the one hand, there is a division of labor and some tasks demand less training and skill than others, and where people, by virtue of their social background, including schooling, cannot compete for anything demanding in terms of know-how. There are, accordingly, jobs that pay well and some that need to be supplemented by food stamps and other forms of subsidy, some implicit like showing up at the emergency room without insurance. This division in incomes is a source of divided interests. The labor movement has always been skewed in its representation of blue-collar workers: so sensitive to the interests of some but not all. Its support for minimum wages has long attracted cynical attention, a way of making a big chunk of the workforce noncompetitive in the labor market and so tightening it up.

These sorts of class division carry over into housing. What you earn dictates what you can afford. If you have the money, you can buy your own house and take advantage of various federal tax subsidies: notably the deduction of mortgage interest and property taxes. If you do not, you are consigned to the rental sector, either public or private, and no comparable federal help: an inequality—no, inequity—that is not widely appreciated. And your chances of graduating up into homeownership are curtailed by the insistence of the more well-to-do on minimum lot sizes, expensive infrastructural expenses for new developments that, by adding cost to a house, turn out to be exclusionary, and who would have guessed? So much for the US not being a class society. The class differences go on and on. They show up in all manner of ways, not to say, social dysfunction: petty crime; incarceration rates; medical conditions like depression, hypertension, infant mortality, malnutrition, and obesity; and self-image and confidence.[2] Poor people have trouble dealing with their multiple oppressions. They lack the money for lawyers, they lack the ability to express themselves in ways that the middle class have defined as acceptable, and their knowledge of the law is lacking. Bottom line, even before we talk about how the city is contested, as we will in the next chapter, we can see how those contesting

2. See, for example, Elliot Liebow's classic, *Tally's Corner* (Boston: Little, Brown, 1967), and Jonathan Cobb and Richard Sennett on *The Hidden Injuries of Class* (New York: W W Norton, 1972).

it are armed with very different resources. The ultimate power in our societies, whether in the US or Western Europe, is that of money, and the money is distributed in highly unequal fashion.

Class Geographies

BACK TO THE FUTURE AND STIFFING THE POOR

To the hundred or so people living there, it came like a bombshell. Bollinger Tower was a public housing development, home to a largely elderly population and close to what would come to be the attractions of the Short North. Alas, it would turn out to be too close. In 2017 came the announcement that the Columbus Metropolitan Housing Authority was selling it to a developer who planned to convert the structure into an upmarket hotel. The residents were to be dispersed courtesy of Section 8 rental vouchers.

There are ironies galore here. Talk about the strip's commercial transformation only started in the mid-'80s. There were some anxieties about displacement, but at that time,

> helping to soften that issue is an 11-story, 100-unit Columbus Metropolitan Housing Authority project for the elderly at 750 N High St. . . . CMHA [Columbus Metropolitan Housing Authority] Development Coordinator Mark Shoemacher said the high-rise was built there because CMHA had a long-term lease on the property, the site of the old Francis Hotel. It will open early next year. "There are a lot of amenities in the area," Shoemacher said. "There's busing, shopping and the downtown. It's an ideal spot. There's a big need for housing in the area." Shoemacher said Columbus officials encouraged CMHA to build there.[3]

But that was then.

A similar story emerged a year later, though this time involving another group that has limited means for housing: college students. This was the case of the Grant Oak apartment complex, next door to and owned by Columbus Public Library. Rents were relatively mod-

---

3. "Short North: A Long Shot for Renovation," *Columbus Dispatch,* December 9, 1984, p. 2B.

est—$500 a month—and the complex was attractive for students attending Columbus College of Art and Design. The library, though, saw a way of making more money for itself by selling it to a developer with plans for demolition and replacing it with studio apartments renting at $1,500 a month. It was encouraged in this by the city, which saw it as consistent with the attempt to make the surrounding Discovery District into an exclusive haunt of the well-heeled—similar to its strategy with respect to Bollinger and the Short North.[4]

What happened to Bollinger Tower, though, is part of the sad and sorry saga that is public housing in the US. Public housing dates back to the 1930s and the New Deal, but it faced a bitter, uphill struggle against private real estate interests. Numerous constraints were inserted in the legislation to make sure that the program would be crippled on arrival. Most notably, there was the requirement that state or local governments agree to creating public housing authorities that could then be the recipients of federal money, and many, of course, refused to do so. And if the various obstacles were overcome, individual projects had to run the gauntlet of neighborhood opposition, with the flames frequently fanned by a local press complaining about federal handouts and the importance of people making it on their own—as if everyone was in a position, by virtue of parental largesse or simply chance, to do so. The red scare of the late '40s and '50s did not help either, with public housing branded as "socialistic."[5] The contrast with West European countries like France, the United Kingdom, the Netherlands, and the Scandinavian countries is quite staggering. Some limited amount of public housing was built, but its image never came close to that in much of Western Europe. It was forever stigmatized as the "projects," and then further stigmatized by virtue of its largely minority residents. Nevertheless, Columbus did have its public housing developments, though largely in what would later be called in another nice piece of doublespeak "the inner city." These are now fast becoming memories, as the experience of Bollinger Tower nicely testifies.

A major benchmark is what is referred to as Section 8. The Section 8 program, a form of rental subsidy for applicants who have been successfully means tested, was created as part of the Housing and Community Development Act of 1974. Vouchers entitling the holder to a

4. See "Developer: 'I Offered Twice as Much for Grant Oak,'" *Columbus Free Press,* March 6, 2018.

5. Parson 2007.

rental subsidy[6] are issued by local public housing agencies and can be used to rent from a private landlord; in fact, at least 80 percent of vouchers have to be so used. There are lots of problems with this program, including the limited number of vouchers available—there is a lengthy waiting list. The one that is relevant here, though, is the way it has intersected with a drive to deconcentrate the poor geographically.

The HOPE VI federal program, initiated in 1992, was a response to calls from academics and policy analysts for the dispersal of the poor from the geographically concentrated form that public housing had hitherto assumed, into other neighborhoods. The way it would work was through federal grants to demolish existing public housing and replace it with a mixed-income housing development. During demolition, public housing tenants would be given Section 8 vouchers, with a view to them returning once the redevelopment had occurred. In practice, though, the number of units available for the poor in the new developments has been much less than those anticipated, so Section 8 has remained a reality for them. This has been regarded by the authorities benignly since regardless of whether the residents returned or not, it was believed that new social networks would be formed that would empower the poor and help them escape their condition.

In practice, HOPE VI and Section 8 have turned out to be very nice subsidies to the real estate industry. The story of Bollinger Tower is one glaring instance. Public housing developments[7] are often proximate to areas that are now experiencing booming demand. If the local public housing authority—in this case the Columbus Metropolitan Housing Authority—can be persuaded to evict the existing residents, then the way can be smoothed to making a lot of money, albeit, as indicated in the quote above, with not a little social distress: a sort of real estate equivalent to the "collateral damage" of war-speak. And the distress continues because finding landlords willing to take Section 8 tenants or locating new housing projects that have agreed to take them can be far from easy, and this, of course, after all the bleating from them about how housing should be a matter for the private market and not something that the state provides.

Bollinger Tower is a case of a private developer spotting an opportunity. In other cases, though, the charge has been led by major institutions like universities or hospitals that want to fortify themselves by,

6. Tenants with vouchers pay about 30 percent of their income for rent, with the difference made up by the federal government.

7. Or developments with large numbers of Section 8 tenants, like Bryden House.

in effect, getting rid of "them" from the surrounding neighborhood. In Columbus, Poindexter Village falls into this category. Poindexter Village was a public housing development dating back to the 1940s but surrounded by the 1990s by an area undergoing severe population decline. What would hasten its demolition, its demise, and the scattering of its tenants was the purchase of a hospital in the vicinity by Ohio State University in 1999; what had been Park Medical Center would henceforth be University Hospital East, a part of the Ohio State University Medical Center. Eleven years later, the university concluded an agreement with the city to invest in "neighborhood revitalization." This was supposedly a quid pro quo for an income-tax rebate that had been granted to the university when it expanded its medical center on campus. But almost certainly the university had its own interests in reworking the area surrounding University Hospital East. In due course, the Village was demolished and the residents dispersed using Section 8 vouchers.

The story of two other public housing developments, Sawyer Towers and Lincoln Park East, would be different and unexpected. They were large developments with 392 and 311 units, respectively. To the CMHA's surprise, which thought them only worth the land on which they were located, they were purchased by a firm called VTT Management, which has proceeded to rehab the units and market them with apparently great success. The original residents were dispersed using Section 8 vouchers. Initially, the new owner accepted Section 8 tenants but has since stopped, which is significant. Strict tenant screening procedures seem to have been one key.[8] It may also be that recent housing shortages in the Columbus area that have made it one of the "hottest" real estate markets in the country are making a difference. But in retrospect what it amounts to is a sort of gentrification: Once strict screening took hold, a more well-to-do clientele was willing to move in. Meanwhile, people were being displaced and dispersed courtesy of Section 8. And what does it imply about the way housing markets are structured in general and in Columbus in particular?

The question is: Where are poor people being dispersed to? The fact is that landlords prefer not to take them. It is more than the image of drugs, crime, and failure to take care of property that dogs voucher holders; it is also that accepting Section 8 tenants means a dose of

8. "Private Owners Clean up Once-Troubled Public Housing," *Columbus Dispatch,* February 23, 2015.

government intervention, like monitoring of property upkeep that landlords would rather avoid.[9] There is also resistance from current residents about their prospective new neighbors (but see "Section 8 and a Voice from the Unjustly Stigmatized.").

The result is that Section 8 tenants tend to cluster (figure 8.1): exactly counter to the original intent of those advocating the dispersion of public housing tenants, therefore. They also tend to cluster in areas where landlords are willing to take them, which means those experiencing social change, like Northland[10] or the area surrounding Eastland Mall (zip code 43232 on the map). The CMHA, to its credit, has tried to counter this by cosponsoring new housing developments in which Section 8 tenants would be welcome, but the results have not been auspicious.

One instance concerned a development in Hilliard school district, though not in Hilliard itself. A private developer had agreed to sell land to a nonprofit, the Columbus Housing Partnership. The plan was to construct 54 three-bedroom units. The CMHA would then provide Section 8 vouchers for forty of the units. There was, to put it mildly, neighborhood uproar, and the developer withdrew from the contract.[11]

The assumption, of course, is that the state should not be pushing its nose into the provision of housing—apart, that is, from providing subsidies to homeownership in the form of the tax deductibility of mortgage interest and property taxes, and to hell with the renters. The private housing market functions perfectly adequately. And it is true that over much of the US, there is no shortage of housing, and in fact, in the Columbus area, housing costs remain remarkably low. In fact, until very recently,[12] there has been an excess of supply, but from the standpoint of the masses, it is an excess that they could do without since they suffer its consequences in terms of the devaluation of older housing.

Markets are not, of course, supposed to function like this; excess supply is supposed to be tempered by less building. According to the

9. "Some Landlords Say They're Pulling out of Section 8 Due to CMHA Inspectors," *Columbus Dispatch,* December 6, 2015.

10. "CMHA Relocations Ruffle New Neighbors: Some Areas Wary of Section 8 Renters," *Columbus Dispatch,* June 13, 2010.

11. "Dominion Backs out of Low-Income Housing Project," *Columbus Dispatch,* April 22, 2010.

12. "Central Ohio Homebuilders Far Shy of Meeting High Demand," *Columbus Dispatch,* March 11, 2018.

Section 8 and a Voice from the Unjustly Stigmatized

Two articles in the *Dispatch* on Section 8 renters,[1] elicited a quite massive twenty-six comments, the vast, vast majority of which spewed forth bile. Most of the comments were two or three lines of unqualified stereotypes and ugliness. Significantly, those who spoke out in defense of Section 8 recipients were much longer and more thoughtful. One is particularly worth recording for both its passion and its insight:

> Okay I know I'm late, but I just seen this and have to say. That this is a prime example of one bad apple giving everyone a bad name. Truth be told those of you that are down talking people you don't even know should be a shame of yourselves. I am from the hood but had great things instilled into me, I work very hard for my family and pay 950 a month for rent in a very nice neighborhood. But I have a lot of people I grew up with that isn't as fourtunate as me right now any way, but their blessings will come, they do have section 8 but they work hard for their money paying like 450 to 500 in rent and section 8 pays the rest of the 300 or 400 that they can't. But they are good people that work 8 hour days and they PAY TAXES! As well they too are trying to work and provide for their families the best way they can. It's the young people that are aloud to hang out and sell drugs, gang bang, and whatever else who have no guidence, a record and no way to get a job because they turn them down, so speak on what you know. One of my close friends just moved from lincoln park projects into a beautiful home with her section 8 and is doing well. PAYING HER TAXES! And working hard everyday. We all weren't born with a silver spoon in our mouths we had to make it the best way we can. I agree the street life is not the way. But don't down my people when y'all have never walked in our shoes! We came from a struggle, something y'all no nothing about clearly or y'all wouldn't have been doing the things y'all did when y'all start getting laid off. Y'all know what I'm talking about. So many do need to get it together I agree, but there are so many that do have it together, but can't help the hand they were delt. So know the facts before you judge everybody with section 8 isn't a bad person nor are y'all just paying for their rent with your TAXES! They pay TAXES too! God Bless all of you judgemental people. *A Dumas signing off*

1. "CMHA Relocations Ruffle New Neighbors: Some Areas Wary of Section 8 Renters," *Columbus Dispatch*, June 13, 2010; "Voucher Users Scatter County after Housing Projects Close," *Columbus Dispatch*, November 21, 2011.

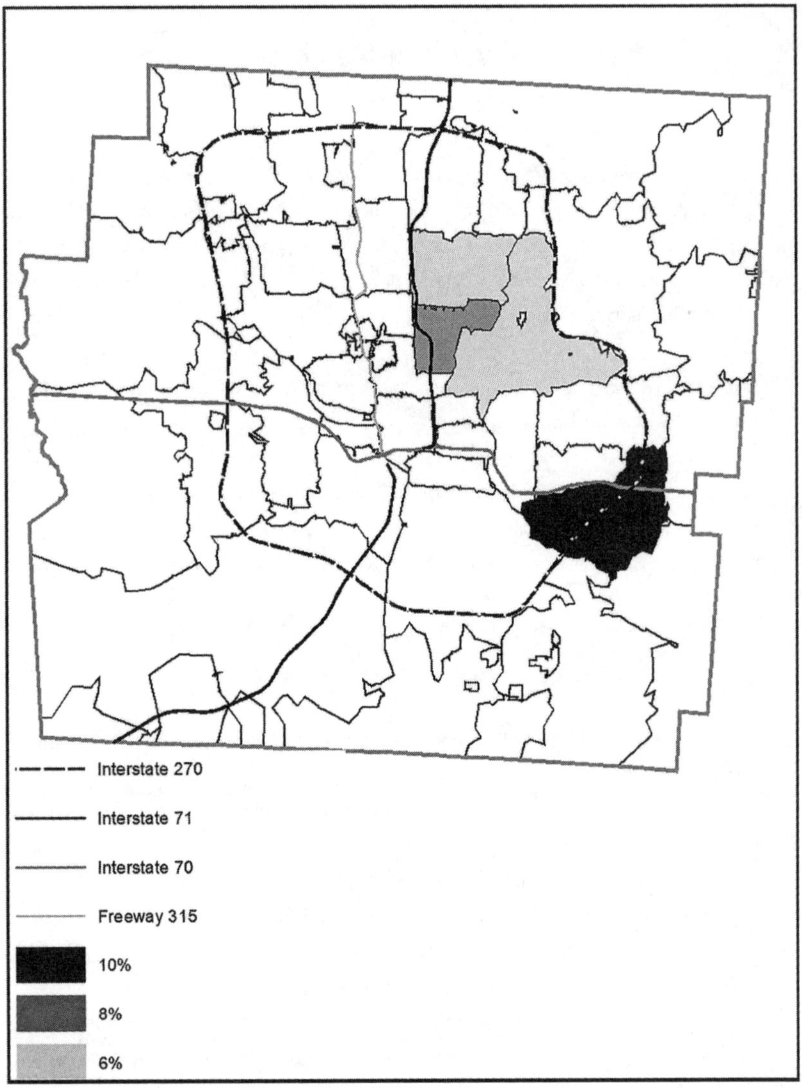

FIGURE 8.1. Distribution of Section 8 housing vouchers by zip code in Columbus, 2015. Source: Columbus Metropolitan Housing Authority. Map by Jamie Valdinger.

conventional wisdom, markets provide a nice balance of supply and demand so that everyone is housed in accordance with their preferences and, say it quietly, ability to pay. This assumes, though, that supply and demand are independent forces, and on closer examination, this assumption is hard to sustain. Rather, the development industry, broadly understood, works at both ends at once: It supplies housing, but it also structures the demand for it, without individual developers necessarily being aware of how their decisions combine to have those effects.

UNEVEN DEVELOPMENT AND THE CHILDREN

In its most abstract form, class refers to a vertical structuring of society. Nevertheless, how we imagine it tends to emphasize the geographic, the horizontal, the territorial. A common view is of "good" and "bad" areas: areas, therefore, but with a strong class inflection of a distributional sort. "Good" areas are where the "successful" live and "bad" areas where you find the "failures." Regardless of whether they are "successes" or "failures," these class relations are vividly on display in the way the wider metropolitan area is so unevenly blessed—unevenly developed, even, since those with money are those with the more diverse experiences and, whether they take advantage of it or not, by virtue of a favored formation, the intellectual capacities to develop themselves further. Oh lucky people, even while many of them have difficulty seeing farther than the latest SUV and purchasing the most recent in architectural ugliness!

Poverty in Columbus, moreover, is far from a monopoly of African Americans. By no means is it the case that all African Americans are poor or that there are no white families below the poverty line. Quite to the contrary. While just short of a third of African American families in Columbus were estimated to be below the poverty line in 2016, over two-thirds were not. In the suburbs, as defined by the remainder of Franklin County, the rates were lower (table 8.1). Likewise, when one looks at all the families under the poverty line, while half in Columbus are African American, just short of 40 percent are white (table 8.2), which is a lot of people. This is not to diminish the magnitude of these figures; that so many fall under the poverty line is a damning comment on society in this day and age. But it is not just an African American issue, despite racist propaganda to the contrary, and poverty has serious consequences, including for children, which is where I want to place the emphasis in this section.

TABLE 8.1. Percentage families under poverty line

RACE	COLUMBUS	REMAINDER, FRANKLIN COUNTY
African American	29.1%	19.4%
Hispanic	30.5%	14.3%
White	10.0%	4.4%

Source: 2016 community survey estimates.

TABLE 8.2. Percentage of total population under poverty line

RACE	COLUMBUS	FRANKLIN COUNTY	RESIDUE
African American	51.3	46.9	25.8
White	38.0	42.5	63.8
Hispanic	9.4	8.9	6.5
Total number	29,680	35,838	6,158

Source: 2016 community survey estimates.

Not the least of these impacts is infant mortality.[13] Poverty makes a real difference (figure 8.2). Some of the figures are borderline Third World: places like Peru, Uzbekistan, and Barbados (figure 8.3).

How poverty works is through the poverty of something else: that of the American welfare state. Poor people are the least likely to have health insurance, and this will obviously have effects on the birth and after-birth experience (figure 8.4). Despite the Affordable Care Act, there are still people who lack health insurance, and they tend to be poor.[14] So again, the proportion of families remaining uninsured is elevated in the poorer areas of Franklin County (figure 8.5).

If the children of the better-off are the ones more likely to survive, the inequality of opportunities continues into childhood through the massive inequalities among school districts: one more effect of geographically uneven development and one that is bound to reproduce unevenly developed people with highly variable prospects for the

13. Rates of which, presumably in some parts of the city, have been described by an editorial in the *Dispatch* as "shameful" ("Make It Easier to Follow the Money at City Hall," *Columbus Dispatch,* April 29, 2018).

14. "Even under the ACA [Affordable Care Act], many uninsured people cite the high cost of insurance as the main reason they lack coverage. In 2016, 45% of uninsured adults said that they remained uninsured because the cost of coverage was too high" ("Key Facts about the Uninsured Population," *The Henry Kaiser Family Foundation,* November 29, 2017, https://www.kff.org/uninsured/fact-sheet/key-facts-about-the-uninsured-population/; last accessed April 30, 2020).

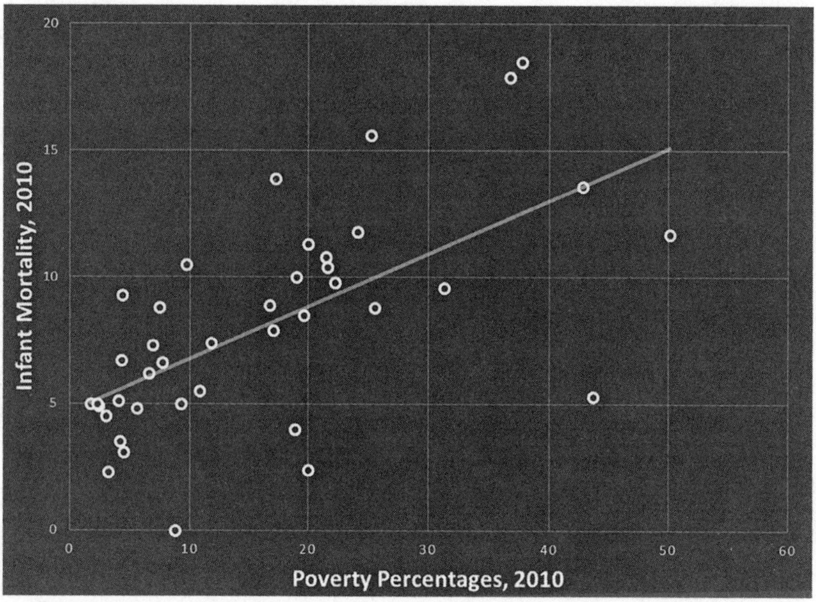

FIGURE 8.2. Poverty and infant mortality for Franklin County zip code areas. R = 0.724. Figure by Jamie Valdinger.

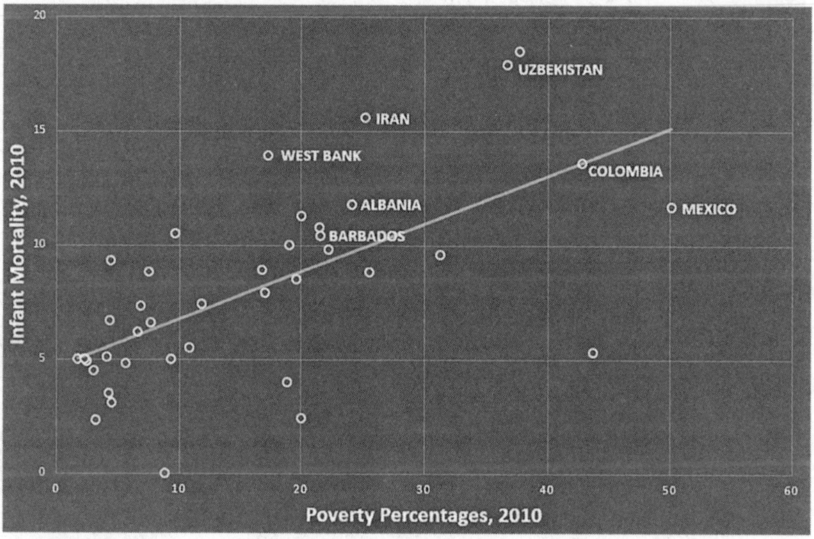

FIGURE 8.3. Poverty and infant mortality for Franklin County zip code areas projected onto infant mortality rates for select countries of the world. Figure by Jamie Valdinger.

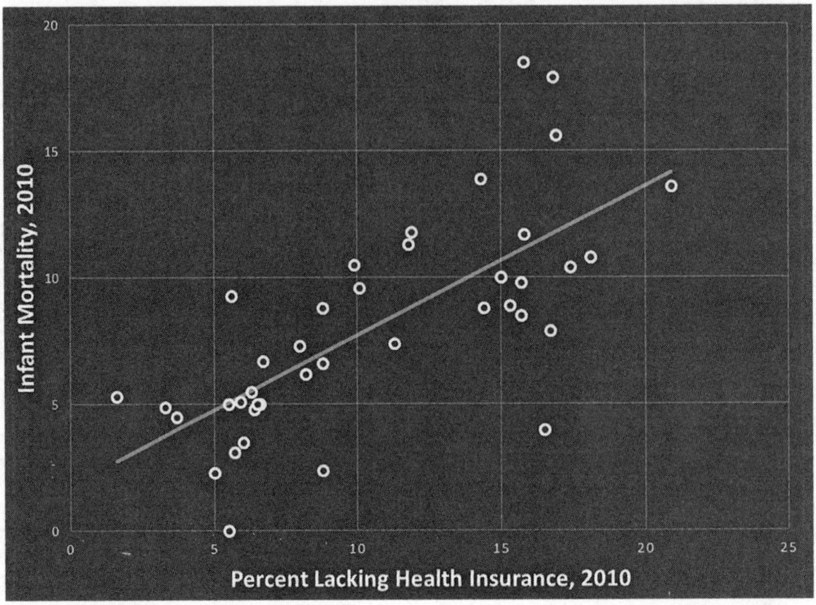

FIGURE 8.4. Lack of health insurance and infant mortality rates for Franklin County zip code areas. R = 0.719. Figure by Jamie Valdinger.

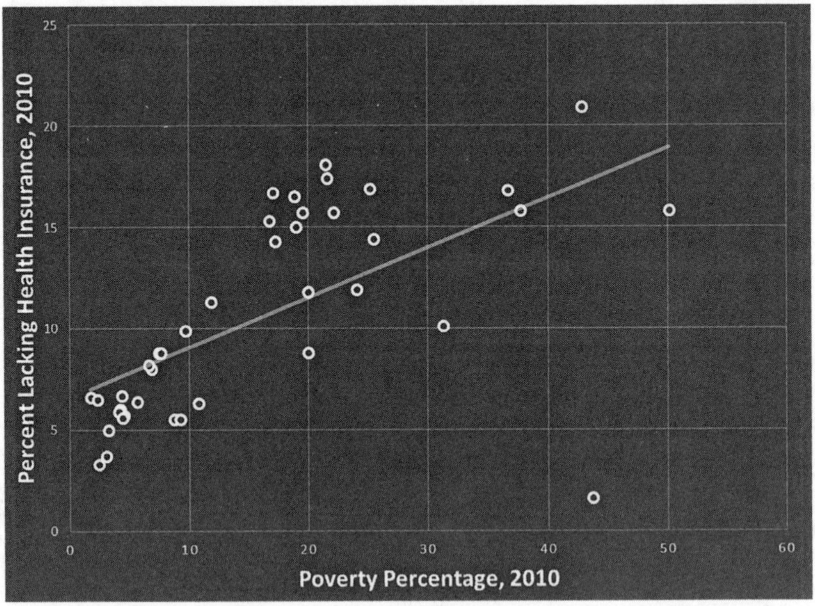

FIGURE 8.5. Poverty and lack of health insurance for Franklin County zip code areas. R = 0.804. Figure by Jamie Valdinger.

future, not least incomes and therefore life expectancy. In other words, we are talking about damage to the poor of a highly structured sort: structured because of the institutional setup governing schooling, in Franklin County as elsewhere.

In Ohio, school districts remain very unequal in terms of the resources they have at their disposal. Given the reliance of the schools on local property taxes, much depends on the assessed value of property per student: Given higher values, the same tax rate will raise more money per student than in a district with lower values. This can be rectified by raising taxes in the poorer districts, but it is a politically fraught process, since poor people, however much they might care for the education of their children, struggle to make ends meet. This particular way of funding schools in Ohio was actually declared unconstitutional in 1997, but the equality implicit in the judgment remains a pipe dream. There *has* been change. Since the judgment, more state aid has been directed to the poorer school districts in the state, and this is reflected in the Columbus area. But as table 8.3 shows for some sample and contrasting school districts in Franklin County, how much is spent per pupil in teacher salaries still varies considerably and in accordance with tax resources. This is not just because some areas can afford to pay for more experienced teachers; it also means that they can hire more teachers with a subsequent and beneficial effect on student-teacher ratios. Again, on these contrasts table 8.3 is eloquent.

Even so, I remain skeptical of the "resources = better educational outputs" thesis, common as it is in the media and among many of the pundits. It is easy to reject the conservative view that throwing money at problems is not necessarily the solution, but in this case, and as far as school funding is concerned, they might be right. Table 8.4 presents some statistical correlations between different features of school districts, on the one hand, and math and reading test scores, on the other. The values of these correlations for teacher salaries and student-teacher ratios are derisorily low, suggest that they have very, very limited effect on test scores. But poverty rates make an important difference. The correlation is close to 1.0, which would be a perfect correlation and negative, meaning that the greater the poverty rate, the lower the test scores. Care clearly has to be used in interpreting these figures. What we cannot conclude is that it is children from the poorer families who

TABLE 8.3. Comparative statistics for three poorer and three wealthier school districts

SCHOOL DISTRICT	TAX BASE/ PUPIL	% POOR	SALARIES/ PUPIL	% CHANGE, STATE FUNDING, 1998–2016/2017	STUDENT–TEACHER RATIO	% FAMILIES FEMALE HEADED	CHURN	MEAN MATH TEST SCORE	MEAN READING TEST SCORE
POORER									
WH	$56,296	27.1	$7,083	+94.0	18.9	22.2%	21.3%	61.2	77.0
GR	$113,470	16.7	$5,804	+45.1	20.6	27.0%	21.9%	71.5	89.4
HAM	$69,913	13.9	$5,026	+51.6	17.4	9.9%	22.2%	84.6	84.9
WEALTHIER									
UA	$297,406	4.1	$9,931	–28.2	16.1	1.5%	3.0%	93.7	95.6
WORTH	$187,191	3.5	$8,312	–2.0	15.2	3.9%	3.0%	84.7	92.8
BEX	$207,080	3.3	$9,083	–28.2	15.8	4.2%	7.1%	93.1	95.6

Note: Abbreviations for school districts—WH: Whitehall; GR: Groveport–Madison; HAM: Hamilton Local; UA: Upper Arlington; WORTH: Worthington; BEX: Bexley.

Sources: Tax base per pupil (real property tax base per pupil): https://www.tax.ohio.gov/Portals/0/tax_analysis/tax_data_series/school_district_data/sd1/SD1CY16.pdf. % poor (proportion of families with children, below the poverty level, 2009): http://proximityone.com/acs/dpoh/dp3_3904702.htm: based on 2009 Community Survey. Salaries per pupil (teacher salaries per pupil 2012): http://www.usa.com/school-district. % change, state funding, 1998–2016/2017: "Twenty Years after DeRolph: Ohio School Funding Remains Mysterious," *Columbus Dispatch*, September 22, 2017. Student–teacher ratio, 2012: http://www.usa.com/school-district. % families female headed, 2009: http://proximityone.com/acs/dpoh/dp3_3904702.htm, based on 2009 Community Survey. Churn (Churn rate 2010): http://kirwaninstitute.osu.edu/reports/2013/2013-Franklin-County-Childrens-Report.pdf, p. 35. Math and reading test scores (2013: Ohio Achievement Assessments): https://webapp1.ode.state.oh.us/proficiency_reports/Data/csvtoasp.asp?filename=G8_Public_0613.csv.

score poorly on these state assessments, true as that might well be.[15] All that the data are telling us is that children in areas where there are significant concentrations of poor people tend to do not so well on these standardized tests.

Just why poverty has such dramatic effects is debatable. One common hypothesis is that it is a matter of cultural enrichment, or lack thereof. In middle-class homes, there will be reading matter, parents eager to teach their children to read before they go to school, travel, and other experiences that poorer families will struggle to provide. Poverty can also mean malnutrition, and malnutrition, believe it or not, does exist, and it affects mental development. These conditions of poor academic achievement are hard to document quantitatively. There is another, though, where there *are* data. This is what is known as "churn": the movement of children from one school district to another and something that one might reasonably expect to interfere with the academic learning process. Churn is strongly associated with poverty[16] and with achievement scores (table 8.4). This gilds the lily, though, since churn is measured only *between* school districts and not within, and in a large school district like Columbus, where stable housing is precarious for a very large poor population, movement between one school and another can be expected to be high.

TABLE 8.4. Educational outcomes across all school districts in Franklin County and "explanatory" variables as measured by coefficients of correlation

VARIABLE	MEAN MATH TEST SCORES	MEAN READING TEST SCORES
Salaries/pupil	.142	.217
Student–teacher ratio	–.209	–.171
% Poor	–.921	–.904
% Families, female headed	–.870	–.888
Churn	–.781	–.810

For sources, see Table 8.3.

The other mediating factor—"mediating," that is, between poverty and achievement scores—is family structure. In school districts with

15. This is the problem of the so-called 'ecological fallacy': correlations among data aggregates—percentages or means—tell us only a limited amount about the individuals on the basis of whose characteristics these statistics are computed. The classic reference is W. S. Robinson (1950).

16. The correlation is 0.845, which is respectably high and demands our attention.

relatively large numbers of families under the poverty line, the proportion of families with children that are female-headed is also unusually high.[17] This is actually almost as effective a predictor of achievement scores as poverty levels (table 8.4).

In this regard, the Columbus area is just a microcosm of the country as a whole: far more unequal in the distribution of wealth and income than its peers among the advanced capitalist societies. This has been further aggravated by the shift from an industrial to a postindustrial society, from the sort of unionized, assembly-line work that prevailed, for example, on Columbus's west side to nonunionized work for companies that supply janitorial and security staff to the burgeoning office sector or for the growing warehouse sector on the far south, west, and east sides (see figure 4.4).

UNEVENNESS AND THE DEVELOPERS

Developers are far from nonchalant about these differences; they cannot afford to be, and in fact, they help reproduce them. But to start at the beginning, they do not operate in a geographic vacuum. In making their decisions as to where to develop, they confront a highly uneven geography. For housing developers, schools and perceptions of their quality are a major element. They also confront a market equipped with a heightened perception of class difference as a result of its geographic expression in the form of "bad" areas or "the inner city" and the mayhem that the media are quick to publicize. This is in addition to the availability, or otherwise, of the sorts of sites they prefer for developments that are commonly highly land-extensive and so suitable for major mixed-use developments: cases like Easton or residential developments like Muirfield and the need to accommodate a golf course so as to enhance its attractions to the buyer.

In the search for enhanced rents, this differentiation is something that can be taken advantage of. For sure, developers typically appeal to the wealthy in the form of class-homogeneous developments. Social mixity is an innocent indulgence of planning theory—the planners themselves long realized its futility, and it is in fact sharply

17. A very high correlation of 0.907: the higher the poverty level in an area, the greater the proportion of families that are female-headed.

hemmed in by zoning designations: to zone for a single family leaves little room for the less well-off who, because they are unable to afford to buy a home, are limited to apartments. There is also the variable perception of school districts and their "quality." On the other hand, small rural districts can be turned around and rescued from their mediocrity, so long as you have the necessary influence over them and the money to invest. Think of the New Albany Company and Plain Local schools.

What I want to emphasize here are schools and local government. The significance of schools and how they are generally perceived—something now stoked by the newspaper publication of state test scores broken down by school district—has been referred to numerous times in this book. Busing for racial balance put the cat among the pigeons and stimulated a real estate boom in school districts not subject to the court order—that is, anywhere other than the Columbus school district. The developers poured money into those areas of the city of Columbus that, therefore, had access to city water and sewer but were in suburban school districts. They were then caught with their proverbial pants down when Columbus city schools moved to annex those areas into the school district, as discussed in chapter 2. As the controversy raged, housing starts in the disputed areas came to a standstill. An alliance with the school districts affected—teachers, superintendents, and school boards—then fortified their opposition, resulting in the standoff that would set the stage for Win-Win. The subsequent case of the Villages at New Albany and its goal of securing Columbus water and sewer while remaining outside of the Columbus school district would underline just how significant schools are in developer calculations. This does not mean that housing investments in the Columbus City School District are precluded. Not everybody has children to see educated. In fact, there has been a rash of developments specifically targeting the retired and empty nesters, particularly in areas abutting the fancier independent suburbs: Take a drive north along Linworth Road from where it branches off from Olentangy for some good examples, or even off Olentangy River Road beyond that point; or more quickly, check things out on Google Maps. Much of this area falls within the boundaries of a particular census tract, and the figures as to who lives there are revealing: a relatively older, white population, therefore, in owner-occupied housing, and relatively few children of school age (see table 8.5).

For housing developers, sensitivity to school district issues does not mean simply investing in those that have already arrived. Rural school districts on the urban periphery are typically quite small in their enrollments, and for a big developer, a fertile field for transformation.

TABLE 8.5. Census Tract 69.50: Older, white people, living in their own homes and in two-person family households

HOUSEHOLD	TRACT 69.50	FRANKLIN COUNTY
Percentage white	95.2	73.6
Percentage aged 5–17	10.1	16.8
Percentage aged 60 and up	42.5	14.7
Percentage housing units, owned	96.1	59.7
Percentage family households, two-person	65.0	41.8

Source: "Census Tract 69.50, Franklin County, Ohio," *USBoundary.com*. Available at http://www.usboundary.com/Areas/Census%20Tract/Ohio/Franklin%20County/Census%20Tract%2069.50/482635 (last accessed, October 25, 2020).

If you develop on a large scale, then the (usually) more affluent newcomers can swamp the existing residents and vote for the operating levies and the bonds necessary to expand the infrastructure. Such was the case with Muirfield vis-à-vis Dublin school district. It has also been the case with the Villages at New Albany. The school district, Plain Local Schools, renamed New Albany-Plain Local, has been given a totally new look and quickly moved into a position near the top of the local league table of state test scores. Money counted, and not just that of the newcomers. Wexner's New Albany Company has been acutely aware of how significant the school district is, channeling money into it by setting up a special taxing district comprising their developments. This is the New Albany Community Authority which collects a Community Development Charge on all property within the Community District, based on assessed value. Originally the District comprised simply the properties assembled by the New Albany Company but has since been expanded to include all new developments within the school district: a nice way of obviating difficulties about paying for new schools and other infrastructure.[18]

•

18. See the *New Albany Community Authority*. Available at https://newalbanycommunityauthority.org/ (last accessed October 26, 2020).

The title of this chapter is "Whose City?" Apparently the answer is, well, certainly not the poor. Things are not exactly set up to work to their benefit. You need money to access decent housing and decent schools. And if you do by some chance happen to find yourself lucky, it probably will not last, as the hapless residents of Bollinger Towers found out when they discovered that they were in the way of a developer who saw some nice profit from its location in the Short North. Even local government agencies did not come to their aid. The CMHA was actually complicit. The so-called welfare state did not exactly have *their* particular interests in mind. Nor yet those state legislators who simply refuse to do the decent thing that the courts have ordered and achieve some defensible degree of equity in per-pupil school spending. This, though, is not the only way of looking at the question of who gets what and why. There are also territorial divisions within the Columbus area and a struggle for regional hegemony. But don't hold your breath. The same forces are still at work, as we will now see.

C H A P T E R 9

The Contested City

Introduction

Class is the dominant social reality in the advanced capitalist societies of the world, the US included. For many, this is an uncomfortable fact, but the dynamics of our societies depend on it. Without a division between those who monopolize productive property and those who, by virtue of their exclusion from that monopoly, have to work for them and fork over some of the value that they produce, things would be very different: not least, more egalitarian and spared of the incessant drive to make money. Class, though, is a complicated category since it can also refer to social stratification: the fact that a particular fraction gets a privileged share of that portion of the product appearing as salaries and wages.

These are facts of life that tend to get occluded, and one of the reasons for that is that class relations tend to be experienced through space and territorial relations: defending and excluding. Classes are divided geographically. This is because people, whether capitalist or worker, whether a better paid or a less well paid worker, tend to have stakes in particular places. This is very clear with developers, as we have seen. In the Columbus area, they all have stakes in the future of the metropolitan economy since, on the one hand, it helps determine the success of their developments, and on the other, they are substantially locked in—tied down to this particular property market by relations of trust with each other, with lawyers, banks, and architects, and with local government officials: relations that are very hard to reconstruct elsewhere. Further, they have stakes in particular projects: Money is sunk into the ground and nasty things, like an adverse rezoning on nearby land, can threaten the rate of return on that investment. The same applies to the broader mass of the population. People complain about threats to their property rights as a result of some nearby development, but what if they could simply move their houses elsewhere? There again, they are attached to particular neighborhoods because of their familiarity and—hopefully positive—associations.

If there is fixity on one side, though, and interests in the future of particular cities, neighborhoods, and local government jurisdictions, there is also mobility. Developers move money around. They sell projects on to home buyers, insurance companies, and pension funds, and use the proceeds to leverage new projects elsewhere, perhaps in parts of the metropolitan area that promise increased rents. People also move, persuaded, perhaps, by the virtues of a particular school district, the more recent vintage of the housing, and lots more besides. The residential growth of the suburbs, encourages the developers to insert more shopping centers. And so on. This conjunction of fixity and mobility, though, is fraught with consequences for the politics of the city. There are desires to include and also to exclude, and here is the crucial point: They can bring developers and residents together in coalitions of forces, even while what they are looking for can be quite different. Developers may work with residents to oppose a particular development because it is viewed as a threat to, say, the local school district whose merits it is using to sell its housing projects, while the residents equally want to see "standards" maintained, but for their own reasons. In short, the city can often appear to be a battleground of territorial coalitions, bringing together developers and wage workers-cum-residents, defending particular pieces of space—in other words, cross-class alliances. This then generates a geopolitics, which from one angle is about territorial dominance, but from another is about reproducing class relations in the two senses and (hence) accumulation. As we will see, not all cross-class alliances can possibly prevail, and there are underlying structural forces conditioning the outcome: The outer suburbs will, on balance, tend to win out against their inner counterparts.

In this final chapter, and drawing on many of the cases already discussed, I explore how the subsequent geopolitics has worked out in the Columbus area: particular lines of territorial dominance and subordination and how that reflects and affects class relations. But first, we need to look at the agents involved and their particular mixes of class and territorial interest.

Dramatis Personae

THE DEVELOPERS

As indicated earlier, developers in Columbus, like developers elsewhere, tend to be locally embedded. They will come together to contest conditions that threaten their rents rather than moving somewhere else, therefore. But within the Columbus area, their commitment to particular neighborhoods, jurisdictions, varies. There are those who have tended to concentrate on particular parts of the city. Nationwide Realty Investors has been very focused on its massive developments in the Arena District, though it has recently branched out into taking the lead on the Grandview Yard development. While not a developer, Ohio State University has gotten involved in neighborhood redevelopment for its own purposes, but always close to its bases around the campus itself and its east side hospital. Wexner's developments have a similar localizing form. Protecting these bases and the investments made in them is a crucial part of their business. The fight over the casino and the Arena District is a very strong case in point.

There are also those engaged in multiple projects in multiple areas at any one time. Some of these will be what are called "long stay" projects, in which it may take up to ten years to develop, sell, or lease to completion. Developing in different parts of the metropolitan area spreads risks, so that if something goes wrong with one of them as a result of adverse local circumstances, they can afford to be a little more relaxed over the course of neighborhood land-use politics. But their partners can be in a different position, and relationships have to be nurtured.

Regardless of their, often shifting, stakes in particular neighborhoods, the wider Columbus area is their horizon. The metropolitan area as a whole is their opportunity but also their limit. This is by virtue of a dependence on it through their experience of real estate markets there, the connections that they have built up with local lenders and private individuals of wealth over the years,[1] as well as the trust that allows them to enter into joint ventures with other developers; it is an opportunity that they have to protect and exploit. When the *Columbus Dispatch* says, as it has in the past, that if impact fees are imposed then developers will move elsewhere, it is not exactly correct. Transferring their activities elsewhere is not easy, and there are stories of how local developers have tried that route. Building up the local connections and knowledge fundamental to making a success of it is hard, which is why they have fought impact fees so vigorously. And also why they will support any initiative designed to boost demand in the local real estate market. They will make money in the Columbus area by moving to the new frontiers, but the new frontiers will be even juicier if there are more people keen to settle in the wider metropolitan area.

This is not just a Columbus thing. We know who the big developers are in Columbus, and they are not the same names as crop up in Pittsburgh, and the names that dominate in Pittsburgh are absent from the Denver scene. In the US, development is a very, very local, hands-on business, and firms get embedded in particular places. It is not the same in Western Europe, where institutionally, one city is much like the next. In the US, cities vary hugely in their institutional niceties—the Columbus annexation policy is sui generis—so that transferring the experience you get in Columbus to, say, the very different context of Atlanta is fraught with challenges.

THE RESIDENTS

Part of the problem for developers, of course, are the residents willing to do battle with them. Residents have commitments to where they live, particularly if they own their own homes and so have values to protect. One of their responses has been segregation. Strong segregation by income is a major geographic feature of all the advanced capitalist societies. In the US, one tends to associate it with race, but that is of diminishing significance, and there have always been strong tendencies to separation. The stimulus for this has come from the more affluent who seek each other out. They want their children to go to "good," well-funded schools without the distractions of pupils who are

1. "Private individuals of wealth": those willing, for example, to put up money for big projects as limited partners, but who otherwise have no particular preference regarding their investments.

"bad influences" and where the ambition that they have tried to instill in their children will be reinforced by that of their classmates. People like them are more willing and able to pass the operating levies that will keep a school district toward the top of the league in facilities and maintain its ability to attract the more experienced, the more qualified, possibly "better" teachers. In some school districts, on the other hand, budget constraints make the trade-offs for residents more painful. These tendencies are deeply ingrained. Among the more affluent, children are given cues by parents as to who is an acceptable playmate and who is not, and the early age at which these things are learned gives them a powerful emotional charge. This is then reinforced by a press that implicitly ranks people as more or less desirable: a vocabulary of "upmarket" or "upscale," "safe" shopping centers, and "better school districts".[2]

The desired segregation is achieved in part through ability to pay. The housing in "nice" neighborhoods is bid up in value, as in gentrification, and the poor are displaced. But this mechanism can also break down: a developer who spots an opportunity for cheaper housing by virtue of the fact that it will be in a superior school district. Which is, of course, where zoning comes in—a tool for the exclusion of rental or denser housing, which threatens to bring in "them": so a force for exclusion even while not set in stone and the bread and butter of the local residents' association or, in the Columbus case, the area commission.

Changes in the modern family are of huge importance in this: the anxiety of parents for their children to "succeed" on their terms, which means obtaining some sort of formal educational qualification. College preparation becomes an important consideration. And there again, households see the house as an asset whose value is to be protected, even enhanced by attracting a "superior" class of person: in other words, inclusion as well as exclusion, but always selective. Meanwhile, the poor are confined, metaphorically, to the cheaper, less comfortable, seats at the back of the theater.

These propensities are something developers are well aware of. Hence the way they advertise their housing developments not just in terms of the qualities of the housing itself but also in terms of what school district they are in—and if the school district is not worth mentioning, it won't be. Developers know that social mix is abhorrent to

2. An idea reinforced by publication of state test scores by school district: freedom of the press, certainly, but quite pernicious in its effects on people, including their self-perceptions.

their target market, so homogeneity of housing is the rule, though for the more expensive housing, some relaxation is in order. The Villages at New Albany includes some very posh areas, replete with golf course, country club, and lots more. But there is also quite a bit of me-too-ism. This is housing that is still expensive but not nearly as much so, yet sufficient to select a certain sort of buyer: no washing of cars on drives there, RVs parked alongside the house, or garden sheds in the backyard; but a swimming pool might make sense, so long as it is not one of those cheap ones above ground that you can buy in a discount store. There is a reality for developers here. The very expensive housing is where you make the big bucks, but the market for it is quite limited, so you have to make some concessions, so long as you don't scare away the big money. This has to be, and will be borne in mind by the developers in setting standards for those they sell land to regarding the sort of housing that is permissible, as indeed has been the case in New Albany.

Developers can control this, therefore, and the bigger the development, the more they can ensure some compatibility in the housing included or locate discrete barriers—wooded areas or wide highways, or even a carefully designed and tree-surrounded shopping center, to ensure that the less well-endowed do not encroach too much on their social betters. Less under their control are the things that local governments provide, most notably schools. But even here, by making a big splash in a small pond, they can make a difference. As we saw, this was the route taken by both Muirfield and the New Albany Company: big developments that would change the pupil composition of respective school districts definitively, which helps to explain the attraction of the smaller suburban local governments and their often still-rural school districts for this sort of project. The same logics of exclusion and inclusion are apparent in other sorts of development, like the mixed-use ones of Easton or the Arena District, or the way in which Ohio State University has tried to intervene in its immediate area.

LOCAL GOVERNMENT

Local governments share an interest in development and in particular sorts of development. They are, after all, part of the wider social division of labor. But if local government is to provide the schools and the capital improvements like highways and public safety demanded both by business and their employees, it needs dependable streams of revenue, notably taxes and service charges. These can be parlayed into a bond rating that can help finance new infrastructure—water and sewer facilities, new schools, highway improvements—at a relatively low interest rate: one of the secrets of Columbus's success.

But, and to state the obvious, and some state and federal grants aside, for the most part a city has to depend on its own taxable base. By definition, it cannot move elsewhere, like to Silicon Valley. So like the developers and the residents, they tend to be stuck, but to a much greater degree. For the most part boundaries are fixed, though Columbus and some of the suburbs have managed to mitigate that through annexation, particularly Columbus, as we saw in chapter 2. Nevertheless, even Columbus is dependent on the health of the Central Ohio economy. The problem of fixity is compounded by the fact that in order to stimulate development, local governments invest in expensive infrastructure of long life. The bonds they raise are invested in airports, water and sewer plants, highways, and, in the Columbus case, a trash-burning power plant. Again, if the users and their taxes fail to show up, there is no way you can sell the infrastructure to some growing city in need in the Southwest. You are lumbered with it, and you have to make sure that the necessary revenues flow through your boundaries and can be captured in some way.

In short, local governments have their own interest in attracting the expensive housing, the regional shopping centers, and the office parks. In the best of all possible worlds, they would like the land uses with high tax yields and low expenditure demands: shopping centers that require little in the way of expenditure apart from the occasional police run, and low-density housing that is less of an imposition on the school district. This sort of calculation has been raised to a high art in the planner's tool known as cost–revenue analysis. For a fee, the consultants, who do these, will advise a local government on what would work best for them: so, and perhaps, developments for the aged because their child-free status means fewer children for the school district to have to cope with, or one-bedroom rather than two-bedroom apartment developments for the same reason. Exclusion apart, the desire is to pull in the taxables, which is what the Columbus annexation policy has been all about, and with a good deal of success. As I pointed out earlier, all the regional shopping centers in the Columbus area are safely within city boundaries, and there have been additional prizes like the Rickenbacker Air Industrial Park.

"COMING TOGETHER"

In terms of the broader class configurations of contemporary society, capital is inevitably the major driving force in the social process, since it has the money to call the shots, which it does. It is bent on accumulation, and on intervening in all aspects of social life to accomplish that goal, not always succeeding, but on balance, succeeding quite handsomely. But for those with money in the ground, the propensity of other money owners to move it around, taking the people and the customers with them, you have to try to control those movements to your advantage, which of course is what Mr. Jacobs tried to do in protecting his Northland shopping center against a project that was going to draw his tenants away. But in a democracy, trying to mold movements of capital and people to your advantage means entering into coalitions that bring, in this case, the developer together with local government and the masses. And to return to Mr. Jacobs, this is precisely what he tried to do by forming a coalition with residents to the north of his shopping center, fearful of social change and trying, with much less success, to do the same with the City of Columbus, which was paralyzed on the issue by involvement in the throes of a mayoral race.

The metropolitan area is continually contested like this, and to some degree in a quite patterned way. The old versus the new is a constant theme, whether in the claims of the first suburbs for a level playing field with the outer suburbs, which disproportionately attract the developers' money, or those of ones like Columbus's South Side protesting city spending on Polaris, or there again, Northland versus Fashion Place. This is part of a broader geographic bias that works to the advantage of the urban periphery. As I have tried to emphasize, what the major developers tend to look for are the large expanses of yet-to-be developed land that can accommodate their quite massive shopping centers—think Polaris, Easton, and now North Star—and residential developments, like Muirfield and the Villages at New Albany, that can augment rents by internalizing externalities that would otherwise escape to free riders. There is, therefore, a long-term geographic bias in investment in the built environment, countered to some degree by some central city redevelopment, which is analogous to the way in which, in the economy as a whole, money shifts from declining sectors, like textiles and shoes, into growing ones like aircraft and IT.

It is not always so patterned and repetitive. Nationwide and the *Dispatch* fought off the casino and the threat it supposedly presented to the Arena District by forging links with those who had chosen to buy into residential developments there,[3] and with a local government that had initially been quite neutral on the matter. They then found a useful partner on the west side in the form of an auto dealer keen to resuscitate his neighborhood and presumably his market, an auto dealer who would then try to drum up wider support in the area, which he did, though whether Franklin Township needed to be pushed is debatable. Not that all such attempts to reach out and broaden a coalition of forces succeed. One is reminded of the wonderful intervention of Constance Bumgarner, aka Mrs. Gee, who in 1997 (chapter 3) put a spoke in the wheel of the city's attempt to seduce African Americans, through offering a program of neighborhood improvements, into supporting the proposal for a basketball arena and soccer stadium.

There are obvious biases to how these struggles proceed. Not all cross-class coalitions are equal. Developers, those businesses with stakes in particular neighborhoods, can line up against each other, but those who throw more money into the game are likely to come out on top. In the conflict over the rezoning to allow the regional shopping center at Tuttle Mall, the local residents opposed to it were not entirely bereft of resources. This is because another developer, JMB, hoped also to thwart it so as to be able to develop its own regional shopping center some distance to the north. They helped fund the resistance, but the Tuttle developers were much more involved both financially and in seeking the support of the city and the school district, both keen to land the tax dollars, while JMB, aside from its financial contribution, stayed on the sidelines.

The rent seekers can sometimes fail. Those seeking to resuscitate the Northland area, including the auto dealers, would have loved to get the Morse-Bethel connector but were frustrated by a very well-heeled residents' group in Old Beechwold, albeit with the wider support of the Clintonville Area Commission. They can also find the going tough in independent suburbs that are for the most part built out. This is because of a clause in the Ohio constitution, mentioned earlier, that allows city ordinances, like rezoning ordinances, to be put to a referendum. As noted earlier, this is conditional on receipt of a petition that

3. As in the stories drummed up in the pages of the Dispatch at the time: See, for example, "Ellen Weibel Commentary: Casino District Elsewhere Might Satisfy Residents," *Columbus Dispatch,* December 30, 2009.

includes a number of names equal to 10 percent or above of all those voting in the city at the last gubernatorial election. In a smaller city like Reynoldsburg, which has had a number of these, this is not that difficult to do. Moreover, relatively small area means that a development can be easily imagined as having a field of negative effects corresponding to the city as a whole. In the case of Tuttle and the attempt to overturn *that* rezoning, given the sheer geographic magnitude of the city of Columbus, this was much more difficult. Likewise, when it came to the redevelopment of the former Clippers' arena on the near west side into an auto race track, the opposition of the wealthy residents of German Village, who were to be affected by noise, did not count for very much; the city could afford to ignore them.

Even so, it is the very poor who are the most dumped on, victimized by gentrification and neglected by a city that sees greener pastures to be fertilized with its money in the newer, developing areas. They are the least organized. They lack the professionals to give them some leadership and advocacy skills. They often dislike the neighborhoods they live in and want to move out, though Bollinger Tower was clearly an exception. They too would like a better life for their children, but they lack the means. Endless moving around in search of lower rents compounds the problem. There are the absentee landlords who will put their weight behind the possibility of gentrification but who have no other stake in the neighborhood and its residents, and as we saw, they have strategies of making money that can succeed regardless of what happens to it.

The overall picture mirrors that in the country as a whole and regardless of whether we are talking about cities. What rules the roost is big corporate money in alliance with the wealthier social strata. In Columbus, one thinks of the role that Ohio State University has been able to develop with respect to its surrounding area, or that of Nationwide regarding its—sizeable—chunk of downtown.

The Power Grid

This is to work at only the most descriptive of levels. One also needs a framework through which to examine interrelations. We know who the agents are, and we know how they all have to confront the tension between, to put it at its most abstract, mobility and fixity: the mobility of residents and money invested in new developments, the fixity of bricks and mortar in place that stands to be devalued by those movements. How, therefore, to bring them together in a way that can shed light on how class relations and territory combine to reveal the underlying power relations in the area? In this section, I discuss this question from the standpoint of what is known as geopolitics.

Most approaches to geopolitics have tended to be what the social scientists call "politicist": power as something that is struggled for, by governments, political parties, even bureaucracies, for itself and irrespective of its consequences. The focus of these struggles is then territorial: achieving dominance over other areas, as in imperialism—in fact, exactly the way in which suburban local governments might view Columbus as a result of its annexation policy. There are alternatives. Harvey's "Geopolitics of Capitalism" (1985) strikes out in very different directions. Mike Davis, in his book on Los Angeles, *The City of Quartz,* sees territorial struggle there as fundamentally about interests of a material sort: the pursuit of profit and rent. The process of accumulating wealth is at the center of this picture, and it is one pregnant with change. This is because of its contradictory character. Land development at particular times tends to be localized: new frontiers and new nodes of development, which will then become passé. The developers put in the shopping centers and housing and sell them on; for a while, they will fill out this particular set of developments: more housing, some strip centers, perhaps an office park. But then they move on to whatever the greener pastures are: in the past almost entirely on the urban periphery, but now increasingly in the city center, and the owners of the shopping centers and the apartment developers are left holding the can and looking for customers. Think Northland, the unfortunate Mr. Jacobs as he tried to fight off the challenge of Polaris, and then the car dealerships of the area as they struggled to maintain their markets by the creation, courtesy of the city, of the so-called Bethel-Morse connector. Or there again, think of the inner suburbs discussed in the last chapter and their attempts to reverse their fortunes by making the outer suburbs less attractive to the developers—so, many landlords and commercial developments that see their revenues wilting in the face of the ever newer vintages of shopping center and apartment development appearing farther out. And this affects local government through their tax revenues, since they are, by definition, incapable of going somewhere else: a dilemma that Grandview faced when Penn Traffic, the buyers of the Big Bear supermarket chain, went bust and vacated a substantial area that had been making an equally substantial contribution to the revenues of the city and its school district.

In other words, and in sum, what is at the heart of these conflicts, and to put it very abstractly, is a tension between movement and fixity. Within the Columbus area, money and people are constantly on the move. Money is being invested in new developments on the urban periphery while it is being withdrawn in various ways from the inner city. Some of the money returns, as in gentrification. Some shopping centers go out of business and customers shift their patronage elsewhere: from Northland to Polaris, say. People move not just as shoppers but as residents, moving from one neighborhood to another. As employment geography changes, so do commuting patterns. Much of this movement is from one local government to another—people relocating, say, from Columbus to New Albany.

Meanwhile, of course, local governments, businesses, developers, and residents have stakes in the future of particular government jurisdictions or neighborhoods. They have sunk money into shopping centers, housing developments, hospitality districts, distribution centers, and residential neighborhoods. And as movements shift, of shoppers, residents, and money for new developments, so the future of these older investments can be called into question. This is as much a problem for Mr. Jacobs with his money sunk into Northland as it is for the city of Columbus with its investments in fire stations, highways, and water and sewer utilities. As the geography of the Columbus area changes, they can be very exposed. Mr. Jacobs fought and lost. The city of Columbus has tried to counter the possibilities of being left high and dry as the tide goes out by following it through its annexation policy. This is the stuff of geopolitics, whether we are talking about the Columbus area or more generally.

For classical geopolitics was always about territory: extending control over certain areas or those in power there in order to subordinate them to one's own goals. Imperialism is classic, if strongly inflected with the sense of material interest often missing in geopolitical argument: controlling other areas in order to channel the flow of wealth in favor of the imperial country. Neocolonialism is not that different—just that those with investments in a particular country call on their home country to protect them. In these claims, the idea of one place exploiting another, diverting the value generated in one place to another, is never far away, as indeed in the case of Columbus and its wider metropolitan area.

COLUMBUS DOMINANT

Reining in the suburbs: During the 1960s and '70s, urban economists hypothesized what they called the suburban exploitation of the central city.[4] This was in the context of what was known at that time as the problem of central city–suburban fiscal disparities. How was it that central cities did not have the revenues to meet their revenue needs? One answer: They were funding services that were paid for by their resident taxpayers to serve commuters. The commuters from the independent suburbs were using city services, like the police who protected them, and the maintenance of the streets along which they moved on their way to work, without paying for them. To the extent that cultural activities like museums, art galleries, and symphony orchestras were subsidized and then used by those living beyond the city boundaries, the same exploitation effect applied. It was arguments of this sort that originally led Columbus in 1947 to impose a tax on the wages of all those working in the city, regardless of whether they resided in the city or not.[5]

There is, though, a more subtle argument about suburban exploitation of the central city, which also applies to Columbus. Observers of the central city–suburban fiscal disparities problem were not slow to spot the connection with the residential exclusionism of the independent suburbs. A major reason that the suburbs were hogging increases in the property tax base of a metropolitan area was that they were excluding, via zoning and refusal to countenance public housing, the less affluent. The view in the suburbs was that this allowed them to fund their schools more generously; it also allowed home values to be maintained at an elevated level. To open the gates to the less affluent would undermine these advantages. Meanwhile, the wages that fueled the suburban property boom and values there were being paid by firms in the city and in work processes that necessarily also involved the less well-off.

The intent of the Columbus annexation policy was to counter these effects by limiting the expansion of the independent suburbs: to make sure that the wealth did not entirely escape beyond city bound-

---

4. Neenan 1970; Bradford and Oates 1974.

5. "The Commuter and the Municipal Income Tax," *Advisory Commission on Intergovernmental Relations,* Washington DC, April 1970. Available at http://www.library.unt.edu/gpo/acir/Reports/information/M-51.pdf (last accessed October 25, 2020).

aries. The fiscal implications of this, along with what it has meant for the retention of a more affluent population, were discussed in chapter 2. Compared with most other Coldbelt cities, Columbus has been extraordinarily successful in its ability to retain tax base and to keep within the city those major developments, most notably the regional shopping centers, and the annexation policy has been fundamental to this achievement. It also has an income diversity that sets it apart from most of its Midwestern peers. Meanwhile, as in the inner/outer suburb thing, some of the suburbs have come out of it better than others.

There has been some change. The fallout of the schools annexation imbroglio, concluding with the so-called Win-Win agreement, has had repercussions. The Columbus annexation policy, while still in healthy shape, is not quite what it was. It will be recalled from chapter 5 and the discussion of the Villages at New Albany that one of the bargaining gambits of the developers in an attempt to secure Columbus water and sewer without annexation to Columbus school district was to threaten a merger between the Village of New Albany and the surrounding township. This would have meant that annexation by Columbus of land in Plain Township—at that time, still unincorporated, for the most part—would have been impossible. It also meant that annexation beyond in a north-northeast direction, would have been stymied. Columbus caved in and New Albany got an expanded area that it was allowed to annex into, crucial for the interests of the New Albany Company. The quid pro quo was that Columbus could still go on annexing in that northeasterly direction.

But the events in the northeast of the county were like a light bulb going on, as in: If New Albany can get a big expansion area by threatening a city–township merger, why not us? In one of the suburbs, Hilliard, this seems to have been quite explicit. In Dublin, the initiative had different roots, though also drawing from the New Albany case. In both instances, Columbus had to concede bigger expansion areas. But it would also learn a lesson: If city–township mergers actually happened, this could threaten the possibility of expansion into the promised land of never-ending annexation beyond. That had to be discouraged. So in future, water–sewer contracts would last only as long as a suburb agreed not to promote or support the idea of a merger with an adjacent township.[6]

6. Cox and Jonas 1993, 27–32.

Mobilizing the county: Annexation of surrounding unincorporated land has had other, knock-on effects. As a proportion of the county population, Columbus's share has gone down, but it is still quite overwhelming: from about 78 percent in 1940 to around 68 percent in 2010. This gives it an unusual leverage over the county that has shown up in a number of different instances, first with respect to the trash-burning power plant project, and second regarding the creation of a regional airport authority.

The trash-burning power plant was something dreamed up in the '70s and approved by citywide referendum in 1977. It would achieve fruition in the '80s. The idea was to solve an imminent crisis of trash disposal. This was owing to the doubts of the time about the ecological sustainability of landfills, along with a need for an alternative source of electricity for the municipal power division.[7] Trash would be burned alongside coal. The venture was risky. Nothing like this had been done before, and there was business opposition, even while environmental organizations praised the idea. The opposition turned out to have been right. Construction costs were significantly higher than anticipated ($200 million vs. $118 million), and interest rates soared toward the end of the decade, creating a heavy debt burden. It became known as the "cash-burning power plant," and this had repercussions for the ability of the city to sell bonds for other capital improvements.[8] By 1987, Columbus was looking around for a way to spread the costs. A city–county solid waste authority was being mooted to operate the trash-burning power plant, three satellite trash shredding stations, and the county landfill so as to spread the financial burden of the trash-burning power plant. And, despite protests from the independent suburbs, it would happen. The Franklin County Solid Waste Management Authority would come into being, and the cost of the subsidy

---

7. The city had long generated electricity for city lighting, but its existing coal-fired plant was threatened by the implementation of the 1970 Clean Air Act, which restricted the burning of high-sulfur coal.

8. "The trash plant was envisioned a decade ago as a moneymaker for the city. It was to pay its own debt, provide maintenance money and power for street lighting, and produce enough extra money to pay tipping fees for residual ash and non-combustible materials, which must go to the Franklin County landfill. Reality has been far from the dream." And: "Subsidies for the plant come from the 25% of city income tax revenue earmarked for capital improvements. The income tax is 2%. The trash plant will eat up about 40% of the $45M put into the fund this year" ("Capital Improvement Funds Hurt Due to Trash-Plant Debt," *Columbus Dispatch,* February 3, 1986, p. 4D).

would be spread out, albeit through dumping fees that, by virtue of the monopoly thus achieved, were increased. By 1990, Columbus was increasing its demands on the new authority; in addition to helping to pay for the subsidy to operating costs, it should also assume the plant's very considerable debt. This too would happen the following year, and by 1993 it owned the plant too. But the albatross would continue to grow in size because, as a result of growing environmental concerns over the effluent of the plant, it would eventually be closed down, so there were no revenues to offset even a fraction of the debt.

It was also in part a result of limits to the city's bonded debt—not helped by the trash-burning power plant—that Columbus would try to create an airport authority on a broader geographical basis. The goal was to offload some of its debt. The idea of a regional airport authority had been in the works for some time, certainly since before the trash-burning power plant was given the go-ahead. By the mid-'80s, it had risen toward the top of the city agenda, prompted in part by the hunt for a hub airline and recognition that landing one would require significant gate expansion at the airport. The idea was to bring together what was then Port Columbus, with a smaller field used by private plane owners—Bolton Field—with the airfield at Rickenbacker, which was owned by the county but was incurring significant debt. So the county was all in favor, while the same led to some foot-dragging by Columbus as they came to realize the implications, including, of course, the city's loss of control. It took a while, but by 2003 there was a new Columbus Regional Airport Authority responsible for the three airports originally projected, and with its own bonding power.

The problems that a wider geographic authority based in the county were supposed to solve were very practical ones of spreading debt for capital projects, including ones like the trash-burning power plant. What is significant, though, is the way in which a discourse of suburban exploitation was drawn on by the city in order to persuade, even while the details of that discourse might, in some instances, have testified more to the ingenuity of their proponents. The idea of a regional airport authority recalled the way the city has always justified the higher water and sewer rates it charges to the independent suburbs: that it is the city that incurs the debt for the water and sewer works and the expanded water and sewer lines to allow for suburban use. In the case of the airport authority, the argument was that people from throughout the county used the airport; if the bonds taken out to expand it could not be repaid from fees paid by the airlines, those living outside the city would be exempt from the taxation necessary to pay them off. These seem fairly reasonable arguments. The one advanced to justify the county helping out to subsidize the trash-burning power plant was less so: that the plant was subsidizing the county by extending the life of the county landfill.[9] Equally inventive was the claim that by failing to assume plant debt, the county would be limiting capital projects undertaken by Columbus that benefited the wider area.[10] Clever! But bottom line: While it might have been a prolonged process, Columbus has managed to offload a number of its capital costs onto the county as a whole.

THE "-LANDS"

There are also more centralized nodes of power where some power nexus, institutionalized or not, holds sway over the future of a particular part of the urban area. Some of these concentrations of power are more formalized and geared up than others. They have their own armies of lawyers, planners, development experts, even lobbyists, networks of useful contacts, and typically a continuing presence. This is all with a view to making sure that the changing geography of the city works to their advantage; and that their own initiatives with respect to that geography so as to fashion respective backyards to their own purposes carry through: attracting some things into, and repelling others from, what I am calling here their "lands". They can enjoy a good deal of autonomy with their own political bases and have some leverage with respect to the formal political system, whether it is local or state government. And if one avenue fails, they have others that they can fall back on.

Three in particular stand out:

- OSU-land: The university has an enduring interest in making things work for it, regardless of its implications for the rest of the city, as in the basketball arena case discussed in chapter 3. Much of its focus

9. *Columbus Dispatch,* May 29, 1990, p. 1D.

10. "'When the city of Columbus is incapable of funding capital improvement projects for infrastructure that benefits this entire community, then the whole county suffers as well as the city,' [councilor] Portman said" ("Authority Asked to Assume Trash Plant Debt," *Columbus Dispatch,* December 21, 1990). In other words, an old story: "too big to fail."

has been on the immediately surrounding area, where it is the big gorilla: what might be called OSU-land.

- Wexner-land: This is a real estate empire on the northeast side covering, intermittently, an area stretching from Easton to New Albany and taking in the distribution center on the other side of the freeway from Easton.
- Nationwide-land: This is the area where Nationwide has its headquarters and its massive real estate interests in the Arena District.

To expand, while bearing in mind that this goes over some of the ground covered earlier.

OSU-land: The university cannot move. There is a case for it *having* to intervene in the surrounding area. There is no undeveloped area into which it can expand other than the land on the other side of the river, which is a little too remote for much class room or dorm expansion. So when opportunity has come knocking, it has taken advantage of it. The classic case here is the land between West Woodruff and Lane on which now sit the Fisher College of Business and numerous dorms; this was acquired under the Urban Renewal Act of 1949, which facilitated the clearance of supposedly deteriorated properties, and then their sale for redevelopment. In other cases, the university has felt impelled to act to defend its interests. Campus Gateway, another sort of urban renewal project without the formal designation, probably would not have happened without the murder of a student that dramatized a wider security problem for students and, more important, their parents, who pay their bills and keep them at the university. In other cases, its effects on the surrounding area have been inadvertent. The decision to have all sophomores as well as freshmen live on campus is a recent and serious blow to the private student rental industry in the immediate neighborhood of the university.

The university can do these things because it has the resources to draw upon. Some of these are not immediately in the money form. The decision to go ahead with a new basketball arena on campus and the city be damned was in part because of its clout in the state assembly, where there are a number of alumni,[11] and it could then rely on

11. Currently, fourteen of the ninety-nine state representatives and seven of thirty-three state senators are alumni. The Ohio State University Alumni Association also promotes something it calls Buckeye Advocates. According to its website: "Our advocacy program prepares alumni and friends of Ohio State to effectively engage with their representatives and build relationships back home in their districts. As a

its wider alumni constituency to help fund it. It could do without the help of the city; rather, it was the city that needed the university's help if it was to build an arena without a tenant yet in sight. This was an effect beyond the university's immediate neighborhood, and there are others.

The university is a thorn in the city's side as well as a crucial contributor to the city's economy. It is a thorn because the prominence of its athletic programs, particularly football, and the intense local following that it has attracted, make the city a hard row to plough for professional sports franchises. But it is a crucial contributor, not just through its payrolls but also because of the way it produces a highly skilled element in the local labor force. In trying to read the tea leaves of the Amazon short list of twenty cities for its new second headquarters, this has been identified as one of Columbus's advantages over cities that were excluded, like Kansas City, St. Louis, Cleveland, and Detroit; they have universities, but not with the numerical weight of Ohio State, which is usually vying with the University of Texas for the largest number of students in the US. Internship programs, graduates splitting the difference with the partner as to where they will live post-OSU, and it certainly beats small-town Ohio: All of these points have worked to the advantage of major white-collar employers, like Nationwide, and will continue to do so. Ohio State is an indispensable part of the postindustrial city that is Columbus.[12]

Wexner-land: One of the better-known Ohio State alumni who comes to mind is one Leslie Wexner. He is currently the wealthiest person in Columbus—worth a cool $7.7 billion[13]—but, and interestingly, he occupies a more modest ranking among the billionaires of the country.[14] Our Les originally made his money in retail and remains CEO of

---

Buckeye Advocate you'll become familiar with the challenges facing higher education in Ohio. You'll also be the first to know when we need your help to get the word out to legislators." And so it might have seemed.

12. Alas, there is at present no evaluation of the significance of OSU graduates for the area labor market. Anecdotally, they constitute significant fractions of the labor forces of the area's respective major white-collar employers. A nice master's paper project for someone?

13. "The Richest Person in America's 50 Largest Cities," *Forbes Magazine,* 2016. Available at https://www.forbes.com/richest-in-top-50-cities/list/#tab:overall (last accessed October 25, 2020.

14. A "mere" 161st in the latest rank ordering: "The Richest People in America," *Forbes Magazine,* 2020. Available at https://www.forbes.com/forbes-400/#5be75a157e2f (last accessed October 25, 2020).

something called L Brands, which includes the Victoria's Secret, Bath and Body Works, and La Senza chains. But from the mid-'80s on, he started branching out into real estate development. Just how significant this is to his revenue relative to the retail chains is unclear, but it has certainly left a mark on Columbus, particularly in its northeastern quadrant.

Thus far there have been two major—actually quite massive—projects that are still far from completion: very "long stay," in other words. Both have been given extensive attention already in this book: first, the large mixed-use development known as Easton next to the Outerbelt on its east side, and second, the Villages at New Albany, which has been much more singularly focused on residential development. Both of these cover very large areas. Easton includes 1,300 acres—in other words, about two square miles, which is a big chunk. A considerable portion of it is still to be developed. Just how much land has moved through the hands of the New Albany Company as it developed its "Villages" is harder to estimate. Figure 5.3 in chapter 5 provides some sense of the land that had been purchased just prior to the announcement that there would be extensive residential development. Some of that was sold on to other developers, albeit developing within guidelines set by the company. Other land has been acquired since then. For the most part, much of this is very expensive housing indeed—certainly one of the most, if not *the* most exclusive of developments in the whole county. So Les has made a clear mark on the landscape.

As we saw in chapter 5, he has certainly had to fight to impress himself in that way. Obtaining the necessary water and sewer connections for the Villages project was a long and tortuous process in which he had to call on all the guile and savvy of his lawyers, not to mention his own, to turn it to his advantage. Likewise he wanted his own grand entrance to Easton, and getting it over the objections of the federal Department of Transportation needed some string pulling, as we saw in chapter 7. In all these matters, his money has obviously been of crucial significance.

But while his original decision to buy land in Plain Township in an area projected for Columbus water and sewer without being annexed by Columbus schools proved abortive, his subsequent embrace of New Albany and the New Albany–Plain Township school district has allowed him to be a very big player in a small pool. They need him, his money, and his developments far more than he needs them, and he has been able to create a space in his own exclusive, affluent image, acquiring new land for his projects and New Albany's compliance in developing them.

Nationwide-land: The third and final power node, with equally impressive effects on the surrounding physical landscape, has been Nationwide. Its major playground—Nationwide-land—has been the Arena District, a mixed-use development of offices, hospitality, and residential, with the ice hockey arena as its centerpiece. Like Wexner, Nationwide has benefited from the largesse of state agencies and it has also had friends in high places to fight its battles, most notably the *Columbus Dispatch.* This largesse has come in several forms and repeatedly: first, the twenty-year tax abatement for the Nationwide office tower and surrounding plaza; second, a ninety-nine-year lease from the city on the old penitentiary land that Natonwide did not yet own in exchange for 20 percent of parking revenues; $32.8 million that the city agreed to pay for infrastructural improvements and cleanup of the site; then, more recently, the sale to the county of an arena that looked like it might have become a financial albatross, and at public expense. Meanwhile Nationwide is praised to the skies by the local notables for its redevelopment. Nice work if you can get it!

There have been threats to its empire. The most dramatic of these was the attempt of casino promoters to set up shop next door in 2009. Passage of an amendment to the Ohio constitution allowed the creation of casinos in four major cities, including Columbus, and a site next to the Arena District had already been purchased in anticipation by a group called Penn National. As we saw earlier, all hell would break loose. Just how threatened Nationwide felt about this—for there was clearly a trade-off between increased foot traffic in the area and a possible devaluation of residential and even office developments—is not clear. This is because, as we saw in the last chapter, its partner in the Arena District project, the *Columbus Dispatch,* quickly launched a campaign against it, though whether this was on moral grounds, as the then owner had severe views about the corrupting effects of gambling, or strictly business ones has never been determined.[15] In the event, a new site on the west side of the city was found for the casino, but only after a period of brawling, vituperative journalism that the casino promoter, to its credit, refused to answer in kind. But bottom line: If Nationwide did feel threatened, it could safely leave the issue to its

15. Cox 2016, 37–46.

junior partner and its local control of a big part of the local media.[16] In other words, money attracts people who can make a contribution. The *Dispatch* saw the Arena District as a relatively safe investment due to the fact that the lead developer had financial clout in buckets.

There was further fallout from the casino imbroglio. Once it had been dispatched to the west side wilderness, Nationwide moved to buy up the site, presumably with a view to internalizing more of the externalities created by its existing investment. And it has paid off. As discussed in chapter 3, the Crew is moving into a new stadium, and lo and behold, most of the site is on land owned by Nationwide: a nice bonus for its parking garages since there will be no parking next to the stadium itself. But that is not enough. There is more than a bit of evidence that it has played hardball over the price of the land.[17] Certainly the city weakened itself by entering into the bargaining process after announcing how much money it was helping with. But is there no limit to Nationwide's exploitation of the local public purse?

•

There are other nodes, though more transient ones, corresponding to very particular development projects, and hardly with the history or durability of the "lands." These are typically long-stay development projects that, once built out, will lose the developer interest that protected them: Tuttle and Polaris, two major multi-use projects, come to mind. An even shorter "stay" was that of Battelle in the course of redeveloping Harrison West. It is all relative, of course; there is a very, very long-term sense in which Wexner-land will disappear as the New Albany Company ultimately dissolves, its development task done, and

---

16. The only daily newspaper in town and a TV and radio station.

17. "Bret Adams, an attorney and sports agent who has been critical of the project's costs, said the stadium's backers—particularly the Columbus Partnership, the association of the city's largest businesses and organizations that was instrumental in landing the public-private stadium package—should have secured a commitment from Nationwide Realty up front for land costs. 'It was the Columbus Partnership that announced the stadium site without securing an option for a purchase price for that,' Adams told The Dispatch outside the council chamber. 'That deal has not happened yet because, I'm sure, Nationwide is playing very tough from the price point, and there are serious negotiations going on. They're going to overpay for the land,' Adams said" ("Columbus Council Approves $50 Million City Contribution to Crew Stadium Project," *Columbus Dispatch,* July 1, 2019).

the various bits and pieces of Easton pass on to the pension funds, the insurance companies, and other long-term holders of real estate. One can well imagine this happening in the Arena District. From this standpoint, institutions like Ohio State University are unique: They will never "build out" since they are not developers, but they are not going anywhere, either.

THE RESIDENTS

If the geopolitics of any metropolitan area is constituted in its immediacy by tensions between movement and fixity, residents are certainly part of it. As residents, people adjust to those movements by either moving or by staying and fighting to deflect that what they dislike and to make sure that what they want comes to their part of town.

Active contestation typically occurs through a residents' or civic association or sometimes, in the case of Columbus, through an area commission. Some resident groups are quite transient, coming into being to fight a particular threat: often a rezoning or some plan for redevelopment, as in the case of the old Cooper Stadium.[18] From the 1980s on, more permanent ones have emerged. Important in this instance have been developments that were bequeathed by the developer with a civic association whose delegated task is to hire people to attend to the common landscape, including hiring snow-ploughing companies. They often retain lawyers for issues affecting the neighborhood, including the rezoning of adjacent land.

Regardless, the active are typically those fixed in some way in their neighborhoods: commonly a mix of homeownership and school anxieties. Homeownership comes with concerns about maintaining property values and the costs of moving: Selling a home is a bother—not just paying the realtor fees but getting the house in sellable shape and preparing for open days—and looking for another one elsewhere can be time-consuming. There again, if you have children in schools, the general view is that moving them impedes their progress and takes them away from friends. People also get used to where they are: familiarity, a particular neighborhood aesthetic, and particular proximities can be

18. Another example is WOOSE ("We Oppose Ohio State Airport Expansion"), largely of Worthington residents, anxious about increased overflights that would result from the expansion of a small airport.

hard to substitute for. They bought a nice view, they like it and they will defend it. At the other pole are those without these sorts of commitments: more mobile and less likely to get involved, which makes it to some degree a generational distinction.

This overlies a class spectrum. The poor do not fit into this schema at all well. They are fixed but more in the sense of being trapped. They would like to move but cannot afford to. The neighborhood is not one that they can be attached to: poor schools, public safety issues, so why bother? People move within the area—generating the sort of churn for schools discussed in the last chapter—but escaping to something better is rare. A few homeowners may have hopes of "turning it around" through gentrification, but they will be a minority.

There is also an abstract sense in which movement and neighborhood action are closely linked: Movement is a condition for neighborhood action, while the latter contributes to how movements get shaped. They incorporate, modify, or deflect, according to what is seen as some conception of neighborhood interest, though behind that interest is always some class concern: maintaining or advancing a particular social status, protecting home values, maintaining local schools that can help them realize their ambitions of upward mobility for their children. In part this may be because a new land use threatens property values and the return they expect on their investment. In other instances, a lowering of values is a threat because of who it might enable to buy into the neighborhood. Some people are seen as better neighbors than others, and class stereotypes factor into this.

This is to look at the politics of neighborhood as one of inclusion and exclusion. Land-use zoning and zoning fights have often been interpreted in this way. Some land uses, perhaps directly or in highly mediated ways, tend to filter in people of lower income: so apartments in an area of dominantly owner-occupied housing, or any use likely to lower property values in the area and precipitate a process of what is antiseptically called "social change." On the other hand, keeping the neighborhood "pure" also means keeping up property values, which is going to filter in, or "include," the better-off. In a quite complicated sort of way, this is what the politics of Northland has been about. It is not something the media addresses—too politically incorrect—but the northward shift of a dominantly African American population has raised concerns among the homeowners to the north of Morse Road. For a long time, Northland shopping center acted to reinforce the symbolic barrier of Morse Road, which explains in part the support that Northland residents gave to opposing the expansion of Polaris, which would doom Northland shopping center.

Another outstanding case of zoning for exclusion were the blanket rezonings carried out in Clintonville and German Village. For the longest time, both had allowed apartments. The northward creep of campus rentals into the southern fringes of Clintonville raised anxieties—much like those of the Northland residents faced with a different sort of frontier movement—and this led to a request to city council for a total rezoning of the area to single family. This was a sign for the German Village commission to make their own request. Central to how this class interest is conceived is a hierarchy of people as potential neighbors and how the neighbors that one ends up getting are mediated by the shifting contours of the housing market.[19]

Aside from the excluding/including aspect of neighborhood politics, there is a second one that focuses on displacement and resisting displacement. This has been more common toward the center of the city in fights around redevelopment and gentrification. When Battelle moved to rehab the housing it owned to its immediate south, making way for what would be Harrison West, there was lively resistance from those who had been renting the houses, and there was an attempt to frustrate the move, as in opposition to the small shopping center through the development of which Battelle hoped to make the area more residentially attractive. Some other cases are more complex. If parking becomes an issue that it was not, and in a residentially attractive area, you are likely to fight for some resolution that will work to your advantage, which is what is happening in the Short North, as corporate money moves in to cash in on the image.

In all of this, the role of money always catches the eye, not least the ability to hire lawyers, but also the way in which what urban economists call the competitive bidding process has always worked in urban property markets. Housing goes to the highest bidder. If people of money lose interest in a neighborhood, for whatever reason—age of housing, changing proximities to employment—then values go down

---

19. Thus Zane Miller in talking about Cincinnati: "After the mid-1960s, then, the metropolitan area seemed to be composed of a mélange of service and economic areas, varied in size, which existed to foster pursuit by individuals of personal goals and objectives. Each of these areas competed for economic resources, power and 'top-notch' citizens, and the competition not only pitted Cincinnati against its suburbs but also big city neighborhood against big city neighborhood, suburb against suburb, and neighborhoods within a particular suburb against one another" (Miller 1981, 239).

and who gets to live there changes, much to the anguish of those who want to stay. On the other hand, where values are increasing, housing can give way to commercial, and with all sorts of obnoxious implications for the residents, which is what is happening in the Short North.

What works best for residents pursuing what they believe to be their interest is the patronage of a developer. There are the people in the new residential towers springing up around the Arena District, but when the possibility of a casino next door loomed large, threatening what they saw as the quality of their lives, not to mention the values of their recently purchased condos, they had influential benefactors: not least the *Dispatch,* which had its own reasons for opposing it but was happy to relay the tales of woe of the residents to galvanize popular opinion.

On the other hand, being enrolled by a developer anxious to support their cause does not guarantee doing the trick. The Kilbane–Shannon Heights group opposing the rezoning that would allow the Tuttle Mall shopping center got financial support from the developer JMB, which had its own reasons for nipping it in the bud, but they were totally outgunned financially by the mall developers. The publicity war was misnamed, it was a massacre. The struggle of the Northland owner to fend off the Polaris challenge likewise went down in flames, even while it might have encouraged the Northland residents who had their own anxieties about imminent closure.

If either Tuttle or Northland had not been in the city of Columbus but in one of the smaller, suburban jurisdictions, things might have turned out differently. The smaller the local government, the greater the pressure a residents' group can exercise. It is not just their relative numerical weight and how the negative externality field of what is opposed can cover a large part of the jurisdiction; it is also the way the referendum petition works, as discussed earlier. In a city like Reynoldsburg, with about 37,500 people, putting together a number of names equivalent to 10 percent of those voting in the last gubernatorial election is much easier than in a city like Columbus, which has 23 times the population. So while in the early years of a suburb on the periphery, the developers can find it plain sailing, particularly as they hook up with local landowners heavily represented in city government, once it starts filling up and the residents begin to get used to the empty spaces that are left, it can be quite another story.

•

The constant backdrop to the geopolitics of any metropolitan area is the swirl of movements, of money moving into new real estate developments, of people moving to different parts of the city, of shoppers patronizing different shopping centers, and how that comes up against existing commitments to particular places: commitments that real estate investors can have, quite as much as residents. This is the origin of attempts to exclude and to include, of territorial embellishment and hegemony over the rest of the city or at least parts of it: Think in particular of how Columbus's annexation policy, through the inclusion of juicy additions to tax base, has allowed it to call the shots in the rest of the metropolitan area, and continues to do so; and this, despite some shift in the balance of power over negotiating the water and sewer contracts.

Commitments to particular places can make odd bedfellows: A neighborhood organization teams up with a big real estate developer in order to preserve an exclusionary zoning that works to the advantage of both; or a developer appeals to people in a wider area, perhaps on the grounds of the increasing tax revenues that they can expect by virtue of a new development, in order to do an end run around the opposition of a residents' organization anxious about noise and traffic. Developers team up with one group of residents against another, therefore, something facilitated by the fact that the population is residentially stratified; households come with different sorts of tax contributions to, and burdens on, local schools, along with various sorts of what have been politely referred to as "behavioral externalities" (Downs 1973).

The result is a tapestry of coalitions, constantly forming, and then dissolving as developers shift their attention elsewhere, or as a neighborhood undergoes some social change, but then re-forming on the new development frontiers. The way it works, of course, gives support to those who see the city as contested by various sorts of territorial coalitions that bring together very diverse sets of interests: a university, a set of real estate developers, and a residue of middle-class homeowners hoping for a neighborhood turnaround, as the university seeks to fortify its boundaries against "them." Or a local government, an older suburb, perhaps, in alliance with a developer to strengthen its tax base but with the result of a transfer of jobs from some newer, outer suburb as the developer draws on its institutional affiliation, perhaps with an insurance company (?!), to make sure that there will be a stream of rents.

But this is misleading. These are all marriages of convenience. The underlying dynamic is the relentless accumulation of money in the form of profits and rents. This plays itself out against a background of fixities on the one hand, and a stratification of the population on the other. The latter is the condition for resident willingness to enter into coalitions: not just keeping out "them," but fortifying property values by bringing in the "right sort" of resident. Fixities, meanwhile, affect both the developers and the residents; they both have them, even while in their substantive form they are quite different.

So while there are territorial hierarchies and hegemonies, Columbus over the whole metropolitan area, particular neighborhoods with respect to others—Clintonville and particularly Old Beechwold against Northland—they by and large hew to class lines. On the one hand, the developers tend to prevail over the broad mass of the population, not least through their domination of Columbus city council but also through their dogged resistance to impact fees, among other things. Small bottom-feeders renting out property in the inner city, perhaps speculating on gentrification, can lose out, but the general tendency is clear. If it was not thus, the money would eventually be diverted into other sorts of investment, and perhaps not in Columbus. It is then through playing off one set of residents against another that they manage to get their way in particular cases. And underlying this is always the social power of money, and not just that of the developers with their clever attorneys and campaign finance.

Wealthier neighborhoods tend to be bastions of stability. Poorer neighborhoods with older vintage housing are more vulnerable and tend to be dumped on by land uses that, while significant to the development of the city as a whole—they have to go *somewhere*—are obnoxious neighbors: Think trash-burning power plants, new freeways, parking lots for school buses. Not least, the land there is cheaper. There is also less likely to be opposition; people tend to be more transient, with less attachment to the immediate area. These are also the neighborhoods deemed most likely to be in need of "improvement" or "redevelopment," but all that does is move the poverty elsewhere. This is far from arguing that the wealthier parts of the city are always able to steer the obnoxious uses someplace else; the (unsuccessful) opposition of the German Village Commission to the redevelopment of Cooper Arena as a motor racetrack suggests otherwise. But the overall trends are clear.

AFTERWORD

AS I WAS GIVING this book manuscript a final revision in late 2019, some items in the news reminded me of old themes in the politics of development in the Columbus area. The first concerned the city of Pataskala, adjoining Franklin County on the east, experiencing fairly rapid population growth, though not as rapid as in the '90s, when it grew by over 200 percent. The news was that the city had imposed a six-month ban on development in order to study the problem of raising money for the highway improvements that development had necessitated.[1] Impact fees were one of the solutions mentioned. This has not sat well with the development community and its allies, and the usual discourse was wheeled out. According to Jon Melchi of the Building Industry Association of Central Ohio, the lobby for developers, "The fear is that policies are being crafted to prevent people from coming into communities. Our hope is that is not the case in Pataskala, but recent history would lead you to believe otherwise." In other words, it is not a matter of money lost but of serving a wider public interest. One city council member refused to support the ban, citing the hurt that this would impose on those planning to sell their land for development—but no mention of the fact that it is sheer luck that allows them to cash in on their inflated property values: the sheer luck of being on

1. "Pataskala Decides to 'Hit Pause Button' on New Homes for Six Months," *Columbus Dispatch,* October 9, 2019.

the edge of an expanding metropolis. But rhetoric aside, Pataskala is booming, and this should give pause. It is, after all, a good seventeen miles to the east of the center of Columbus, which is a very long way indeed, but quite appropriate to the American pattern of urbanization.

The other item concerned the construction of a new downtown stadium for the soccer franchise, the Columbus Crew, discussed at greater length in chapter 3. This raised, like the Pataskala case, old fears about the development behemoth, but now, and unlike Pataskala, a city council committed to development and the public be damned. As I related, what had emerged was that unbeknown to the public, the amount of money that the city was putting into the project was double the $50 million originally planned. This echoed the secrecy surrounding the closure of a freeway ramp to benefit OhioHealth, which was discussed in chapter 7. It has, though, another significance. This is the determination of the city to hang on to what major league franchises it has, something apparent earlier in the purchase of the Nationwide Arena so as to mitigate the financial position of an ice hockey franchise looking for pastures new. As I emphasized earlier in the book, as a latecomer surrounded by cities that were big before Columbus was barely small, the city has struggled to achieve a (major) league status appropriate to its size.

Columbus shares a great deal with other large US cities. It has the same expansive urbanization. Developers love the ease of assembling land on a periphery that is forever moving farther out. Big acreages allow regional shopping centers with their massive parking lots, and new housing developments on a scale that can incorporate a golf course, a lake, even a shopping center to enhance the rents to be generated. Meanwhile, the expansion of employment at nodes around characteristic outer belts brings employment closer to the periphery: nodes in the Columbus case like Easton, Polaris, Pickerington, and Dublin, all with flourishing employment opportunities. It bears emphasis that this is a very American pattern.

So too is the urgent push for major league status. City administrations, supported by their developer friends, want it because it promises increased growth, increased tax revenues for the city, and increased rents for the developers. Back in 1976, the sociologist Harvey Molotch talked about the city as a growth machine, but this is a very American idea and one that applies to cities in this country, but to cities elsewhere only with considerable difficulty.[2]

2. Cox 2017.

Like the Western European countries, the US is subject to the same capitalist logics, but how things work out in major cities seems different. Partly this is because of a peculiar and distinct state structure. The American state is extraordinarily decentralized. Cities need to find most of their own revenue, which is a major reason why Columbus embarked on its annexation policy; it saw what was happening in Cleveland, where the taxables were flowing toward the independent suburbs, leaving behind a relatively dependent population. This is also a major reason why the independent suburbs and their school districts are keen on attracting development and are so happily complicit with the plans of the developers—so long, that is, that they are fiscally attractive: developers planning low-income housing developments, please note. One result has been a competition between different local governments for major developments: as in the struggle between Columbus and Delaware County to snag Polaris.

American cities are different from West European counterparts, and Columbus shares in that difference. Yet there is something else about American cities. Unlike those of the different countries of Western Europe, they are all quite distinct. Dependence on their own tax base, and then providing them with the powers to carve out a strategy to cope with that constraint, has meant a huge institutional diversity. No city is like Columbus and no city is like Los Angeles. Los Angeles has the Lakewood Plan, through which the county contracts to supply local governments with police and fire services. In the Columbus area, police and fire service are local responsibilities. What Columbus has, though, and I am not aware of anything quite like it in the US, is the annexation policy: a means of safeguarding its fiscal position through a lassoing of suburbanizing business—as indeed in the pattern of regional shopping centers, which are all within city boundaries. All this is in sharp contrast to the more monochrome, predictable character of cities in France or the United Kingdom: a standard institutional template laid down by strongly centralizing governments that stand in sharp contrast to the decentralized state that is the US.

Cities and regions within countries develop unevenly. Columbus is an anomaly: a rapidly developing city in a region that has suffered deindustrialization and an economy that, in contrast to much of the West and South—compare California, Florida, Texas, and Washington—has expanded only slowly. Columbus, therefore, has more in common with Austin and Denver than with Cleveland or Cincinnati, and if it was in a more rapidly growing part of the country, it would have shown even more rapid growth than it has. Nevertheless, it is the closest that Ohio has to a Sunbelt city—something it shares with very few other Midwestern cities, Indianapolis, Kansas City, and Minneapolis apart.

Nevertheless, history matters in ways other than a regional economy that could be more prosperous. By virtue of its location, surrounded by other major cities that were, in a sense, there first, Columbus has had to struggle to get the airline connections and the major league franchises that the development lobby and city council believe are significant to its further growth, and it has had very qualified success in these regards. It remains, therefore, both out of place and out of step: in short, both blessed and cursed.

BIBLIOGRAPHY

Blackford, M. 2016. *Columbus, Ohio: Two Centuries of Business and Environmental Change.* Columbus: The Ohio State University Press.

Bradford, D. F., and W. E. Oates. 1974. "Suburban Exploitation of Central Cities and Governmental Structure." In *Redistribution Through Public Choice,* edited by H. M. Hochman and G. L. Peterson, 43–92. New York: Columbia University Press.

Buzzelli, M., and R. Harris. 2006. "Cities as the Industrial Districts of Housebuilding." *International Journal of Urban and Regional Research* 30(4): 894–917.

Clavel, P. 1986. *The Progressive City: Planning and Participation 1969–1984.* New Brunswick, NJ: Rutgers University Press.

Cox, K. R. 1973. *Conflict, Power and Politics in the City.* New York: McGraw-Hill.

———. 2002. *Political Geography: Territory, State and Society.* Oxford: Blackwell.

———. 2016. *The Politics of Urban and Regional Development and the American Exception.* Syracuse, NY: Syracuse University Press.

———. 2017. "Revisiting 'The City as a Growth Machine.'" *Cambridge Journal of Regions, Economy and Society* 10(2): 391–405.

Cox, K. R., and A. E. G. Jonas. 1993. "Urban Development, Collective Consumption and the Politics of Metropolitan Fragmentation." *Political Geography* 12(1): 8–37.

Curry, T., K. P. Schwirian, and R. Woldoff. 2004. *High Stakes: Big Time Sports and Downtown Redevelopment.* Columbus: The Ohio State University Press.

Davis, M. 1990. *City of Quartz.* New York: Vintage Books.

Downs, A. 1973. *Opening up the Suburbs.* New Haven: Yale University Press.

Dyer, S. 1998. "'Holding the Line against Philadelphia': Business, Suburban Change, and the Main Line's Suburban Square, 1926–1950." *Business and Economic History* 27(2): 279–91.

Evans-Cowley, J. 2006. "Development Exactions: Process and Planning Issues." Working paper, Lincoln Institute of Land Policy, Cambridge, MA.

Gaffney, M. 1973. "Tax Reform to Release Land." In *Modernizing Urban Land Policy,* edited by M. Clawson, 115–52. Baltimore: Johns Hopkins University Press.

Gendron, R., and G. W. Domhoff. 2009. *The Leftmost City: Power and Progressive Politics in Santa Cruz.* Boulder, CO: Westview.

Gill, H. L. 1983. "Changes in City and Suburban House Prices during a Period of Expected School Desegregation." *Southern Economic Journal* 50(1): 169–84.

Graff, H. 2008. *The Dallas Myth: The Making and Unmaking of an American City.* Minneapolis: University of Minnesota Press.

Green, R. K., S. Malpezzi, and S. K. Mayo. 2005. "Metropolitan-Specific Estimates of the Price Elasticity of Supply of Housing, and Their Sources." *American Economic Review* 95(2): 334–39.

Haig, R. M. 1927. "Major Economic Factors in Metropolitan Growth and Arrangement." In *The Regional Survey of New York, Vol 1.* New York.

Harris, R., and R. Lewis. 2001. "The Geography of North American Cities and Suburbs, 1900–1950: A New Synthesis." *Journal of Urban History* 27(3): 262–92.

Harvey, D. 1985. "The Geopolitics of Capitalism." In *Social Relations and Spatial Structures,* edited by D. Gregory and J. Urry, 128–63. London: Macmillan.

Hunker, H. L. 2000. *Columbus, Ohio: A Personal Geography.* Columbus: The Ohio State University Press.

Jacobs, G. S. 1998. *Getting around Brown: Desegregation, Development, and the Columbus Public Schools.* Columbus: The Ohio State University Press.

Jonas, A. E. G. 1998. "Busing, 'White Flight,' and the Role of Developers in the Continuous Suburbanization of Franklin County, Ohio." *Urban Affairs Review* 34(2): 340–58.

Lipset, S. M., and R. Bendix. 1959. *Social Mobility in Industrial Society.* Berkeley and Los Angeles: University of California Press.

Mair, A. 1986. "The Homeless and the Post-Industrial City." *Political Geography Quarterly* 5(4): 351–68.

———. 1988. "Private Planning for Economic Development: Local Business Coalitions in Columbus, Ohio: 1858–1986." Unpublished diss., Department of Geography, The Ohio State University, Columbus, OH.

Mair, A., R. Florida, and M. Kenney. 1988. "The New Geography of Automobile Production: Japanese Transplants in North America." *Economic Geography* 64(4): 352–74.

Massey, D. 2007. *World City.* Cambridge: Polity Press.

Miller, Z. 1981. *Suburb: Neighborhood and Community in Forest Park, Ohio, 1935–1976.* Knoxville: University of Tennessee Press.

Mishan, E. J. 1967. *The Costs of Economic Growth.* Harmondsworth, Middlesex: Penguin.

Mollenkopf, J. H. 1983. *The Contested City.* Princeton, NJ: Princeton University Press.

Molotch, H. 1976. "The City as a Growth Machine: Toward a Political Economy of Place." *American Journal of Sociology* 82(2): 309–22.

Neenan, W. B. 1970. "Suburban-Central City Exploitation Thesis: One City's Tale." *National Tax Journal* 23(2): 117–39.

Parson, D. 2007. "The Decline of Public Housing and the Politics of the Red Scare: The Significance of the Los Angeles Public Housing War." *Journal of Urban History* 33(3): 400–417.

Preteceille, E. 1976. "Urban Planning: The Contradictions of Capitalist Urbanization." *Antipode* 8(1): 69–76.

Puentes, R. "The State of Organizing in Midwestern First Suburbs." *Opolis* 2(1): 53–64.

Robinson, W. S. 1950. "Ecological Correlations and the Behavior of Individuals." *American Journal of Sociology* 15(3): 351–57.

Saiz, A. 2010. "The Geographic Determinants of Housing Supply." *The Quarterly Journal of Economics* 125(3): 1253–96.

Schelling, T. 1971. "On the Ecology of Micro-Motives." *The Public Interest* 25: 61–98.

Schumpeter, J. A. (1942) *Capitalism, Socialism and Democracy*. New York: Harper and Brothers.

Shermer, E. 2013. *Sunbelt Capitalism: Phoenix and the Transformation of American Capitalism*. Philadelphia: University of Pennsylvania Press.

Stone, C. N. 1987. "Summing up: Urban Regimes, Development Policy, and Political Arrangements." In *The Politics of Urban Development,* edited by C. N. Stone and H. T. Sanders, 269–90. Lawrence, KS: University Press of Kansas.

Weiss, M. A. 1987. *The Rise of the Community Builders*. New York: Columbia University Press.

Newspapers and Periodicals

Business First of Greater Columbus, Columbus, Ohio.

Capitol Magazine, Columbus, Ohio.

CityLab, Columbus, Ohio.

Columbus Alive, Columbus, Ohio.

Columbus Citizen Journal, Columbus, Ohio.

Columbus Free Press, Columbus, Ohio.

The Columbus Dispatch, Columbus, Ohio.

The Columbus Monthly, Columbus, Ohio.

The Columbus Guardian, Columbus, Ohio.

The Lantern, Ohio State University, Columbus, Ohio.

Neighborhood News Northwest, Columbus.

The Other Paper, Columbus, Ohio.

This Week in Worthington, Worthington, Ohio.

The Worthington News, Worthington, Ohio

Worthington Suburbia News, Worthington, Ohio

INDEX

abandonment: in Columbus, 116n8; unintended consequence, 108, 116, 150–56. *See also* mall wars

agricultural land: tax privilege, and how the developers take advantage of it, 113, 113n6

airline service: longing for a hub, 48–52; low-cost airlines, 51–52, 52fn13; relative weakness of, 11, 50, 50 table 3.1, 52, 52 table 3.2; relative weakness explained, 72–73; significance of hub status, 48–49; wooing TWA, 50–51; wooing America West, 51

airport: renaming to reinforce provinciality, 47n6; shifting the costs to the county, 230

American city: different from West European cities, ix–xi, 1–6, 109, 165–66, 192, 197, 210, 244–45; institutional variation, 10, 218, 245; middling cities, xi; predominance of corporate urban regimes, 131

AmeriFlora, 56; fails the attendance test, 57; fails the financial test, 57

annexation: agreements with independent suburbs, 17–20; city government divided, 30–31; city services in exchange for, 16–17; city versus the neighborhoods, 25–31; city versus the townships 22–25; developers to the rescue, 25; encirclement the name of the game, 18, 156; fiscal implications for Columbus, 41–42, 221; policy, 15–44; pro-developer, 42; schools annexation, 16–17, 33–38; successes, 20–21, 41–42, 44, 119, 228. *See also* central city-suburban fiscal disparities; Columbus Board of Education; Columbus Department of Utilities; suburban exploitation of the central city; water-sewer contracts

area commissions: functions, 172–73, 223, 237, 239, 242; in lieu of wards, 172; overridden by development interests, 173–74

Arena District, 53, 86, 91, 143; city subsidies, 62–63, 63n36, 133; creates downtown office vacancy problem, 71, 91; snags Columbus Crew stadium, 70; snags Columbus Clippers baseball arena, 92

attracting the wanted downtown. *See* Columbus Crew; Columbus Clippers

Banc One: growth, 87–88; relocation of headquarters, 88–89, 89n16

Battelle Memorial Institute, 79; convention center, 53; impacted by adverse court decision, 95–96; promotes gentrification, 95–96

bidding wars. *See* jurisdictional fragmentation; Polaris; Villages at New Albany

Board of Elections in question, 175–76
Bollinger Tower, redeveloping: to hell with the residents, 196
Brewery District, 87, 91
Buckeye fever, 46–47
busing for racial balance, 32–33

campaign finance, 171, 174n7, 175, 175n11, 176, 177n18, 179, 190, 242; Easton, 190; Villages at New Albany, 126
Campus Gateway, 96, 96n34, 232
Capitol Square, 87, 88 fig 4.2
casino: diverting public revenues to save Nationwide Arena, 65–66; from polecat to financial savior, 65–67; snagged by Columbus, 20; uproar, 184–85, 235; victim of rhetorical rant, 184–85
central city, redevelopment of, 117
central city-suburban fiscal disparities, xii, 14, 156, 227
citizen initiatives, 43, 223–24. *See also* Morse-Bethel connector; resident organizations; Tuttle Mall
City Center, 133, 141–44; bone to Lazarus, 143, 176n13; stiff competition, 142
city-township mergers, 124–26, 168, 228
class: in the USA, 193, 193n1, 195–96. *See also* social stratification in Columbus
Clintonville, 43n54, 172, 223, 242; zones out apartments, 239
coalitions, 241. *See also* Campus Gateway; Morse-Bethel connector; Northland; Polaris; Tuttle Mall
code enforcement (or lack of), 155, 155n50
Coldbelt cities, xii, 228
Columbus Blue Jackets, 62–65; dubious financial proposition, 65n41; public subsidy, 66
Columbus Board of Education: anxieties about white flight, 32; opposes water and sewer agreement with New Albany, 124, 126; pushes for retroactive schools annexation, 33–38
Columbus, City of: corporate urban regime, 132–34; indulges developers, 132–34; indulges Nationwide, 70–71; northward bias to city expansion, 100, 105–6; subordinate to developers. *See also* postindustrial city; Sunbelt cities
Columbus City council, 56, 60, 62: annexation, 26, 29; antagonizes *Columbus Dispatch,* 187; area commissions, 173–74; Battelle gentrification, 96; blanket rezonings, 239; complaints about bus queues, 90; elected at large, 171–72; Fashion Place, 146; generous tax abatements, 168n2; opposes Ford plant rezoning, 83; pressure for change in electoral system, 172. *See also* Villages at New Albany
Columbus Clippers, 92, 100, 184, 224
Columbus Coalition for Responsive Government, 175. *See also* Represent Columbus
Columbus compared, 11 table 1.4, 13 table 1.5, 42 table 2.3, 50 table 3.1, 52 table 3.2, 52fn13, 84 table 4.5
Columbus Crew, 68–72; attendance problems, 69, 72; public subsidies, 69–71, 244; Nationwide plays hardball over site, 69–71, 236, 236n17; threat of relocation to Austin TX, 69
Columbus Department of Public Utilities: big winner from the annexation policy, 43–44; defensive about expansion plans, 28–29; position on Villages at New Albany controversy, 126
Columbus Dispatch: anxiety about 'unwise' policies, 132; boosts Blue Jackets, 62–63; forgets history, 40–41, 185–86; interests in development, 181; joins in the chorus, 91, 138, 148; newspaper monopoly, 188; ownership transferred to Gatehouse Media, 67n46, 188; pro-developer 26–27, 132, 148–49, 149n44; stokes Buckeye fever, 47; tries to stifle debate, 38fn46
Columbus downtown: lacks cohesion, 86–87, 86n14; emergence of residential towers, 87, 88 fig. 4.2. *See also* expelling the unwanted from downtown
Columbus Ford Dealers 500, 56
Columbus image: absence, 45–48, 72, 73n54; competing for investment, 45–46
Columbus Police Department: police chief's position on annexation and use of 'asinine,' 31
Columbus School District. *See* Columbus Board of Education; schools annexation; tax abatements

conflicts of interest, 115–16, 116n7; *Columbus Dispatch,* 187; Kass, Frank, 91; McCoy, John, 147

Continent, The, 142n26

Convention Center, the, 53–56; benefits from Battelle 'charitable' donation, 53; dogged by city image, 53; dogged by poor airline service, 53; hotel rooms problem, 73, 73n55

Cooper Stadium, 91–92, 237

cost-benefit analysis, 186, 186n30

cost-revenue analysis, 221

crocodile tears: developers shed them for homebuyers, 25, 28, 113, 138; Old Beechwold sheds them for those standing to be displaced, 162. *See also* Weiler, Robert

Davis, Mike: xiii, 225

Delaware County, 145; Fashion Place, 145; Polaris, 118–19, 127–28, 167

Delco: 129; and Polaris, 118; and the Villages at New Albany, 125

democracy: a problem, 171; how to get around it, 171–80. *See also* money, power of; ward elections

developer discourse: development is good for everybody, 181–83; it's the business climate, stupid, 146–47; no outsiders, please, 147–48

developer-resident coalitions: the logic, 216; the casino, 223; Morse-Bethel connector, 223; Northland, 222; Tuttle, 223. *See also* Gee, Gordon

developers in Columbus: anxious about retroactive schools annexation, 36–38; attention to detail, 128; campaign donations, 128; caught with pants down, 37, 123–24, 124n21, 136, 211; chutzpah, 136–37; consumer's 'friend,' 140; dealing with democracy, 136–38, 138n15; defending annexation policy, 25; exploiting fragmentation in public provision, 129, 210; local economic development 6; local embeddedness, 4–5, 216–18; misinterpretation when it helps the cause, 140; paying—or not—for water and sewer line extensions 28–30; product innovation, 2, 18, 20; reaping where others have not sown, 53fn16, 133; schools, 201, 212; significance in urban development, xiv; subordinating local government, 109; suburbanizing bias, 222, 225; versus the planners, 26–27; take advantage of tax law supposed to benefit farmers, 113n6. *See also* conflicts of interest, crocodile tears, developers in the United States, development industry, impact fees in the Columbus area

developers in the United States: pushing costs on to others as part of the logic, 113

development industry: complexity, 107–8; historical emergence, 3–5, 108–11; innovation, 111, 112, 127, 152; local embeddedness, 113, 218; local government, importance of, 115–16; logics, 108, 111–13, 117–18; multi-use developments, advantages of, 120, 127, 142, 210; peripheral bias, 112, 116; rezonings, 114; space-extensive, 112, 127, 155, 158, 159, 244; speculative, 111, 156; suburbanizing bias, 222; tax abatements, 114. *See also* conflicts of interest; developer discourse; development 'speak'; inner suburb problem

development 'speak': 180–89; beware 'community groups,' 187–88; 'development' as something for everybody, 182–83; expertise, 186; a public primed, 181; role of the *Columbus Dispatch. See also* outsiders

discourse: *See* developer discourse; development 'speak'

discrepant areas, 33–38; mapped, 35 fig. 2.3; tabulated, 34 table 2.1

displacement: Bollinger Tower, 99n41, 196; gentrification 98–99; Grant-Oak, 196–97; Renaissance District, 239

distribution centers, 102, 103 fig. 4.4

Duffey, Mike: makes an issue of Win-Win, 39, 39fn49; unclear why, 39; wants to help wealthy suburbs avoid Win-Win payments, 39–40

Easton, 119–21; faux architecture, 119; freeway access issue, 120–21; massive tax break, 169

exclusion, residential, 219, 238–39

expelling the unwanted from downtown: homeless shelters, 90; bus stops, 90–91. *See also* attracting the wanted downtown

expertise: versus community groups, 187. *See also* cost-benefit analysis; development 'speak'

Fashion Place, 145–50
First Suburbs Consortium, 158
fiscal disparities problem, xii, 227–28. *See also* suburban exploitation of the central city
fixity: developers; local government, 221; residents, 237–38. *See also* OSU-land
Ford plant that could have been, 83
Franklin County: assumes costs of trash-burning power plant, 230; Columbus leverage, 229–31; Cooper Stadium fiasco, 92; New Albany fiasco, 123
Franklin County Convention Authority: hapless owner of Nationwide Arena, 66
Franklinton: 92; abandoned by the county, 92; abandoned by Mount Carmel hospital, 98

Gee, Gordon: co-chairs referendum campaign for a downtown arena, 60; unease at professional sports franchise competition for Ohio State University, 58n29; wife puts spoke in the wheel, 60–61
Gentrification, 155; bottom-up style, 94; competitive bidding, 239–40; conflicts around, 96; corporate style, 95–98; defined, 93–94; discursive gloss, 95, 97, 99; displacement, 98; moving the poor around, 99, 155, 224. *See also* Bollinger Tower; German Village; Renaissance District; rustbelts; Victorian Village
geopolitics of the city, 215–42
George, Henry, 166
German Village: gentrification, 94; opposes Cooper Stadium redevelopment, 92n26, 100, 242; zones out apartments, 239
Golden Arc. *See* northern arc; office parks
Grandview Heights: tax base problems mitigated, 158–59
Grant-Oak apartment complex, redeveloping: to hell with the students, 196–97

Harrison West: anxieties about arena parking, 60
Harvey, David, 225
Honda, 79–80, 80 fig. 4.1
horse trading: reviled, 176; used when it suits, 143, 176n13. *See also* Lazarus
housing subsidies: middle class gets lion's share, 200. *See also* Section Eight housing vouchers
housing vacancies: segregation, 152, 152n9; speculative housing development, 152–53
housing values, 150–52; role of supply and demand, 152–53; winners and losers, 153–55

impact fees, 134–41, 183; developer opposition, 28, 113; their logic, 28, 113, 134; in the United States, 134n7. *See also* schools annexation; impact fees in the Columbus area
impact fees in the Columbus area: developer recourse to spurious arguments, 138–40; opposition of developers, 136–40, 243; the perfect storm, 134–35
industrial employment: in surrounding counties, 79–80; major industrial employers, 81, 82, 83; plant closures in Columbus 102–3
inner suburb problem, 157–63; ambivalent situation of Columbus, 162–63; connectors, 161–62; mitigating strategies, 157–63; real estate innovation, 157. *See also* First Suburbs Consortium; Grandview Heights; Upper Arlington; Worthington
inward investment policy, 82–84; opposition to, 82–84
Italian Village, 100; anxieties about convention center parking, 54

Jefferson Township: and the Villages at New Albany, 125–26, 129
jurisdictional fragmentation, 2–3, 44, 166–70; competition for development, 129; confronting congestion issues, 136. *See also* Polaris

landlords: neighborhood decline: 141, 150, 153, 155, 155n50, 224–25; Section Eight housing vouchers, 198–200
latecomer. *See* particularity
Lazarus: gets on board with convention center location, 143; opposed branch plant policy, 82; participates in cratering of Northland Mall, 145
local economic development, 5
local embeddedness. *See* developers in Columbus; development industry
local government, 5; size and the power of resident associations, 240; stakes in local

development, 115–16; vulnerability to developers, 166–69

major league franchises: National Hockey League as 'junior varsity,' 65n41; relative absence, 11, 58, 72–73; St Louis Cardinals show interest, 46fn5. *See also* Columbus Blue Jackets; Columbus Crew; Gee, Gordon; major league status; Nationwide Arena; OSU-land

major league status, 85; Columbus as major league city, 85–86, 244. *See also* airline service; convention center; major league franchises

mall wars, 141–50

Mid-Ohio Planning Commission. *See* MORPC

money, power of, 176–78, 189–92; secures closure of freeway ramp for OhioHealth, 190–92; secures freeway ramp for Easton, 190; secures Tuttle Mall, 190; the ultimate power, 196

MORPC, 121, 136, 137

Morse-Bethel connector, 161–62, 172, 223

Municipal elections: ward versus at large, 171–72

Nationwide: benefits from presence of Ohio State University, 233; cashes in, coming and going, 66, 71; challenges tax assessment of Nationwide Arena, 66n45; debating headquarters location, 132, 132n3; gets way with City of Columbus, 70–71, 132–33; locked into Columbus, 71–72; plays hardball over new Crew Stadium, 70–71; redevelopment in Grandview Heights, 158–59; stockpiling land, 143

Nationwide Arena: city subsidies, 61–62; competition with new university (Schottenstein) arena, 58–60, 63–64, 64n38, 65; dumping on the public, 64, 65–68; financial incubus, 63–68; plans emerge, 61

Nationwide-land, 235–36. *See also* casino; Columbus Blue Jackets; Columbus Clippers; Columbus Crew; Nationwide; Nationwide Arena

neighborhoods, pitting one against another, 179; the Fashion Place case, 145–46; the Tuttle case, 179–80. *See also* Villages at New Albany

New Albany, 234–35; annexation agreement with Columbus, 122–27

New Albany-Plain Township Schools, 234–35

New World Center, 54–55; opposition, 54, 55n21

northern arc, 101–2, 119, 142. *See also* Easton; office parks; Polaris; Tuttle Mall

Northland: support for Northland Mall, 146. *See also* developer-resident coalitions

Northland Mall, demise of, 145–50

office parks, 105, 105 table 4.6

Ohio Center, 53

Ohio Company, 181

Ohio State University: benefits to the local economy, 233; not keen to share arena with city, 58–60; power, 232n11. *See also* Campus Gateway; Gee, Gordon; OSU-land

OhioHealth: gets its way, regardless, 190–92, 244

Old Beechwold, 153; crocodile tears, 162; not helpful in relieving traffic issues, 162

OneColumbus, 176; master stroke, 177

OSU-land, 232–33

Outerbelt: congestion issues, 134–37

outsiders: suspicion of, 145–50, 183–85; a selective gambit, 184n25. *See* Wexner, Leslie

particularity: theorizing, xiii; of Columbus, xii–xiii, 11–14

Pataskala, 243–44

Plain Township, 22, 22n3, 234; gets shafted, 168, 228. *See also* Villages at New Albany

Poindexter Village, 199

Polaris, 118–19, 132; annexation opposed, 25–26; bidding war, 118–19, 167; comedy show, 119; legal machinations, 118–19. *See also* Fashion Place

postindustrial city, 75–76

postindustrial city, Columbus: emergence, 75–76, 84–85; credentials, 76–81; struggle around, 81–85. *See also* attracting the wanted downtown; expelling the unwanted from downtown

property capital. *See* development industry

public housing: sad saga, 197

redlining, 153, 156
referenda. *See* citizen initiatives
Renaissance District, 95
Rent. *See* developers in Columbus; developers in the United States; development industry
Represent Columbus, 176
resident organizations, 237–40; alliances with development interests, 240–41; class, 238. *See also* area commissions; citizen initiatives; fixity
re-zonings, logic of, 114
Rickenbacker Air Industrial Park, 221; annexed by Columbus, 20–21; logistics nucleus, 102, 103 fig. 4.4
Rinehart, Dana: attracting investment into Columbus, 46; bends to wishes of developers, 136–37
Rustbelts, 104; colonized by those displaced by gentrification, 104–5

schools: importance of, 218–19, 234. *See also* segregation; uneven development
schools annexation: impact fees, 35–37; retroactive, 33–38; role of State Board of Education, 17, 33. *See also* city-township mergers; Columbus Board of Education
Section Eight housing vouchers, 197–98; clustering of clients, 200, 202 fig. 8.1; deconcentration, 198; facilitates unwanted dispersal, 196, 199; gentrification, 97, 199; landlords fought to privatize housing for the poor, and then don't want to know, 198; subsidy for real estate industry, 198; unjust stigmatization, 201
segregation, 218–20; and developers, 219–20
sewage systems in question, 22–23. *See also* Delco; Polaris; Villages at New Albany
Short North, 53, 86, 87, 90, 100. *See also* Bollinger Tower, redeveloping
Skybus, 52fn12
Smith, Harrison, 122, 122n19
social stratification in Columbus, 203–4, 213; injuries caused, 203–10; residential exclusion, 200. *See also* gentrification; uneven development
Son of Heaven: 56; fails the attendance test, 57; fails the financial test, 57; suspicions of cronyism, 57, 57n25
suburban exploitation of the central city, 227–28; shifting costs to the county, 230–31, 231n10
Sunbelt cities, xii, xiii, 8 table 2.1, 9 table 1.2, 10 table 1.3; Columbus as a Sunbelt city, 7–11, 192, 246–47

tax-abatements, 144n31, 192; criticized by *Columbus Dispatch,* 188; implications for school districts, 168–69, 168n2, 170; Nationwide Arena, 67; Nationwide office tower, 235
tax incremental financing districts, 28; defined 70n50; for Nationwide, 132; implications for Franklin County, 169n3. *See* Fashion Place
TIFs. *See* tax incremental financing districts
trash-burning power plant, 15, 55n21, 135, 135n10, 182, 221, 229–31
Tuttle Mall, 21, 142, 147, 149; controversy, 179–80

uneven development: exploited by developers, 36–38, 210; the schools, 204–10
Upper Arlington: tax base frustrations, 159–60, 160–61, 160n56
urban planners: subordination of planners to developers, 6
urban planning: American-West European contrasts, 6; how not to do it, 135, 135n8
urban regimes, 131–34
urban renewal, xi, 2, 94, 232

Victorian Village, 100; anxieties about arena parking, 60; anxieties about convention center parking, 54; gentrification, 94
Villages at New Albany, 122–27; bidding war, 167–68; investing in local school district, 212. *See also* New Albany

ward elections: demand for, 174–79; developer antagonism, 177, 177n16; evaluated, 179–80; history, 174; Mayor Ginther puts in dubious oar, 175n11; neighborhood interests, 175
water-sewer contracts, 17–19, 228; improper influence, possibility of, 126
Weiler, Robert: dubious claims about school district revenues, 149; hostile to outsiders,

147–48; sheds tears for Columbus school children, 149
Weinland Park, 96
Wexner, Leslie, 233–34; critic of downtown land use planning, 86–87, 91, 143–44; Easton, 120–21; jumps the queue for highway money, 120–21; onetime outsider, 122n18; Villages at New Albany, 122. *See* Wexner-land
Wexner-land, 233–35. *See also* Easton; Villages at New Albany
white flight, 32–33, 186; growth of the northern arc, 35; how the independent suburbs benefited, 40; impact fees, 35–37
windfall sites: in Grandview Heights, 158–59; in Whitehall, 161; in Worthington, 161
Win-Win agreement, 38; challenge for developers of Villages at New Albany, 122–27; in the cross-hairs, 39–41; symbolic value, 40; challenge for developers of Villages at New Albany, 122–27. See also *Columbus Dispatch;* Duffey, Mike
Wolfe Enterprises, 52n12, 177, 177n16
Wolfe family, 4n6, 62, 67n46, 82, 83, 122n18, 148n41, 181. *See also* Ohio Company; Wolfe Enterprises
Worthington: expansion thwarted, 18–19. *See also* windfall sites